PIPE FITTINGS

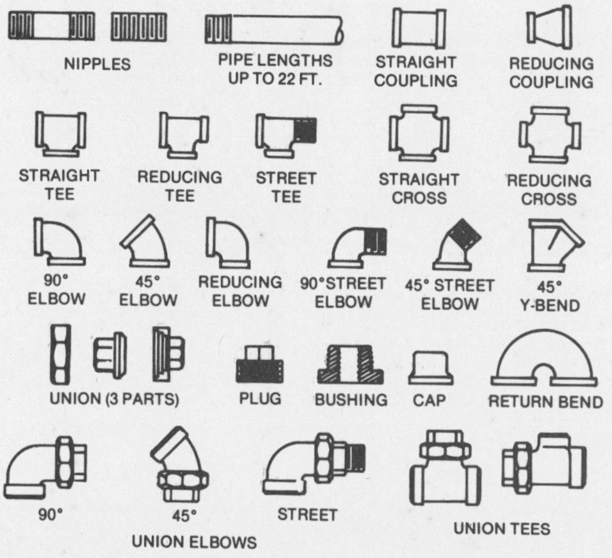

Here are the common steel pipe fittings. Nipples are simply short lengths of pipe threaded on both ends. Reducing fittings join two different sizes of pipe.

Compression fittings of the flared-tube type are the easiest for the novice to handle when working with copper tubing.

STANDARD STEEL PIPE (All Dimensions in Inches)					
Nominal Size	Outside Diameter	Inside Diameter	Nominal Size	Outside Diameter	Inside Diameter
⅛	0.405	0.269	1	1.315	1.049
¼	0.540	0.364	1¼	1.660	1.380
⅜	0.675	0.493	1½	1.900	1.610
½	0.840	0.622	2	2.375	2.067
¾	1.050	0.824	2½	2.875	2.469

SQUARE MEASURE

144 sq in = 1 sq ft
9 sq ft = 1 sq yd
272.25 sq ft = 1 sq rod
160 sq rods = 1 acre

VOLUME MEASURE

1728 cu in = 1 cu ft
27 cu ft = 1 cu yd

MEASURES OF CAPACITY

1 cup = 8 fl oz
2 cups = 1 pint
2 pints = 1 quart
4 quarts = 1 gallon
2 gallons = 1 peck
4 pecks = 1 bushel

WOOD SCREWS

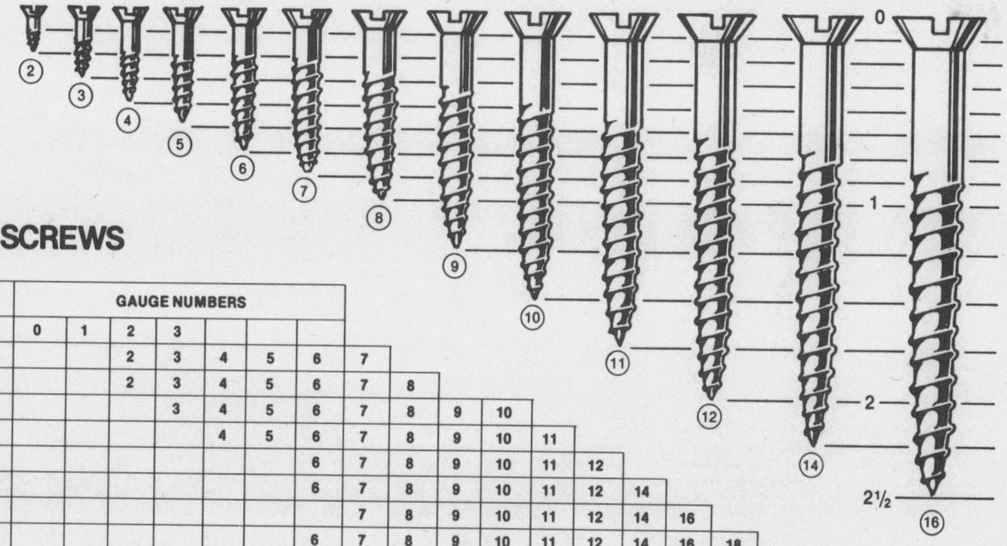

LENGTH	GAUGE NUMBERS																
¼ INCH	0	1	2	3													
⅜ INCH			2	3	4	5	6	7									
½ INCH			2	3	4	5	6	7	8								
⅝ INCH				3	4	5	6	7	8	9	10						
¾ INCH					4	5	6	7	8	9	10	11					
⅞ INCH							6	7	8	9	10	11	12				
1 INCH							6	7	8	9	10	11	12	14			
1¼ INCH								7	8	9	10	11	12	14	16		
1½ INCH							6	7	8	9	10	11	12	14	16	18	
1¾ INCH									8	9	10	11	12	14	16	18	20
2 INCH									8	9	10	11	12	14	16	18	20
2¼ INCH										9	10	11	12	14	16	18	20
2½ INCH													12	14	16	18	20
2¾ INCH														14	16	18	20
3 INCH															16	18	20
3½ INCH																18	20	24
4 INCH																18	20	24

WHEN YOU BUY SCREWS, SPECIFY (1) LENGTH, (2) GAUGE NUMBER, (3) TYPE OF HEAD—FLAT, ROUND, OR OVAL, (4) MATERIAL—STEEL, BRASS, BRONZE, ETC., (5) FINISH—BRIGHT, STEEL BLUED, CADMIUM, NICKEL, OR CHROMIUM PLATED.

WHAT DO THE EXPERTS USE to catch those huge tournament bass? Check their choices on page 1232.

In this volume . . .

HOW DO YOU put out fire in upholstery? In an electrical box? In rubber, grease and gasoline? See page 1218.

REFINISHING FURNITURE is easier than ever. It will pay you to learn about all the new polyurethanes, epoxies, vinyls and alkyds. They offer exceptional beauty and durability. See page 1208.

A BEAUTIFUL FENCE can enhance a home immeasurably. The right fence seems to flow right out from the home, indeed to be a part of it. On page 1202 you'll find complete information on how to build fences, from unique designs to post-setting know-how and construction tips.

BUILD A FAMILY ROOM that has a personality all its own, whether it's a restful place for browsing through books or a color-splashed playroom for the kids. See the ideas on page 1182.

YOU CAN FIND a good many attractive ideas in this gazebo. And we show you complete plans for building still another outdoor entertainment center on page 1346 of Vol. 9.

Look what you'll find in other volumes!

HERE, IN ONE BRIGHT package, are gifts for everyone in your family, from toys and trays to treasure chests. See page 1352 of Vol. 9.

FOR SOMEBODY SPECIAL in your life we present four valentines from your shop. Find these bright gifts on page 1360, Vol. 9.

Popular Mechanics

do-it-yourself encyclopedia

in 20 volumes

a complete how-to guide for the homeowner, the hobbyist—
and anyone who enjoys working with mind and hands!

All about:

home maintenance
home-improvement projects
wall paneling
burglary and fire protection
furniture projects
finishing and refinishing furniture
outdoor living
home remodeling
solutions to home problems
challenging woodworking projects
hobbies and handicrafts
model making
weekend projects
workshop shortcuts and techniques
hand-tool skills
power-tool know-how
shop-made tools
car repairs
car maintenance
appliance repair
boating
hunting
fishing
camping
photography projects
radio, TV and electronics know-how
clever hints and tips
projects just for fun

volume 8

ISBN 0-87851-073-7
Library of Congress Catalog Number 77 84920

MANUFACTURED IN THE UNITED STATES OF AMERICA

contents

VOLUME 8

How to do an engine overhaul yourself

By MORT SCHULTZ

YOU HAVE A CAR in the 75,000 to 100,000-mileage range that has started drinking oil. You know that oil is not leaking from the engine, but hoping against hope, you check anyway.

You spread some old newspapers on the floor under the engine and flywheel housing, and run the engine with the transmission in neutral or park at about 1000 to 1250 rpm, which is equivalent to 20 to 25 mph. When the heat gauge shows that the engine has reached normal operating temperature, you race the engine for a moment and then let it slacken back down to the 1000–1250-rpm range.

You continue this procedure for at least five minutes after the engine has warmed up. Oil appearing on the newspaper means that there's a leak. A leak that isn't too severe may not make droppings on the paper, but there should be oil wetness on the underside of the engine or flywheel housing.

However, the chances are that you will not find a leak when an engine has reached the mileage

REMOVING YOUR engine for overhaul may be necessary with some cars. You'll need a block and tackle.

REMOVING OIL PAN is necessary for engine overhaul. Clean it thoroughly and, after overhaul, reinstall with new gasket. Tighten to specification.

VALVE GUIDE BORES in cylinder head require reaming to accommodate new valves with larger stems.

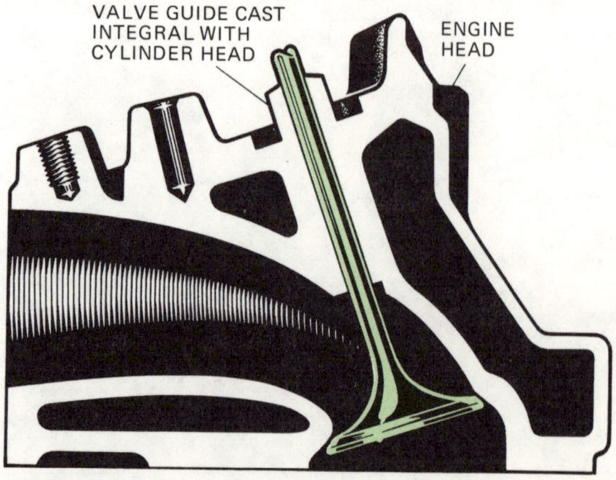

SEE ALSO

Autos, body repair . . . Autos, maintenance . . .
Autos, ramps . . . Gaskets, auto . . .
Lubrication, auto . . . Motor oil . . .
Ramps, auto repair . . . Tune-up, auto

plateau yours has. If not, then the high oil consumption is undoubtedly being caused by oil that is getting past worn parts of your engine into the combustion chambers where it's being burned.

On a hunch, though, let's not overlook one other minor possibility—the chance that a clogged positive crankcase ventilation (PCV) system is responsible for oil consumption.

If your PCV valve is clogged, excessive pressure builds up in the crankcase and forces oil through the valve cover-to-carburetor hose into the carburetor air cleaner housing. Obviously, then, if you find oil inside the air cleaner housing and on the air cleaner filter element you should replace the PCV valve, clean out the PCV system hoses, replace the carburetor air cleaner element and give thanks that you're so lucky.

The usual reason for loss of oil because of internal damage is worn piston rings. However, worn or scored cylinders, worn ring grooves in pistons and/or clogged oil-return slots or ring grooves that prevent oil from returning to the crankcase could also be responsible.

Another internal cause of oil consumption is excessively worn engine bearings. This condition is often easy to distinguish because too much bearing clearance, which allows oil to escape past bearings into cylinders, usually provides low or no oil pressure with the engine warm and idling.

If your automobile is equipped with dash-mounted gauges, you can get a pretty good idea of engine bearing condition by observing the oil pressure.

If the car is really losing oil and the oil pressure is low, worn bearings are probably the cause. However, a bearing oil-leak detector may be used to definitely establish bearing condition.

Remove the oil pan and connect the oil-leak detector, which is a pumping instrument, into the engine's lubricating system. With pressure applied, count the drops of oil per minute that each bearing allows to pass.

Generally, if more than 120 drops pass per minute, it means that the bearing is excessively worn.

do a complete job

If any one of the engine problems just mentioned should prevail and work is going to be done by a professional mechanic, he will probably advise that you allow him to do a complete overhaul although some of the parts may not have to be replaced now. Listen to him. If parts in

REMOVING valves requires that valve spring be compressed to get off retainers and locks. Special tool is needed.

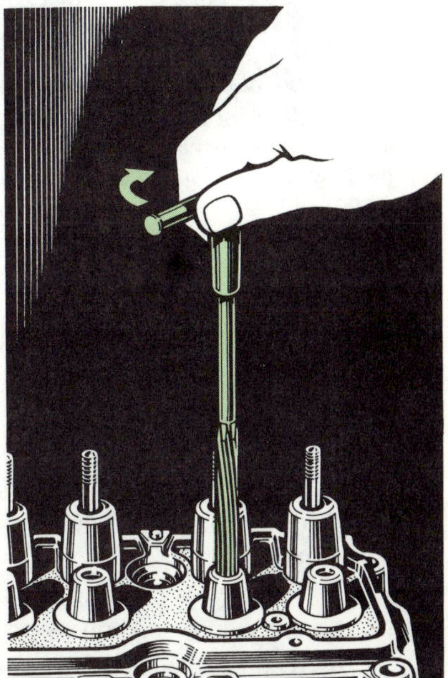

VALVE GUIDE bores are reamed with a special tool costing under $10.

MEASURE valve-guide wear with dial indicator. Reading should be within manufacturer's tolerance. If there's too much play, valves must be replaced and valve guide bores must be reamed.

CYLINDER BORES must always be carefully measured before the correct piston-ring size can be determined.

CHECK RING GROOVES by inserting feeler gauge between ring and land. Gauge should slide freely. Do this around piston's entire circumference and for all ring grooves to determine high spots.

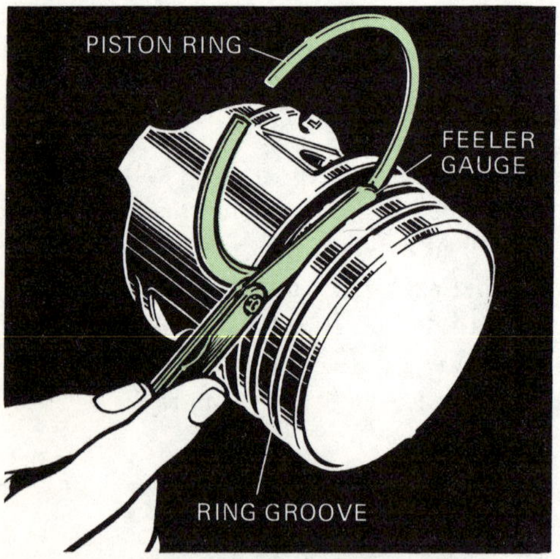

TO CHECK RING set size, position a ring in a cylinder bore by pushing it down carefully with the head of a piston. Measure gap between ends of ring. If ring gap is greater or less than specified limits, it is time to get new piston rings.

A RING COMPRESSOR will be necessary to reinstall the piston back in the cylinder, as shown here.

one area of the engine are worn—rings, for example—parts in another area (bearings, for instance) will probably wear out soon.

The same advice holds if you're going to tackle this work yourself—it is practical to do a complete overhaul job when work in one area is required.

However, you still may have an "out" that will permit you to postpone overhaul. There is always the chance that your old engine has worn valve guides. Repairing worn valve guides, although not a snap job, isn't in the same class with doing a ring job.

You can get a good idea what your course of action will have to be by noticing a few things. First of all, pull the sparkplugs after running the engine at idle for about 10 minutes.

If plugs are oily, there is no longer any doubt that oil is getting into the combustion chambers. You can discount external leaks and the PCV system.

But is oil getting into the chambers because of worn valve guides?

To find out, reinstall the plugs and drive the car about 10 miles. Pull the plugs again. If they are now dry, you can proceed with valve guide repair. If sparkplugs are still wet with oil, an engine overhaul is needed.

If you need more evidence, test engine compression. Warm the engine to operating temperature, shut it off, and remove all sparkplugs.

Take off the carburetor air cleaner and block the carburetor throttle linkage in full open position. Insert the compression gauge in a cylinder and crank the engine until the gauge's pointer no longer rises. About six or seven compression strokes are needed. Record the reading and proceed to take readings for each of the other cylinders.

You will probably find readings below normal in several or all cylinders (check the service manual for the engine's "normal" compression reading). Inject about two tablespoons of SAE 30 or 40 motor oil in each low-reading cylinder in turn and test again. An increase in the reading means that loss of compression (and oil) is past worn piston rings.

Keep in mind that a compression test will not tell you if oil loss is the result of deeply scored cylinder bores. Injection of oil into a cylinder with a damaged bore will not seal the cylinder. Thus the compression gauge reading will remain the same as it was before you injected oil. In this case, you don't know if your problem is damaged bores or worn valve guides. But it's logical to assume that valve guides are to blame and proceed to tackle them first.

Before you do an overhaul yourself (you may figure you have nothing to lose but time and sweat) let me fill you in on a few details.

First, you can lose money if you get discouraged and give up halfway through the job. Engine work requires special tools. Special tools can cost you over $100, and most of them will not be used again unless you do another engine job.

Second, ask yourself whether you have the facilities to take an engine apart, especially if it has to be removed from the car. How are you going to do this if, say, you live in midtown Manhattan?

If you decide to go ahead, you will need the service manual to guide you. It contains the essential instructions and specifications.

valve guide repair

Valve guides in modern engines are an internal part of the cylinder head and in most cases cannot be replaced.

When valve stem-to-valve guide clearance becomes excessive, the normal procedure is to replace valves with new ones having oversize stems. For example, valves are manufactured for Chrysler Corp. engines having oversize stems of .005 inch, .015 inch and .030 inch. Chevrolet engines can be served by valves having oversize stems of .003 inch, .015 inch and .030 inch.

Valve availability information is contained in your service manual.

To repair valve guides, you have to remove the cylinder head(s) and valves. The valve stem guide clearance should be measured. If it is determined that valves with oversize stems are needed, guides have to be reamed out (made larger) to accommodate those stems.

Some special tools you will need for this job and their approximate costs are as follows (prices quoted are from Kent-Moore Tools at the time this article was written):

- Valve guide reamer—$7.50.
- Valve spring compressor—$17.
- Valve seal installer and tester—$10.50.

facts about engine overhaul

- It is important in doing a ring job that the cyclinder bore be examined closely for ridges. Run your fingernail over the bore. If a ridge can be felt, it will be necessary to ream the ridge out. A reamer costs about $60. Any attempt to install a piston having new rings in a cylinder having a ridge would probably result in new rings being broken.
- When removing connecting-rod caps it is important that you identify them to the cylinder. In some cases, caps and connecting rods are numbered for easy cylinder identification. But if they aren't, use a punch to make identifying marks. For example, one punch mark can serve to identify parts belonging to No. 1 cylinder; three punch marks, No. 3 cylinder and so forth.

  Do *not* use a file to make identifying marks.
- Since rods move up and down in pairs, it is convenient to disassemble them in pairs. Rotate the crankshaft until a pair of rod caps are in position, remove rod-bolt nuts and take off the caps. Push the pistons up through the bores, but be careful not to damage the journals.
- Piston rings are available in a variety of sizes to accommodate worn bores. Bores should be measured accurately with a cylinder-bore checking gauge, so the correct size rings may be selected.
- If cylinder bores have a taper of more than .015 inch, you should rebore them and install new pistons and rings. If bores don't have to be honed, a glaze buster should be used to remove glaze before pistons are reinstalled.
- Some special tools you will need (or may need) when you're at work on the piston area of an engine and their approximate prices as of the time this article was written are as follows:

1. Piston ring compressor to compress rings when installing pistons in bores—$10.
2. Piston ring expander for removing and installing rings—$5.
3. Cylinder bore gauge—$65.
4. Cylinder bore honing tool—$30.

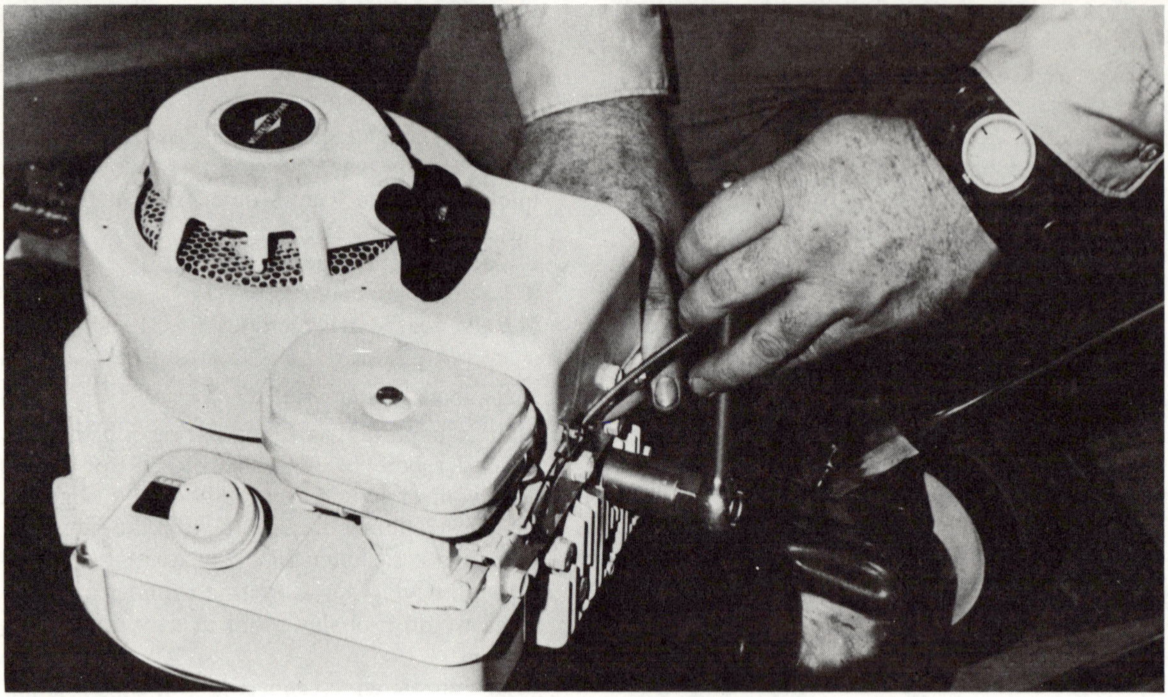

THE SPARKPLUG IS one of the first places to check when you're troubleshooting on a small engine. In replacing it, seat it by hand, then give it another half turn by wrench.

How to service small engines

By MORT SCHULTZ

These handy little power packs perform a multitude of chores for us—and we're obliged to care for them in return. You need only to follow a sensible system to master the big three: troubleshooting, repair and maintenance

ONE-LUNGERS—small, single-cylinder gasoline engines—are a proliferating breed of lightweight power supply that more and more householders are finding handy. These reliable little beasts are depended on by more of us each year. So it's wise to understand their troubleshooting, maintenance, and—as it becomes necessary—repair.

These engines power yard and garden equipment. The range includes everything from self-propelled and riding mowers to tillers, leaf blowers, sweepers, tractors, chain saws, trimmers and snow blowers.

Let's start by defining terms. *Troubleshooting,* the single most useful skill to master, means to zero in on a malfunction. Before you can solve a problem, you must find its cause. Even if you don't want to tackle the repair, knowing what's causing the problem allows you to be specific in dealing with a mechanic, thus assuring yourself that unnecessary repairs won't be made.

Maintenance, which includes tune-up, is the care you give a small engine to minimize the chance of breakdown. Replacing parts and making adjustments to forestall a breakdown will be considered as maintenance.

Repairs includes replacing parts and making adjustments to solve a problem. We won't get into engine overhaul. Practically every case of engine failure can be resolved with minor repairs; we'll concentrate on those.

Two other terms you will encounter are *two-cycle* and *four-cycle*. Your single-cylinder engine is one or the other.

SEE ALSO

Chain saws . . . Mowers . . . Snowblowers . . . Sparkplugs . . . Tractor lifts . . . Tractor trailers

engine types vary

Two-cycle engines take in fuel, compress it, burn it, and exhaust waste gases in two strokes

HARD STARTING in a two-cycle engine often comes from ignoring specs for the fuel mix.

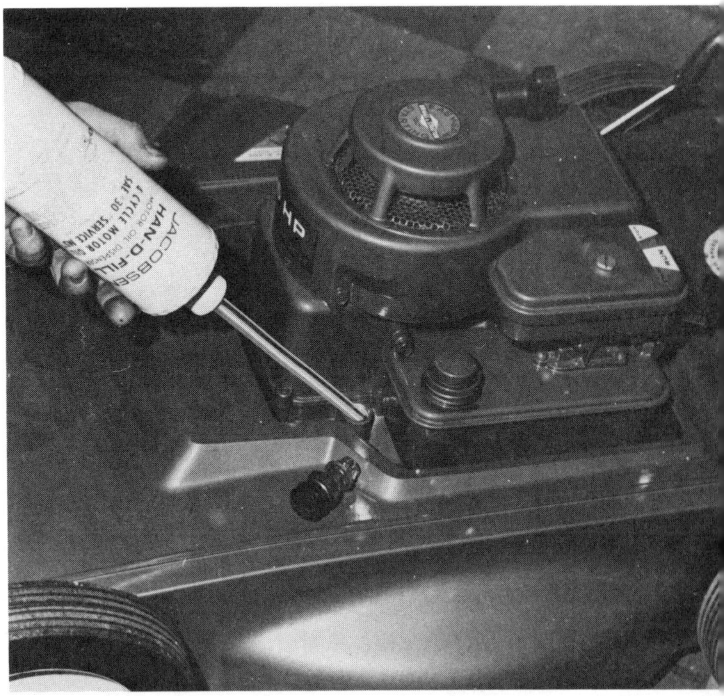

FOUR-CYCLE engines need good oil to guard against scoring cylinder walls.

of the piston—up and down. There's an ignition (power) stroke during every revolution of the crankshaft.

Four-cycle engines accomplish intake, compression, ignition and exhaust in four piston strokes. If you're not very well acquainted with small engines, here's how to tell two- from four-cycle quickly: You mix oil with the gas for a two-cycle; a four-cycle has an oil sump and filler pipe. If your engine is made by Briggs & Stratton, Kohler or Wisconsin, it's four-cycle. If it's a Jacobsen engine, it's two-cycle. If your engine is made by Clinton or Lauson-Tecumseh, it could be either a two- or four-cycle.

Jacobsen, incidentally, is one of the few manufacturers that makes two-cycle engines for its own equipment. However, where four-cycle engines are used in Jacobsen mowers and other equipment they are made by other companies, such as Lauson-Tecumseh. The manufacturer of the equipment and the manufacturer of the engine are not usually the same.

Two-cycle engines used in Lawn Boy mowers are manufactured by the company that makes the mower—Outboard Marine Corp. But Lawn Boy riding mowers use either a Briggs & Stratton or Lauson-Tecumseh four-cycle engine.

Engines that power chain saws, such as McCulloch, Homelite and OR (many Sears chain saws have OR engines) are two-cycle.

the major problems

Troubleshooting. Here is a list of eight major problems that affect small engines:

1. Engine doesn't start or is hard to start.
2. Engine overheats.
3. Engine vibrates excessively.
4. Engine stops running and won't restart.
5. Engine misses under load or lacks power.
6. Engine knocks.
7. Engine surges (gallops).
8. Engine backfires.

Each of these problems, with the exception of numbers 3 and 6, engine knock and excessive vibration, comes primarily from trouble in one of four areas: ignition, sparkplug, fuel or compression. The sparkplug is, of course, part of the ignition system, but it's considered separately for two reasons. First, sparkplug trouble alone is often enough to create your difficulty. Second, plug problems may betray more serious trouble—more than a new plug alone can cure. But examining the plug will help you find the real problem.

Except for knocking and extreme vibration, engine troubleshooting should begin with a look at the ignition. Most small engine problems start there.

But you could face either of two types—a magneto or ignition coil system—and they're quite different. Most small one-lungers use mag-

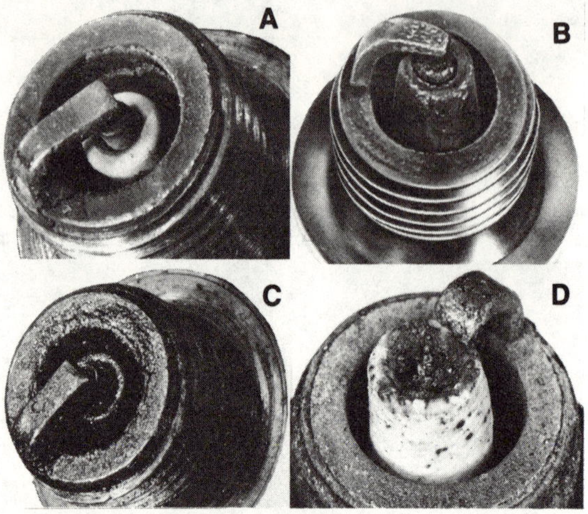

PLUG CONDITION tells tales: (a) grayish deposits and normal wear; (b) carbon fouling; (c) oil fouling; (d) badly burned sparkplug electrodes.

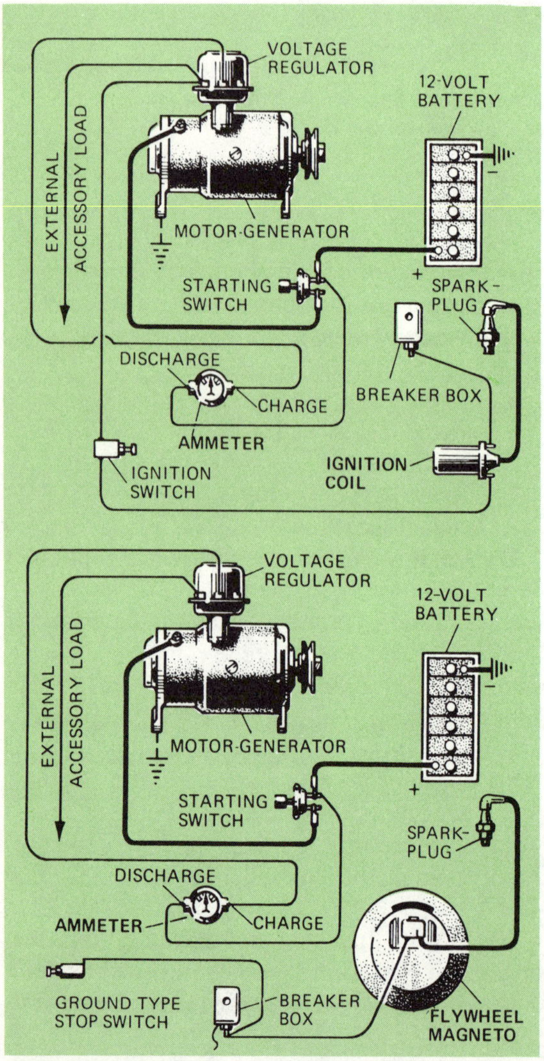

IGNITION COIL system (top) is common on garden tractors with big four-cycle engines. Most others rely on magneto ignition systems (bottom).

netos. Exceptions include some of the larger horsepower Wisconsin, Kohler and Lauson-Tecumseh four-cycle engines that are used in garden tractors.

The difference between magneto and ignition coil, simply stated, is that once the engine is running, a magneto makes its own electricity. A properly operating magneto system provides about 15 kilovolts to the sparkplug.

In the ignition-coil system, a regular automotive-type ignition coil (basically a transformer), replaces the magneto. A modern system has a 12-volt battery (charged by an alternator) providing current to the ignition coil. It steps the 12 volts up to approximately 25 kilovolts at the sparkplug.

Both magneto and ignition coil systems use breaker points. They work like switches to concentrate full voltage at the sparkplug precisely when that juice is needed to fire the fuel mix. Some recent garden tractors with Wisconsin, Kohler or Lauson-Tecumseh engines use a breakerless ignition, one that depends on solid-state devices instead of breaker points.

Breakerless ignitions provide almost 50 kilovolts at the sparkplug. And spark timing is permanently set. With mechanical points, timing can get out of adjustment. That will bring engine problems until the timing is reset.

testing a magneto

To test a magneto system, buy a 14-mm or 18-mm sparkplug at a gasoline station or auto parts supply store. Open the electrode gap to 5/32 to 3/16 in. Take the high-tension lead from the engine sparkplug and attach it firmly to the test plug. (You can leave the engine plug in place during the output test.)

To avoid a shock during this test, don't hold either the test plug or lead in your hand. Put it on the engine next to a clean ground such as a bolt. Tucking the plug under something like the choke cable or attaching it with a pair of vise-grip pliers will keep it from slipping.

Now crank the engine. If spark jumps the gap on the plug, magneto output is fine. Ignition isn't the cause of your engine problem. But if there's no spark, ignition breakdown is the source of your trouble. The magneto will probably have to be disassembled and each part tested.

Why use a separate plug for testing magneto output? Why not just pull the plug from the engine and use that? Because the wide gap of the test plug gives a more accurate indication of magneto output.

A 14-mm sparkplug gapped to .028 in. requires a magneto output of only 7 kilovolts for spark to jump the electrode gap. (Most single-cylinder small engines use 14-mm sparkplugs.) But when you open the gap to 5/32 to 3/16 in., about 10 kilovolts are required for a spark to jump the gap.

A magneto in good condition supplies approximately 15 kilovolts to a sparkplug. Thus, if your magneto cannot provide a wide-gapped test plug with sufficient voltage to make spark, it tells you that the magneto has broken down or is in process of doing so.

coil system test

A less accurate indication of output is given with the test for the ignition coil system. It's the same test, but uses the engine's sparkplug instead of a test plug.

The ignition coil system is supposed to put out about 25 kilovolts. The comparatively small amount of voltage required to make spark with a wide-gap test plug doesn't justify use of this plug for the test.

If you get any spark at all as you crank the engine, you can assume for the time being that the ignition system is okay. However, if other tests (sparkplug, fuel and compression) show these areas to be in good condition, then suspect ignition trouble and come back to it. If spark doesn't appear at the plug, try a new plug before ripping into the ignition system.

For solid-state ignition such as a breakerless system, you need a spark intensity tester. Spark occurs so rapidly that you can't see it. Grounding the plug strains solid-state components and may damage them. A spark intensity tester needn't be costly.

To use one, disconnect the lead from the sparkplug and attach the test instrument's lead to the cable's metal terminal. Touch the point of the test instrument to ground as someone cranks the engine. If the test light flashes, the ignition system is okay.

check sparkplug condition

If your engine won't start, is hard to start, or misses or lacks power, check the sparkplug. Get a new one if you find a cracked insulator, burned electrodes or heavy carbon deposits.

Make sure that electrode gap conforms to the maker's specifications. For two-cycle engines, gap is set at .028 to .033 in.; for four-cycles, it's .025 to .028 in. Check your engine manual.

Critical examination of a plug's firing end can lead you to the cause of a problem. Here are

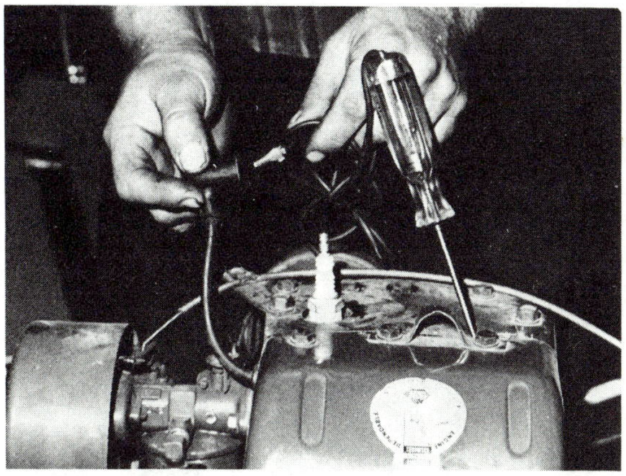

TESTING BREAKERLESS ignition systems takes a spark intensity tester hooked to the plug lead.

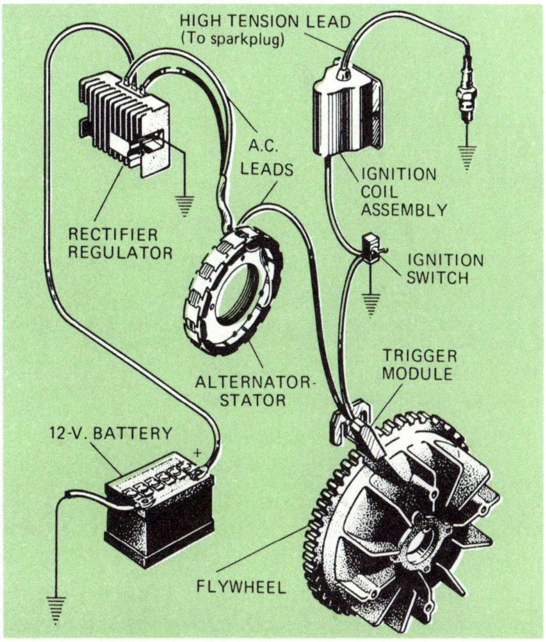

BREAKERLESS ignitions, using electronic devices, are featured on some Wisconsin, Kohler and Lauson-Tecumseh engines. The timing is thus set permanently and needs no adjusting.

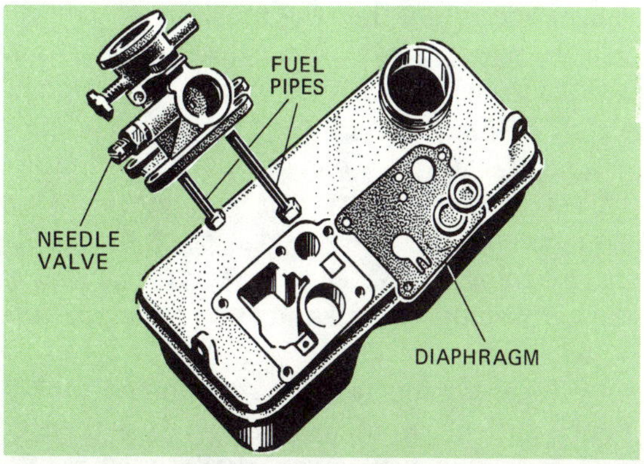

THIS DIAPHRAGM carburetor is coupled directly to the fuel tank. If the fuel's flow seems restricted, check the screens in the fuel line.

IF SQUIRTING fuel into the sparkplug hole brings a brief cure, fuel blockage is the problem.

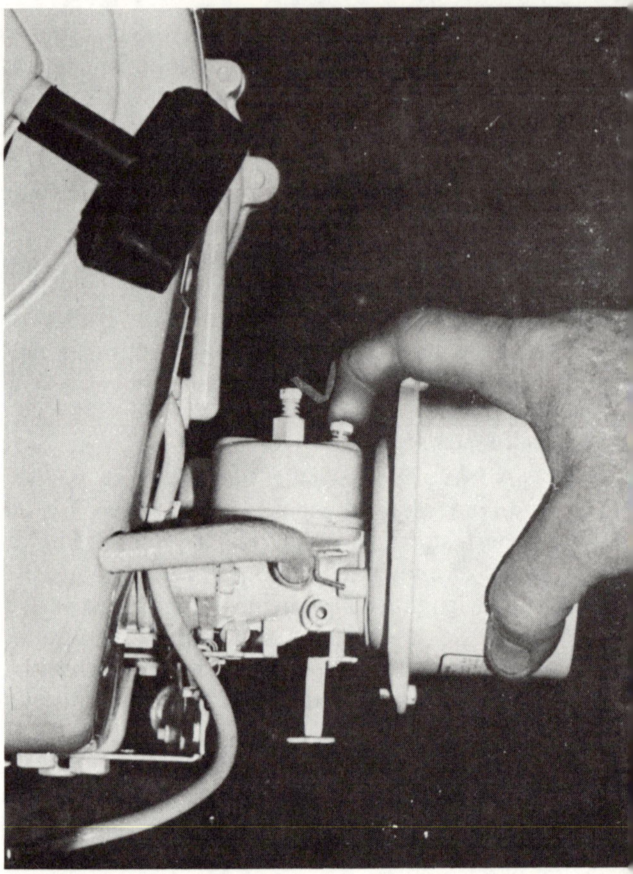

PRESSING the drain valve (arrow) on carburetor bowl shows whether fuel got that far.

some most common conditions and what they mean:

• *Normal wear.* If the sparkplug has brown or grayish-tan deposits and there is some electrode wear, the plug is wearing normally. Clean off deposits with a small wire brush, file the electrodes square and bright with an ignition point file, set electrode gap with a sparkplug feeler gauge, and return the plug to service.

If the plug shows extreme electrode wear and a pitted insulator, it's worn out. Get a new one.

• *Carbon-fouled.* A carbon-fouled sparkplug will have dry, fluffy black deposits on the tip. This is the usual result when the engine is fed an over-rich fuel mixture. It's caused by overchoking, by a clogged air cleaner restricting air flow to the carburetor, or by an incorrect fuel-mixture adjustment.

Another reason for a carbon-fouled plug is poor ignition output that results in a reduced voltage condition to cause misfiring. Check for bad breaker points, a weak coil or condenser, or a worn ignition cable.

• *Oil-fouled.* An oil-fouled sparkplug spells internal engine trouble in the form of worn piston rings or valve stems. Oil has gotten into the combustion chamber. The engine isn't meant to burn this mix, so gunky deposits build up on the electrodes.

• *Burned electrodes.* The chief cause here is an overheated engine; also check for improper ignition timing and a lean fuel mixture.

To install a sparkplug, seat it by hand. Then tighten it one-half turn with a socket wrench.

check fuel system

Make sure that fuel is getting to the carburetor and, if so, through the carburetor into the cylinder. For a quick check, crank the engine and then remove the sparkplug. If the tip of the plug is wet with fuel, your engine problem is being caused by something other than a fuel-system malfunction.

A more accurate way to see whether the fuel system is functioning is to squirt some fuel into the cylinder from a clean, trigger-type can. Only

ADEQUATE COMPRESSION? Only a gauge can tell you just what compression you're getting.

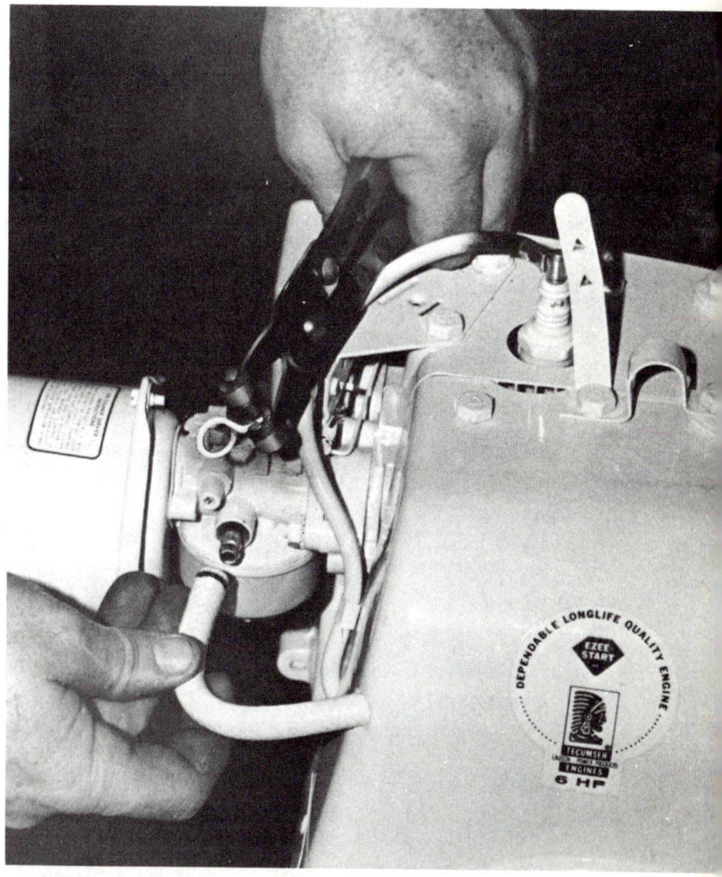

FUEL BLOCKAGE is within the carburetor if an unhooked fuel line shows fuel got that far.

two or three squirts are needed. Insert the sparkplug and try to start the engine. If the engine starts, runs for a few seconds or so, and then stops, trouble is indicated in the fuel system.

Now, where's the stoppage—upstream from the carburetor or within it? Many carburetors with bowls have a drain valve in the base of the bowl next to the main adjustment screw, which is larger. Press the drain valve. If fuel doesn't leak out, there's an obstruction in the tank or fuel line.

If there is no drain valve and the fuel line connects the tank (or fuel pump) to the carburetor inlet, simply unhook the line at the carburetor. If fuel dribbles out, it is getting to, but not through, the carburetor.

If your fuel system is the type in which carburetor and fuel tank are coupled together, fuel is fed directly from tank to carburetor through pipes attached to the carburetor. This is done by the creation of low pressure in the carburetor while the piston is moving on its downward stroke.

If the sparkplug or cylinder-loading test indicates a fuel failure, the carburetor will have to be disconnected from the fuel tank. Check the screens in the fuel pipes to determine if they are clogged. If they aren't, it's evident that the carburetor needs overhauling.

Engine trouble will also result if the fuel system floods the cylinder. If the engine doesn't start after cranking, examine the tip of the sparkplug. If it's wet with fuel, either the engine is flooding or an ignition or compression failure exists. Make ignition and compression tests to determine the problem.

test compression

If your engine has an A-1 ignition and fuel system and a brand-new sparkplug, it still won't do much unless it has compression. This is the ability of the piston to compress fuel to a point where it will ignite and burn to provide maximum power.

Compression in a single-cylinder engine is extremely important. Without the specified

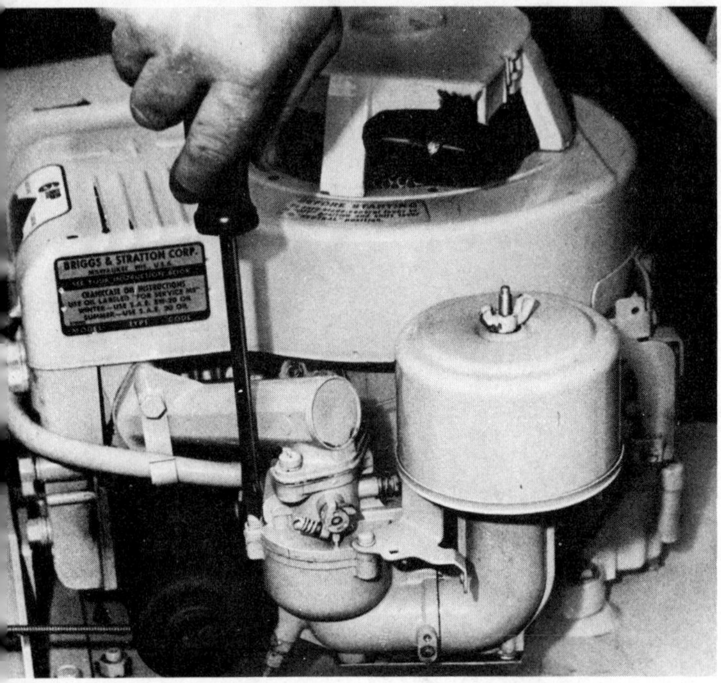

LOOSE BOLTS on the carb let extra air lean out the mixture and make starting difficult.

The fuel pump isn't suspected often, because trouble there is rare. That's why fuel pump gremlins are hard to identify when they do attack

amount, the engine will prove hard to start and will not develop maximum horsepower.

Good compression depends on engine "tightness." An engine loses compression when it loses its ability to seal. Leaks around worn rings and the piston, cylinder or valves; or a ruptured gasket, for instance, will destroy the seal and cause loss of compression.

An accurate check of compression can be made only with a compression gauge. Remove the sparkplug and hold or screw (depending on the type used) the gauge into the sparkplug hole. Crank the engine several times until the gauge gives a maximum reading.

If you are working on a two-cycle engine, the reading should be at least 60 pounds per square inch (p.s.i.). If you have a four-cycle engine of 4½-hp or less, the compression reading should be 65 to 70 p.s.i. If it's above 4½-hp, minimum compression should be 70 p.s.i.

Once the problem area has been isolated, the part (carburetor or magneto, for example) may have to be disassembled and each component checked. But if you're lucky, perhaps only an adjustment is needed.

But if repairs are required, you'll save both time and effort by following a logical sequence. Engines and cases vary, of course, so you'll have to choose the advice that applies to you.

Most problems with these simple engines, luckily, call for only simple repairs. Even so, they may be beyond either your experience or your stock of tools. Then it's time to get the help of a small-engine repair shop.

But before you do anything else, be sure the sparkplug is in good condition and properly gapped. That may be the only step necessary.

no start or hard starting

When the difficulty involves getting started, begin with the simplest, most commonly needed fixes and procede to more difficult ones as necessary. But don't pass up the things you think are obvious; check them all.

The problem generally is with either fuel or ignition. If fuel isn't getting to the engine, here's the sequence to follow:

- Is there fuel in the tank?
- Do you follow maker's instructions when starting the engine?
- Is fuel contaminated? Drain an eyedropper amount from the tank and drop it into your hand. If water or dirt remains after the fuel evaporates, remove the fuel tank, dump old fuel, and slosh the tank clean with kerosene.

Suppose you have a two-cycle engine. Naturally, the oil in the fuel mixture won't evaporate. But the gas will. And if there's water still present, it will be apparent as droplets. Dirt will make the oil feel gritty.

Never use last year's fuel in yard and garden equipment. It may not vaporize and could leave varnish on carburetor parts. Avoid trouble—always fill the tank with fresh fuel.

- Is the fuel line damaged? Replace one that's kinked. Remove the line and blow through it. If it's obstructed, clean it out or get a new one.
- Is air leaking into the fuel system because of loose bolts? Tighten all carburetor mounting bolts and fuel line connections.
- Does the choke plate fail to close fully as you start the engine? Then clean dirt from around the plate and shaft with a carburetor cleaning solvent. Make sure that the choke cable, if there is one, is neither kinked nor broken.

Some model engines, such as the Briggs & Stratton 92000, built since August 1968 and Wisconsin's ACN and BKN, feature an automatic choke. The B & S system is fully automatic. With the Wisconsin setup, you must close the choke plate by hand, but it opens by itself when the engine starts.

If the choke shaft and plate are clean and these chokes still don't work right, dismantle the carburetor to get at the internal choke elements. They should be cleaned and some may have to be replaced.

• Is the fuel filter clogged, obstructing fuel flow? Engines that employ float-type carburetors generally have a wire-mesh screen fuel filter in the tank-to-fuel line adapter. Remove it by unscrewing the adapter and wash it in gasoline.

On large engines, the standard filter is a sediment bowl housing a ceramic element. Shut off the fuel valve, drop and clean the bowl, and swish the element in clean gasoline.

• Is the fuel pump shot? If your engine has a fuel pump (it will unless it has a gravity-feed fuel system), it can be either a mechanical type that works off an eccentric on the engine crankshaft or what's called a diaphragm type that operates in relation to engine vacuum. Don't let terminology mislead you; mechanical pumps also have diaphragms.

Fuel pumps are usually found in the fuel line between fuel tank and carburetor. Engines with diaphragm carburetors, however, have the fuel pump built into the carburetor. You can't see the diaphragm element unless the carburetor comes off, which is what has to happen if you suspect fuel-pump failure. The fuel pump isn't suspect often, because trouble isn't common—that's why it's tough to find when it does crop up.

Pumps fail mainly when bolts work loose, and the pump starts to pull in air that leans out the fuel mixture. Pump diaphragms can develop leaks, but you'll rarely find one that abruptly quits pulsating so the engine won't start. Rather, an engine with a faulty fuel-pump diaphragm will stall when revved up as a result of an insufficient delivery of fuel at higher speeds. Replace the diaphragm. Once the cover comes off, replace the gasket.

• What about the carburetor? If you haven't yet discovered why the engine is starving for fuel, it's probably in the carburetor—dirt-clogged parts or passages. Disassemble and clean it thoroughly in carburetor solvent. The task is easy enough with proper instructions from the manufacturer of your engine; give him the en-

SIMPLY CLEANING the choke plate and carburetor linkage may well solve hard starting problems.

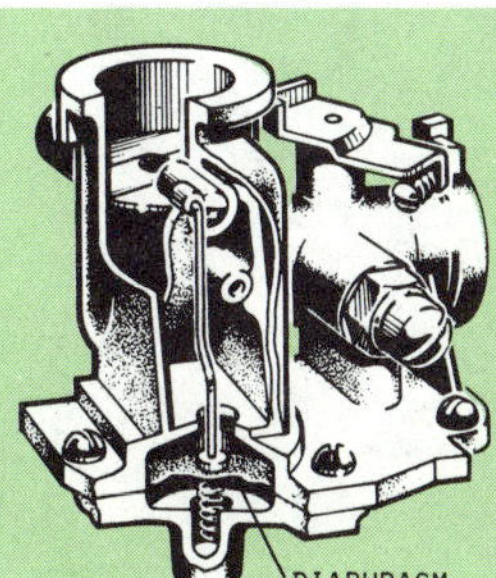

BRIGGS & Stratton 92000 and Wisconsin ACN and BKN engines have automatic chokes. B&S carb (left) has diaphragm inside. Cleaning, replacing parts requires you to strip the carb.

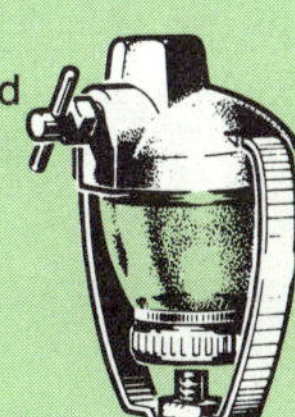

SEDIMENT BOWL is often used as a fuel filter. Its ceramic element, other parts can be cleaned and reused.

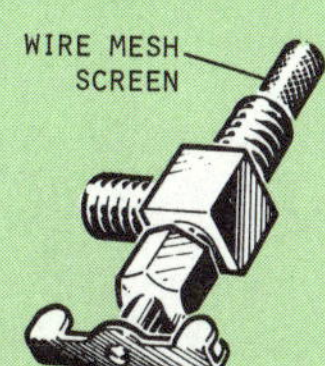

SHUTOFF ADAPTER (left) has cleanable mesh filter, most common with float-type carburetor set-ups.

LAUSON-TECUMSEH carb has an internal fuel pump. To cure trouble here, you remove the carburetor, clean the cavity and replace the element.

EXTERNAL FUEL pump "failure" may come simply from loose bolts that admit extra air.

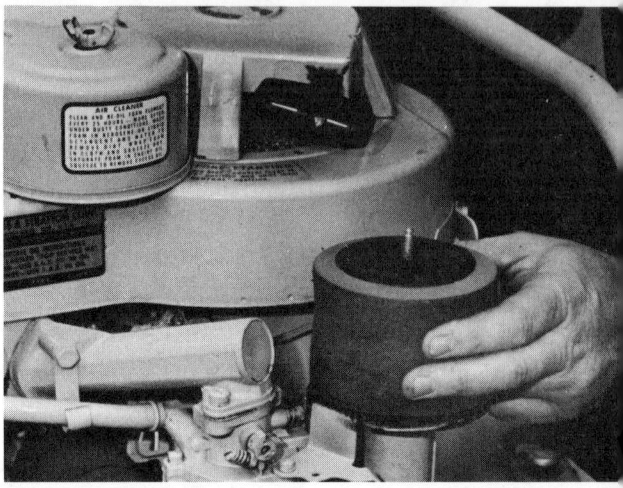

ENGINE FLOODING can often be traced to a dirty air cleaner that acts like a choke.

TRY LOOSENING a stuck needle valve by rapping the carburetor bowl smartly.

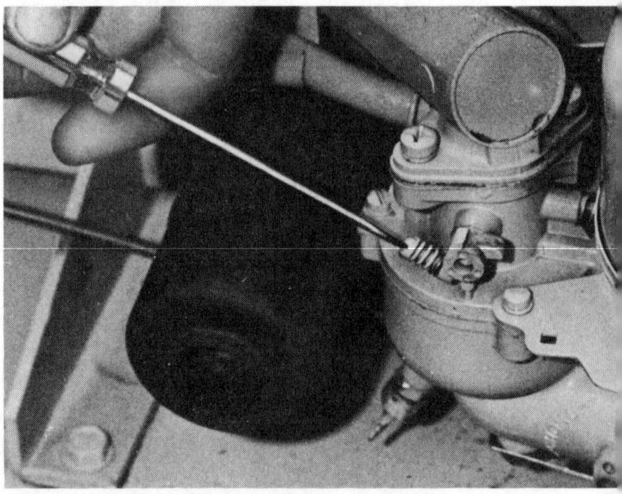

ADJUST IDLE speed by backing off the screw. Return it just to the throttle—plus one turn.

gine's model and serial number. They're on the nameplate.

too much fuel?

Fuel starvation isn't the only danger. The fuel system can also keep the engine from starting by flooding it. Check:

1. *Does the choke open fully as soon as the engine starts?* If not, repair as described above.

2. *Is engine flooding caused by a dirty air cleaner?* This is common and should be checked before you start twirling carburetor adjustment screws. Clean it if that's needed.

3. *Is dirt holding the needle valve open?* This is likely if fuel drips from a float-type carburetor. Often, rapping the bowl lightly with a screwdriver handle will remedy the problem. If not, dismantle and clean the carburetor.

4. *Is the carburetor out of adjustment?* Specific adjustment details will have to be obtained from the manufacturer. Meanwhile, an approximate adjustment is possible if you don't have fixed jets.

Turn the main-mixture and idle-mixture needles in until they're finger-tight—then back off one turn. To adjust idle speed, back the screw free and turn it back in until it just touches the throttle lever—and continue for a full turn.

how about ignition?

Ignition failure usually comes from a bad plug or breaker points. Often, getting at the points is the big part of the job.

There's no sweat if you have external points under a cover attached to the engine. If breaker points are internal (under the flywheel, as in

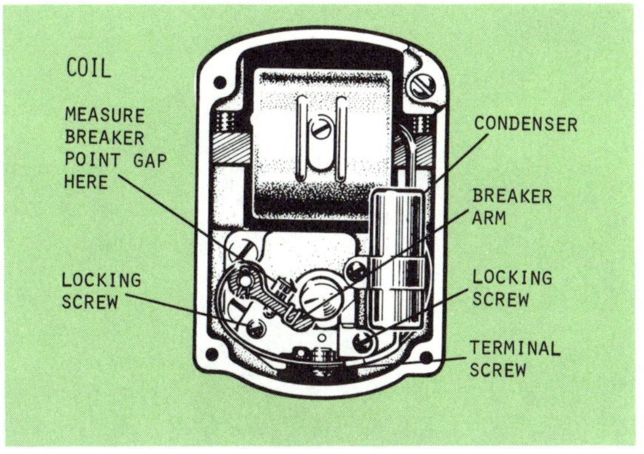

BREAKER POINTS on big Wisconsin and Kohler engines are easy to adjust, repair or replace.

FLYWHEEL NUT comes off with a socket wrench, but you may also need a flywheel holder such as this.

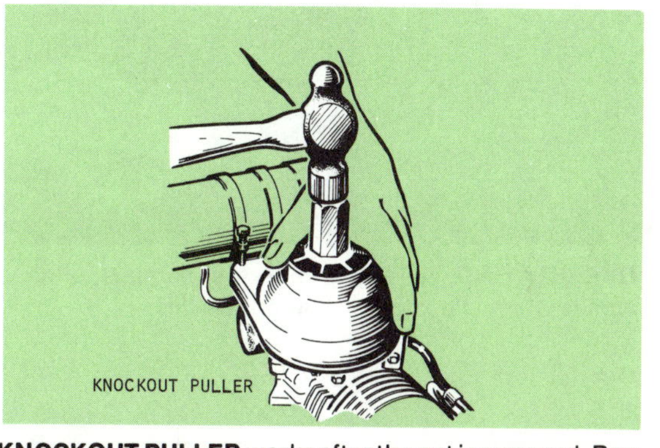

KNOCKOUT PULLER works after the nut is removed. Rap it sharply to jar the wheel loose.

magneto ignition systems), the problem is removing the flywheel. First, make sure the problem isn't some minor thing such as the engine stop device being in the "off" position or a weak battery or bad sparkplug cable.

removing the flywheel

Your flywheel removal method depends on the kind you have. There are two general approaches.

The flywheel nut on most two-cycle engines (you have to check whether it has a left- or right-hand thread) comes off with a socket wrench. If the nut is stubborn, rap the wrench bar with a soft hammer. A flywheel holder will help if the wheel turns with the nut.

A flywheel holder is necessary to remove the nut on most four-cycle engines. Then remove the flywheel. Some take a knockout puller; hold the flywheel firmly and rap the puller with a hammer to jar the wheel loose. Flywheels with holes for the purpose—often on engines of 3½ hp or more—take a special flywheel puller.

Check that all ignition leads are clean and tight and be sure no high-tension wire is shorting.

Check the point gap; usually it should be .020 in., but verify that with the owner's manual. And replace any burned or pitted ignition points. If you find that's often necessary, the condenser needs replacing, too.

If you still don't get a spark, all ignition parts should be tested on an analyzer and timing should be adjusted to specifications.

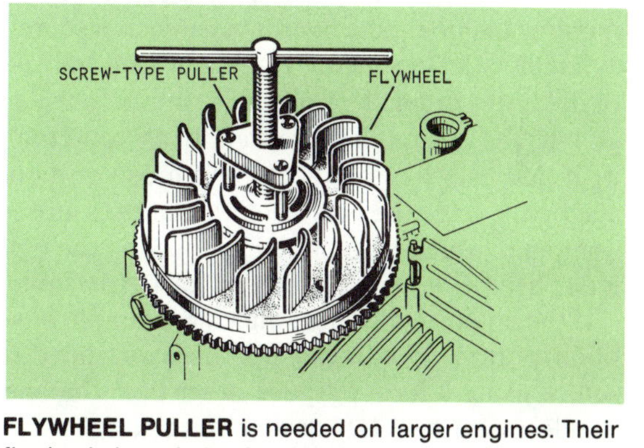

FLYWHEEL PULLER is needed on larger engines. Their flywheels have holes for it to grab.

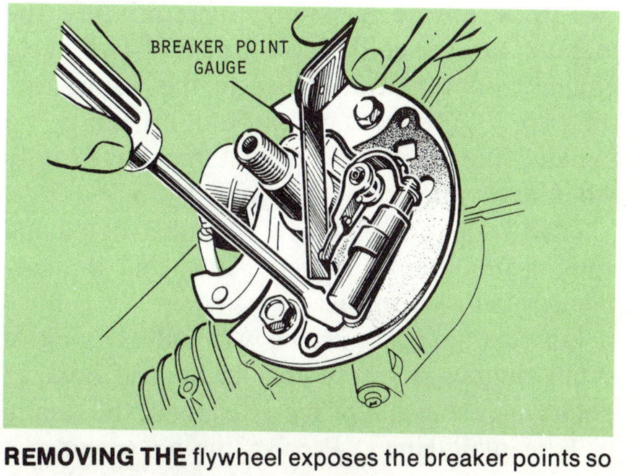

REMOVING THE flywheel exposes the breaker points so they can be replaced or adjusted.

OVERHEATING, especially on mower engines, often comes when clippings pile up on the fins.

TIGHTEN THE cylinder head bolts frequently to close gaps and prevent compression loss.

not enough compression

This is caused most often by a problem that requires major engine overhaul, such as a scored cylinder, sticking piston rings, sticking valves, or defective crankshaft oil seals. But before you go into the engine, listen carefully as you crank it. If you hear a hiss, check for a loose or damaged plug since the hiss could mean pressure is escaping around it. Otherwise it means the cylinder head is loose or the head gasket is shot.

If the engine overheats, check the simple possibilities first. The engine can be overloaded if you're using it for a purpose other than the one it's designed for. Be sure the crankcase of a four-cycle engine is filled with oil—and that a two-cycle engine has the oil-gas mixture the manufacturer specifies. No cause of two-cycle engine trouble outranks use of the wrong fuel mixture. Outboard oil should normally be avoided like the plague, since it thickens heavily when it gets hot.

Then be sure the air flow is unobstructed and cooling fins aren't clogged. Also, that the carburetor isn't set too lean.

Ignition timing could be way off. Timing of small engines is rarely very critical; if breaker points are clean and properly gapped, the timing will be maintained. Precise timing requires a special gauge.

If everything else thus far has failed to cure overheating, carbon has probably built up in the combustion chamber. It will require cleaning.

other engine problems

There are several more kinds of engine problems. When the cause of each is determined, repairs are often simple.

If your engine cuts out while running, check first for ample uncontaminated fuel. Engine heat reaching the fuel line can cause vapor lock. If this seems likely, pour cold water over the fuel line—but don't get any in the carburetor. Be sure the air flow is clear and cooling fins aren't obstructed.

Possible reasons for a missing engine include contaminated fuel, an over-wide plug gap, damaged plug, loose ignition wires, pitted or worn breaker points or compression failure.

A partially or intermittently plugged tank vent can cause the engine to gallop from time to time. Dirty, sticking carb linkage can do that too, if the carb tends to flood at times. Clean the linkage and apply white grease. The same thing may be needed on the governor.

Contaminated fuel or an over-lean mixture can also cause backfiring. If fresh fuel doesn't help, be sure timing is OK. Otherwise you have a sticking valve or valves.

EXCESSIVE vibration from loose mounting bolts can also loosen the muffler hangars.

Any small engine vibrates, but if vibration loosens mounting bolts, it's serious. This can lead to more vibration and even major damage. Tightening bolts and fasteners periodically is always sensible and may do the trick. Otherwise check the balance of such associated gear as mower blades. If that doesn't help, suspect a bent crankshaft.

If the engine knocks, check first for overheating and contaminated fuel. Then be sure timing isn't overadvanced and that the flywheel is tight. If that doesn't work, pull the cylinder head and clean carbon from it and the piston crown. Finally, overhaul the engine. The connecting rod has gone bad.

maintenance is always easier

Giving small engines periodic care is easier than repairing them.

Each time you use the engine, clean out shrouds and exhaust ports. Check oil level in a four-cycle engine.

Every 25 hours of running, change oil in a four-cycle. Tighten all body bolts and fasteners. And clean oil-bath air-filter systems. Other filters should be cleaned or replaced every 50 hours.

Every 100 hours, clean the fuel filter and service the sparkplug and breaker points.

Chain saw saga

WAYNE IS A competent home mechanic. That's often true of people who came off the farm as kids. But he found The Saga of the Chain Saw to be a detective story that almost defeated him, his experience, and his logical attack.

Wayne had bought a new chain saw at a bargain and waited for a chance to put it to work. Then an available Saturday afternoon turned up with a couple of free hours and some trees that needed pruning. Aha!

But the saw wouldn't start.

The tank had just been filled with the right oil-gas mix. The toggle switch was at ON. He flipped it back and forth a few times to be sure nothing was gumming up the contacts. A quick tingle, when he apparently touched something he shouldn't have, at least assured him there was juice in the electrical system.

It's a rule of thumb that the ignition is the better place to start troubleshooting, but that little shock told him electricity was flowing, so Wayne went on to the fuel system. He cranked the engine several times, then pulled the sparkplug. It was almost dripping with fuel, so there was no block between the tank and the combustion chamber.

Pull-cord resistance seemed to guarantee compression was OK. Anyway, poor compression shouldn't account for the refusal to start. Maybe for poor power, but this was a *no*-power situation.

A word about small engines' magneto systems is in order here. The ON-OFF switch is closed at OFF. The principle is simple: This just offers the mag's electrical output an easier path to the ground. The sparkplug circuitry has lots of resistance, so the bulk of the current shifts promptly away from the plug.

Wayne is experienced enough so he checked, repeatedly, to be sure the switch wasn't knocked accidentally to OFF. That it was still open, routing all the mag output to the plug.

But not until he studied the back of the switch did he realize the connector was grounding on the engine cover. In effect, it *was* OFF. That also accounted for the electrical tickle he'd gotten. So Wayne bent the connector post away from the cover and wrapped the connection in tape.

And pruned the offending limbs.

Remodel your entry without remodeling

By HARRY WICKS

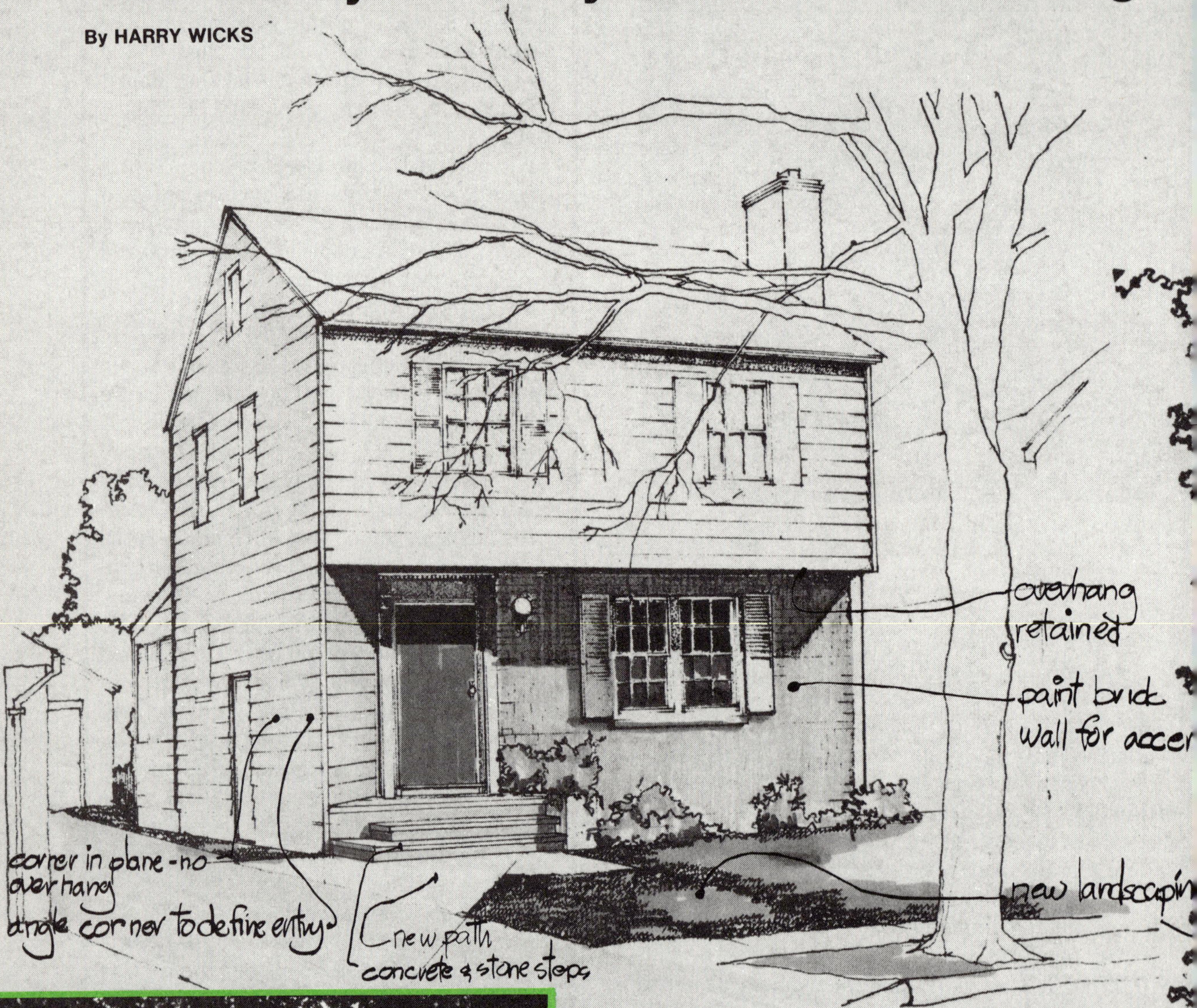

ENTRY NOW DEFINED

This recent-vintage house is of the style called stockade. Photo shows that it is neat and trim, but lacks any visual interest. Grandberg achieves this by painting the brick wall a pastel yellow, extending the corner (left of doorway) to be in same plane as overhang, and installing siding on the diagonal. Wide steps replace narrow ones.

SEE ALSO

Floors . . . Home improvement . . . Measurements . . . Pier sets . . . Quarry tile . . . Remodeling . . . Room dividers . . . Storage walls . . . Tile, floor . . . Tile, wall . . . Wallpaper

"YOU DON'T HAVE to spend a bundle to modernize your house front," says architect Ira Grandberg, AIA. "Dramatic changes can be made by simply concentrating on front-yard landscaping." There are two big advantages to upgrading a house front mostly through landscaping:

- Almost all such improvements can be handled by do-it-youselfers. Not having to call in a professional means saved dollars.
- In most cases, the project can take place in stages—you needn't finish the entire job in one shot. For example, you might put in new steps and walkway this year; add a planter and light, next.

In some cases, carpentry is required. The ranch home, for instance, is greatly enhanced by the front-door makeover. But it is not a must—the landscaping alone provides dramatic visual change.

RETAIN EXISTING CHARM

This marvelous country home has a lot going for it, but its front entry is not clearly defined. Here PM's architect extends the front porch for function as well as esthetics. Seating is built into the deck for outdoor living and large step area is placed to direct attention to the front door (which can be painted for emphasis). The extra-wide, brick-in-sand walkway adds to the house's rural charm. The lamp, though contemporary, blends well. The challenge here was to avoid losing the home's interesting architectural details.

REMOVE A MISMATCHED ROOF

Changes here start with carpentry on the entry module. Original detailing is typical of better-built homes in the '20s. But for a modern look Grandberg replaces the A-roof with one pitched to match the slope of the main roof. For dramatic natural-light effect inside, he suggests using sheet acrylic rather than sheathing and shingles overhead. He accentuates the greenhouse look with a glass side-light to the right of the door. Greenery contained in railroad tie planters replaces large bushes in front. A new walk built of Belgian block retains the home's connection to earlier years.

LET THERE BE LIGHT

This ranch house is only 20 years old, but it also needs some front-entry rethinking. The home immediately ''plugs into its surroundings'' when railroad-tie planters and plants carefully selected to emphasize the entrance replace oversize shrubbery. For the owner who opts to go all the way, windows at right are converted to sliders and some carpenter surgery is performed on and over the door. The glass side-light, clerestory window and sheet acrylic skylight look great from the outside, give that ''open'' feeling from the inside. Notice that wider steps are now in line with the front plane of the house.

REJUVENATE A CAPE COD

The standard Cape Cod with front-to-back roof was, perhaps, the most challenging overhaul. Any house changes would not have been minor cost items, so architect Grandberg confined himself to landscaping ideas. He relocated the front walk to make the property appear larger, placed low plantings along the walk to direct a viewer's eye to the front door, put in a new paving-stone walk to retain the Early American flavor and added a light at the steps to assure the user's safety and convenience.

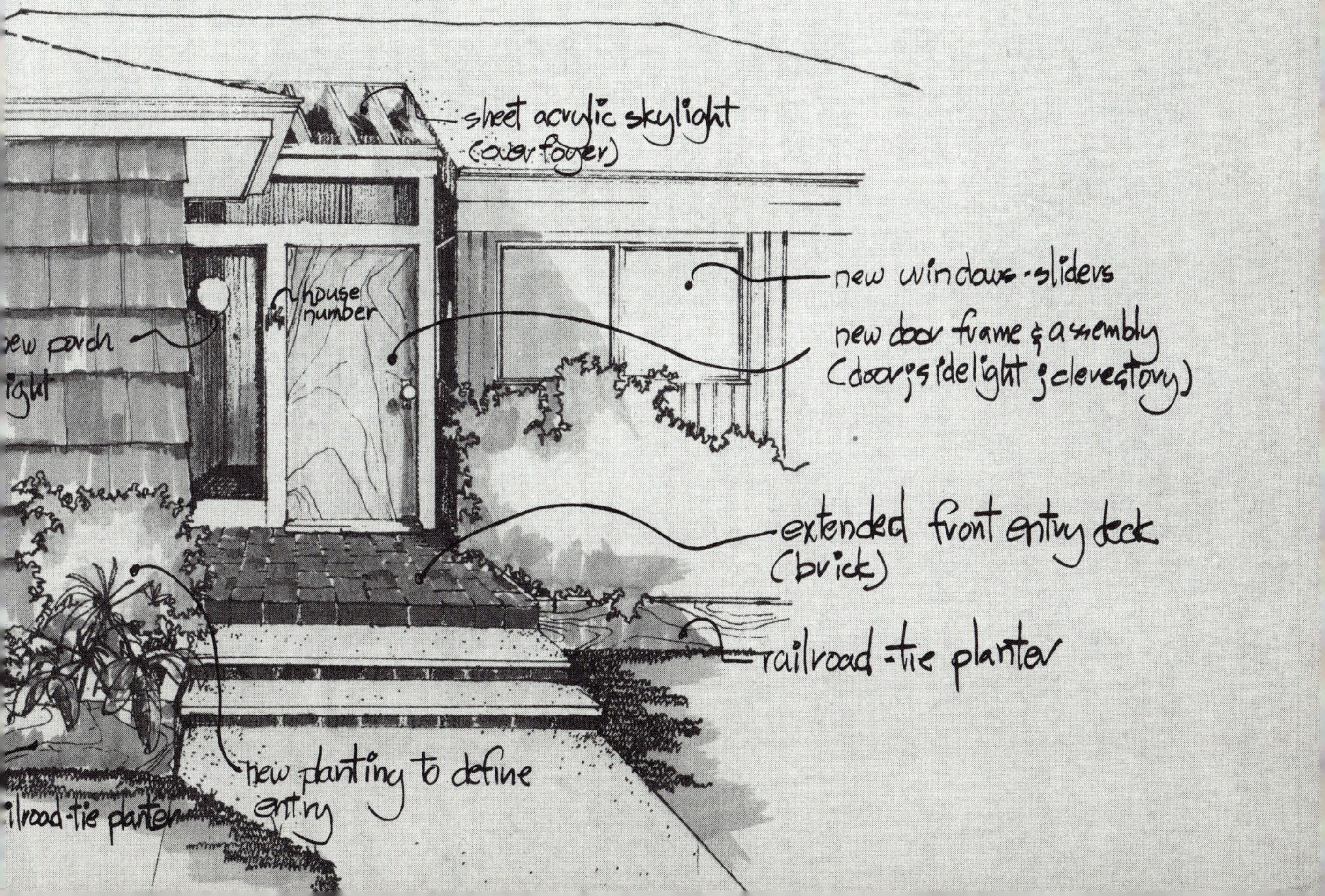

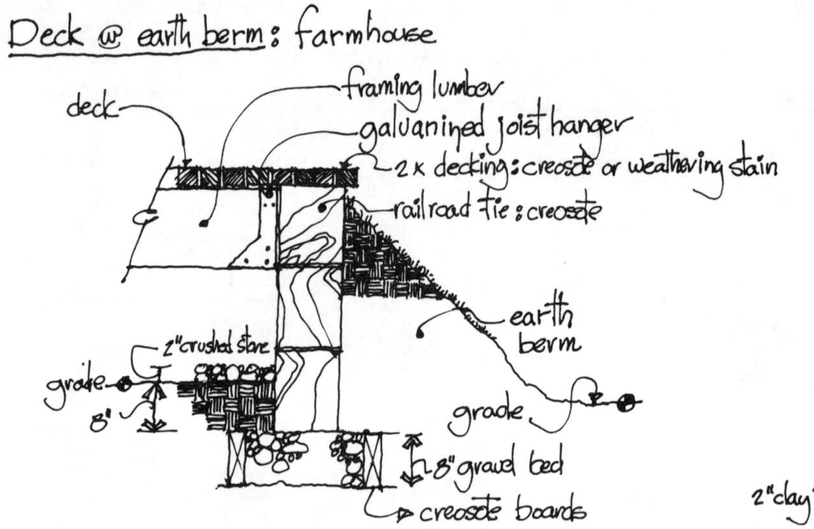

FARMHOUSE DECK gains close-to-earth look because of earth berm sloped against deck's front and side edges. Railroad ties are specified for supporting the wall because they come pressure-treated with creosote penetrating to their centers.

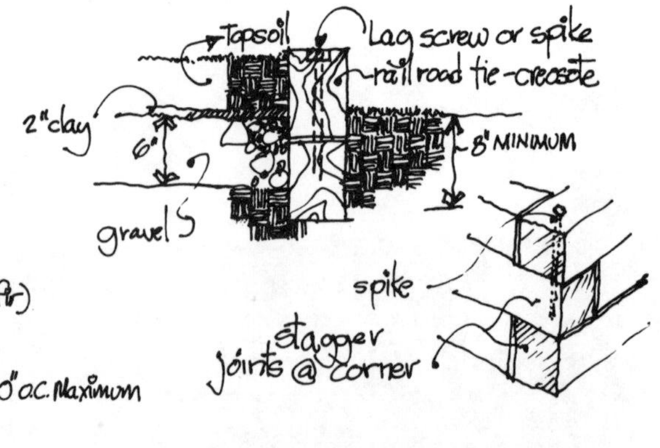

PLANTERS are made by stacking ties as shown. Gravel below the layer of clay assures good drainage. In order to spike ties together, you must first bore pilot holes with a carbide-tipped bit and a bit extension. Bore at a slow speed.

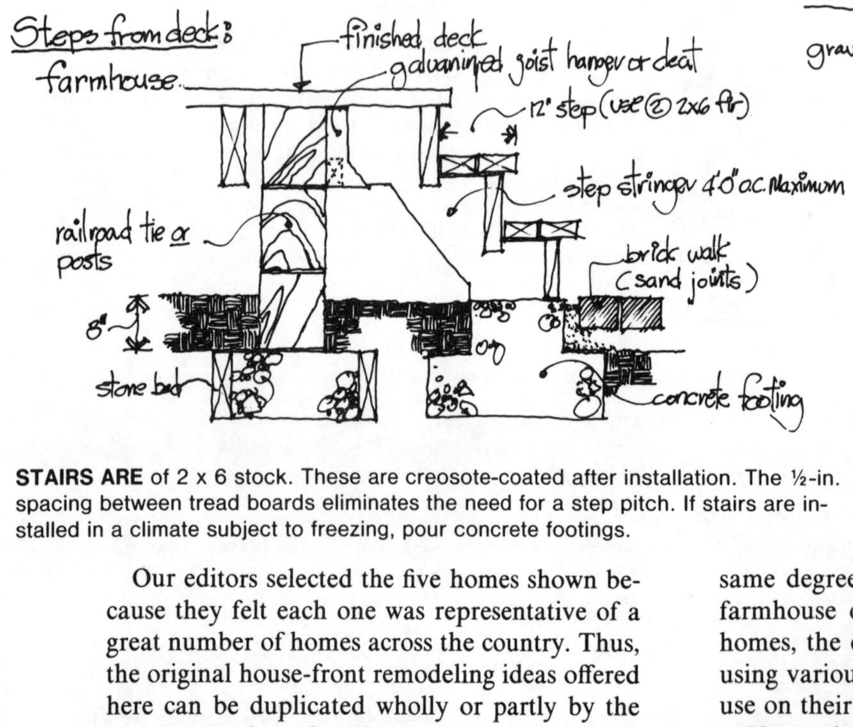

STAIRS ARE of 2 x 6 stock. These are creosote-coated after installation. The ½-in. spacing between tread boards eliminates the need for a step pitch. If stairs are installed in a climate subject to freezing, pour concrete footings.

Our editors selected the five homes shown because they felt each one was representative of a great number of homes across the country. Thus, the original house-front remodeling ideas offered here can be duplicated wholly or partly by the greatest number of readers.

In all of these home types you can accomplish a quick improvement merely by doing some landscaping. This work, of course, can be a 100-percent do-it-yourself effort to keep cash outlay to a minimum. On the other hand, if your house front is in sore need of a remake and your budget and time allow, you can consider making one or more of the carpentry changes shown on pages 1140 to 1143.

Most building and design experts agree that the principal shortcoming in many home designs is the lack of a center of interest on the house front. The ranch house on page 1142, while of fairly recent vintage, lacks this feature to the same degree (if not more) than the century-old farmhouse on page 1141. Thus in all example homes, the challenge was to create focal centers using various design devices—that readers could use on their homes, no matter what style.

If your house closely approximates one of the homes shown, it is simply a matter of more or less duplicating what you see. Or you can customize the suggested changes so they reflect your personal preferences. If your house doesn't match any of those we renovated on the drawing board, study the sketches so you will know exactly what it takes to create a visual focal point.

Here's a quick rundown on suggested changes for the houses shown:

■ **Stockade house.** This typifies those homes built in many suburban areas during the postwar boom. It is clean-looking, trim and without any unnecessary frills or gingerbread. If it is located in a tract of, say, 50 homes, it is one of perhaps

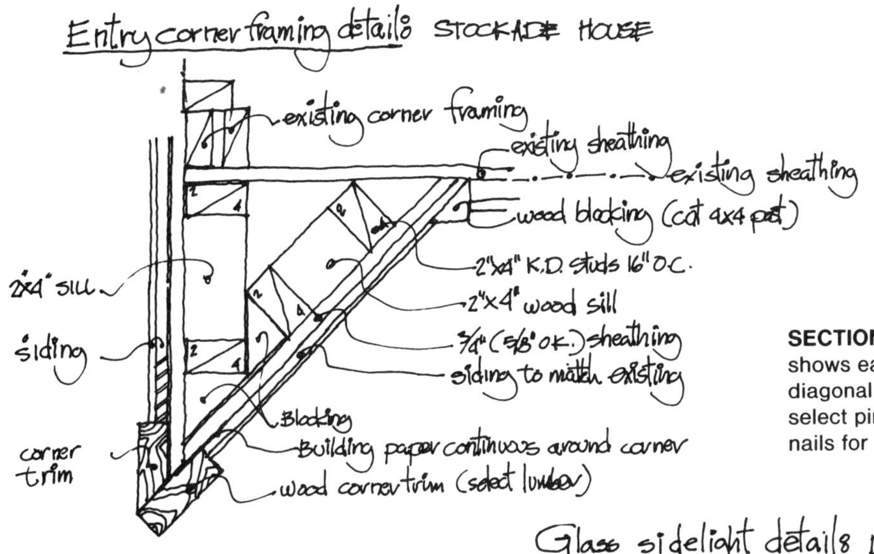

SECTION DRAWING through corner shows easy framing method used to create diagonal corner on stockade house. Use select pine for corner trim and galvanized nails for *all* fastening.

TO BUILD sidelight, rip rabbeted jamb stock on your table saw, then frame opening to suit and have glass custom-cut. Set wooden stop in caulk for draft and waterproof joints.

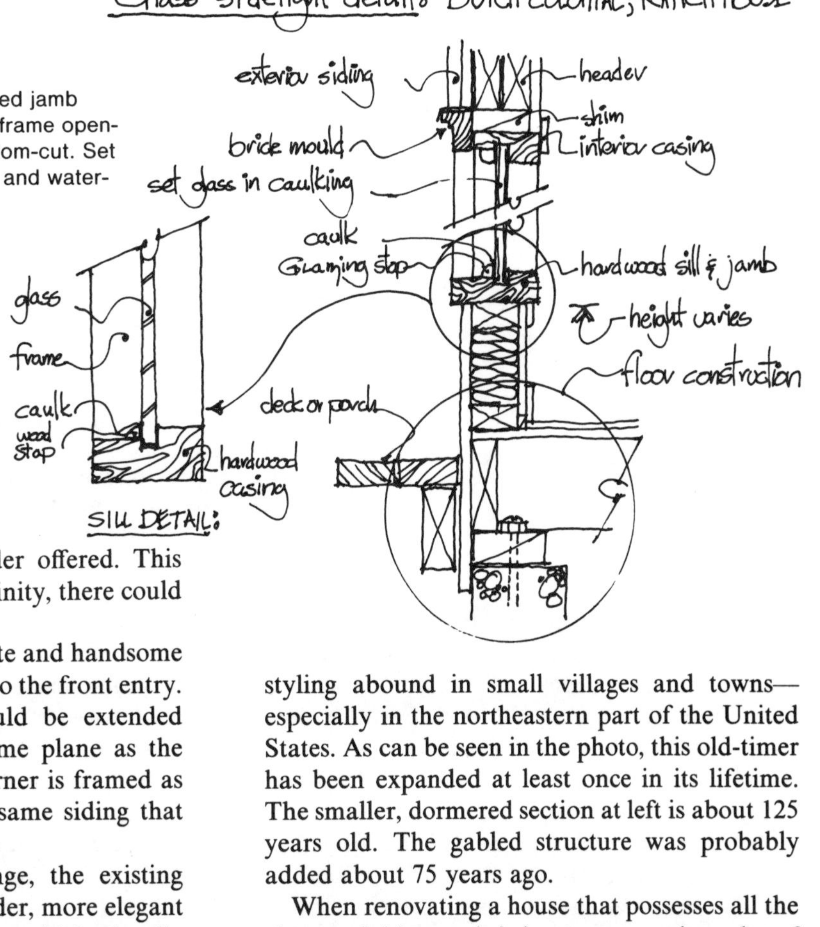

three or four models the builder offered. This means that in the immediate vicinity, there could be 15 or so look-alikes.

One way to effect an immediate and handsome change is by directing attention to the front entry. Here the left front corner could be extended forward so that it is in the same plane as the overhang corner above. The corner is framed as shown and then clad with the same siding that covers the overhang.

Along with the corner change, the existing narrow steps are replaced by wider, more elegant ones. The old walk to the front—which visually breaks up the small front yard, is removed and a new walk is installed from steps to driveway. The final touch is to paint the brick veneer a pleasing pastel color for accent.

All changes channel your attention to the entry with the result that the house now has a focal center of interest.

■ **Farmhouse.** Though this dwelling is situated in the country, homes of this type of architectural styling abound in small villages and towns—especially in the northeastern part of the United States. As can be seen in the photo, this old-timer has been expanded at least once in its lifetime. The smaller, dormered section at left is about 125 years old. The gabled structure was probably added about 75 years ago.

When renovating a house that possesses all the charm of this one, it is important to give a lot of thought in advance to what *should not* be changed at all. For example, the feeling achieved by the various design elements is good: Dormers are interesting, windows are well placed and the porch adds a charm that you would be hard-pressed to improve. As a result, our suggested "changes" aren't really changes, but add-ons.

A wooden deck is added at the front right at the same elevation as the existing porch. Instead

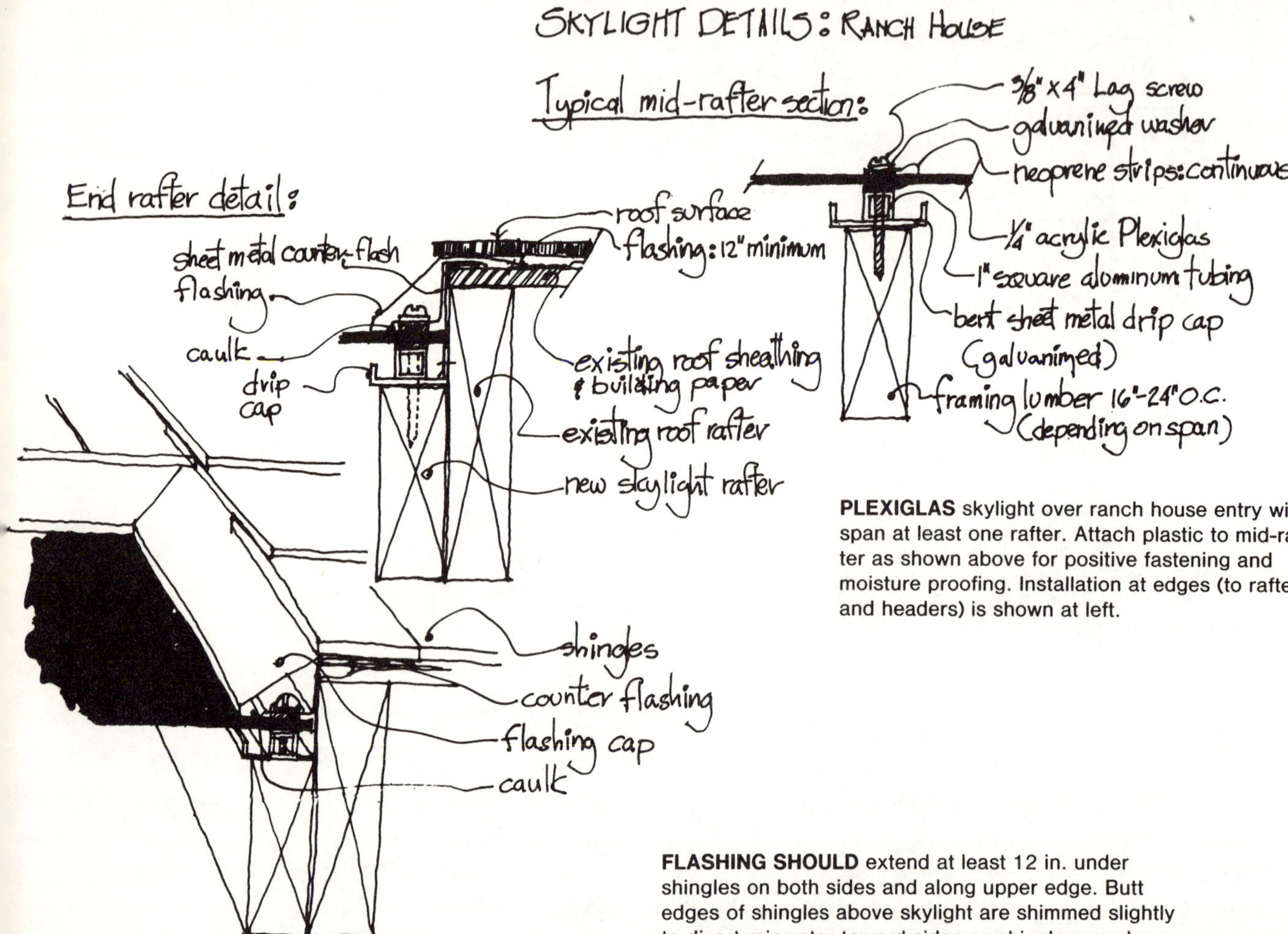

PLEXIGLAS skylight over ranch house entry will span at least one rafter. Attach plastic to mid-rafter as shown above for positive fastening and moisture proofing. Installation at edges (to rafters and headers) is shown at left.

FLASHING SHOULD extend at least 12 in. under shingles on both sides and along upper edge. Butt edges of shingles above skylight are shimmed slightly to divert rainwater toward sides so shingle granules will not wash over—and scratch—the plastic skylight.

of having the porch underpinnings exposed, an earth berm gently slopes up to cover ties. Grand-scale steps added to deck and porch direct the eye to the front door—which heretofore was anonymous, thus hard to spot. Again the change is simply a matter of routing attention to the front entry.

■ **Two-level colonial.** You needn't be an architect to realize that the front entry on this house is not the best match possible with the house proper; its oversize A-roof line visually fights the other two roof lines. The new plantings and walkway here make an impressive change all by themselves. However it might be a good idea to consider modifying the entry's roof along the style shown here. In PM's version the A is replaced with a shed-type roof. The shingles disappear and in their place we find sheet-acrylic plastic installed to give a greenhouse effect. A rectangular flush door replaces the old one (with its half-moon top) and a sidelight complements the skylight.

■ **Ranch house.** This home is improved almost instantly with some common-sense plantings and planters. For many, these changes would suffice. Others, however, may elect to go all the way and install a sidelight and skylight as shown.

As can be seen in the before photo, the front entry is dark and receding—really just the opposite of what a good entry is all about. The three areas of change—carpentry to the house, new landscaping and a large front step moved in line with the house front plane, changes that look by 180°.

■ **Cape Cod house.** Changes suggested for this cozy and familiar house all have to do with landscaping. Here it is a matter of rerouting the front walk—to make the yard appear larger—and to add plantings that blend with the house and serve to direct the viewer's eye.

Seeding after tree removal

The city removed a diseased elm tree from my curb early in spring and the stump was shredded. I removed shreddings, then lifted and leveled the sod about the stump. I put about 4 in. of black soil in the hole, mixed in fertilizer and seeded the area. But the seeding, even with regular watering, is yellowish colored, appears stunted and looks as if it may die out. What's wrong?—S.H., Ill.

Perhaps you did not remove all shavings or shreddings. This usually is necessary when you seed immediately after tree removal. Refill the hole a little over-full with fresh, new soil mixed with an organic fertilizer, such as sheep or cattle manure, and tamp lightly with the garden rake to pulverize all lumps. Make sure the surface soil, especially, is uniformly fine. Then spread seed evenly (not too heavily) over the surface with the fingers and pat it in with the palm of your hand. Don't rake seed in; this tends to bunch it, leaving bare spaces. Cover with an even, rather open layer of wheat straw or burlap, then ring the seeded area with white stakes and cord or light chain to warn passersby not to walk over the new seeding. Sprinkle the area at regular intervals using a fine spray and sufficient water to soak the soil to a depth of 5 or 6 in. Pull out any weeds that appear and don't use your mower until the new seeding is 1½ to 2 in. high.

Tricky plaster patch

A plaster break has me stumped. It's in a corner where the ceiling and two walls meet, the opening being a little over half-fist size. There seems to be no backing; the patching falls out as fast as I apply it. Should I hire a pro or is there some simple trick for this sort of thing?—R.N., N.M.

I know of no sleight-of-hand method, but I once patched a similar opening with a fold of paper, some heavy thread and lots of patience. This opening, similar to the one you describe, was apparently caused by a blow from some heavy object which broke the wood lath.

Inexperienced at that time, I tried several procedures without success. Then I hit on the idea of wrapping several thicknesses of heavy paper around a card strip cut wide enough to cover the opening with some to spare. I bent this to a right angle and needled two short lengths of thread through the paper and cardboard near the center of each flap. With the thread I held the improvised backing in place while I built up the plaster patch to a depth slightly less than that of the original. I let this set, clipped the threads, troweled on a finish coat and then smoothed the surface with sandpaper thumbtacked to a small block. So far as I know, that patch is still there.

Fuel-oil stain on concrete

I've replaced my oil-burning furnace with a gas-fired unit. A fuel-oil stain remains on the floor just in front of the new installation. It is about 2 sq. ft. in area and although it is in a small room separate from the rest of the basement, the stain bothers me because of its unsightliness. Can I remove or conceal it?—T.S., Ind.

A fuel-oil stain on concrete, especially if it's more than a month old, is difficult to remove entirely by any ordinary procedure safe for use in the home. Solvents that will do the trick, as a rule, are highly volatile, flammable, and usually toxic in a closed room, so I hesitate to suggest their use in the home. I once had a problem like yours, although the area involved was somewhat less. I used a liquid household cleaner and solvent sold under the trade name of "Amway," applying it full strength with a vinyl sponge and rinsing the area with clean water after each of the several applications necessary to reduce the stain to near invisibility. The procedure appears to have been successful as the stain has not reappeared in several months. At least I'm satisfied with the result. Of course, it takes lots of scrubbing and cleanup and the time necessary to carry out several applications.

Peeling paint at picture window

Paint peels on an inside wall just under corner of my picture window. Plaster is discolored and feels damp. The window does not sweat. Can this be condensation, or a leak?—Robert Henry, Alliance, Neb.

It's quite likely a leak, or leaks. Water may be getting inside the framing and running down to the lower corners of the window opening. I suggest that if you caulk these particular areas, your troubles should be over.

Winter mold

This spring my lawn turned up a number of patches of dead grass—and I mean dead. I've been advised to rake off all the residue, rework the soil and reseed, but I don't want to do this until I'm sure of the cause. Can you name it and tell me what to do?—R.Y., Minn.

The cause is probably what's known as "winter mold," or perhaps more properly, "snow mold." Usually it's traceable to a fungus, so you'll need to remove the dead grass, plants and roots. Burn these and then treat the soil with a suitable fungicide. The latter, with instructions, will be available through your local dealer.

Translucent panels transform your entry

By ROSARIO CAPOTOSTO

If the foyer in your home looks a little drab, you can perk it up easily and inexpensively by remodeling the door and adding a filigree-paneled archway. You can do it yourself with a minimum cash outlay

■ ARCHITECTURAL STYLES have been changing dramatically since the post-World War II building boom, but there's one design feature that's found in nearly every home built in the last two decades. It's the lackluster front-door foyer. Fortunately, it doesn't take much effort, imagination or money to brighten up a drab entryway.

Starting with the conventional front door shown at right, we ended up with a bright, cheerful entry (above) that really does *welcome* people to our house.

The job can be tackled in two stages, if you desire. But, to assure continuity of design, lay out the *total* project at one time. If you don't, you may be tempted to change style slightly when you start the second stage. The result then is almost certain to show that you changed your mind in mid-project.

Once we settled on our overall design, material selection was a snap. Translucent panels in the door and arch and the filigree are manufactured by Masonite Corp., 29 N. Wacker Drive, Chicago, IL 60606. Walls in the foyer were skinned with Tuscany Travertine planks made by Marlite Paneling, Dover, OH. All products used in the project are available at well-stocked lumberyards.

SEE ALSO

Closets . . . Doors . . . Hinges . . .
Home improvement . . . Locks, door . . .
Moldings . . . Remodeling . . . Room dividers . . .
Storm doors and windows

• *Customizing the door.* To start, knock out the hinge pins and set the door on sawhorses. Clamp or tack-nail a straightedge to guide your saw and make the four cuts to drop out the opening. A sabre saw will cut right up to a corner; with a portable circular saw, you'll have to stop short of each corner and finish them with a handsaw. If you decide (as I did) to panel the door's interior, let the saw blade project as much as possible and cut with the inside of the door facing upward. Paneling will hide the extended corner kerfs. Finish the preparation by scraping off any loose paint.

Apply a piece of ⅛-in. luan plywood (or your own choice of paneling) with an insert opening 1 in. smaller *overall* to the door with panel adhesive. Do as the pros do and drive a few small brads at random to prevent the panel from sliding. Use clamps or ample weight to make good contact overall. But, do *not* use excessive pressure with the clamps.

framing snugly fits opening

The insert plastic-panel framing is made of solid mahogany to match the new interior panel of the door. Make a rectangular frame, butt-jointed and dimensioned to fit snugly into the door opening. Cut the rabbet in the frame members before gluing and screwing them together. Exact angles of the cross pieces will be determined by the size of your door opening (this varies with different doors). Inasmuch as the plastic panel inserts used are designed for interior use only, we inserted plate glass over the entire insert panel on the exterior. Thus, you must allow for the thickness of the glass (or plexiglass) when figuring the depth of the insert frame lumber.

The easiest way to lay out the crisscross members is to begin with an X from corner to corner. Draw the angles indicated at the center and the corners and cut them. The center gets a crosslap; the ends require a stepped-lap to fit into the rabbet. Drop the X into the frame and repeat the procedure with the smaller Xs.

Number all of the pieces so that they don't get mixed up, then disassemble them and cut a ⅛ x ⅜-in.-deep kerf along all the sides to contain the plastic inserts. Reassemble the parts and apply a router to both edges of the inside face with a shaped cutter. Filler strips which lie in the rabbet between the cross pieces should be included in the routing operation.

Cut the plastic inserts oversize so they rest in the grooves and the rabbeted setback of the outer frame. Use a fine-tooth saw blade and sand off any burrs before the final assembly. A dab of General Electric's Silicone Seal is used in each groove to keep the plastic inserts from shifting about. This material is pure rubber, which remains flexible, thus preventing any expansion problems. Varnish the inside, paint the outside and then add the plate glass which is secured with a molding frame.

• *New archway.* Similar procedures are used to build the archway. The oak framing is a stock building-supply-house accessory item grooved to accept either the filigree or plastic panels. It is available in 8-ft. lengths and 2-ft. cross pieces. The cross pieces have tongues at both ends to fit into the uprights. Our units require smaller cross members so it will be necessary to cut them down to size and form a new tongue on the cutoff end.

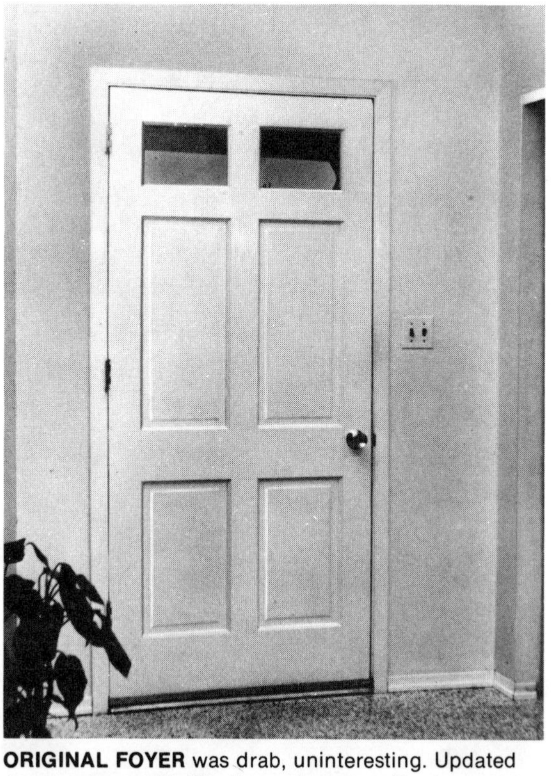

ORIGINAL FOYER was drab, uninteresting. Updated door, arch and Marlite Travertine on walls changed it.

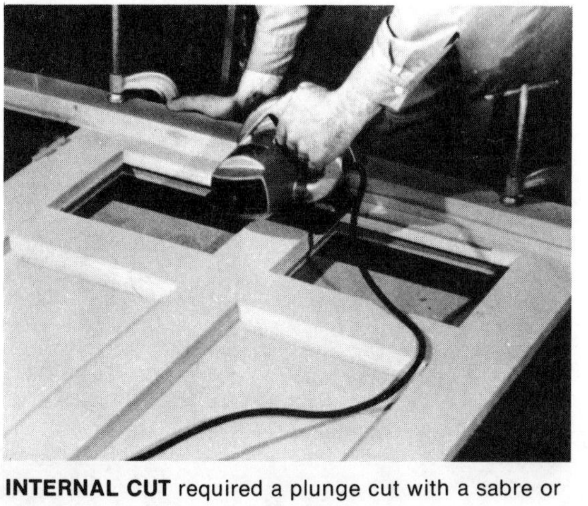

INTERNAL CUT required a plunge cut with a sabre or circular saw. Use a straightedge for accuracy.

PANEL ADHESIVE simplifies facing the door interior with flush panel. Apply a thin, flat coat to the door.

POSITION PANEL and drive a few brads to prevent it from shifting. Use weights until the glue is dry.

PRECISE ANGLE required for each diagonal piece is determined by positioning before cutting the dado.

COMBINATION SAW BLADE can be used for dadoes by making a series of cuts. Shift work with each pass.

ROUTER AND SHAPED cutter dress the strips. Make sure that all parts are numbered before you disassemble.

PLASTIC INSERTS are labeled for reassembly identity. GE Silicone Seal keeps the pieces from shifting.

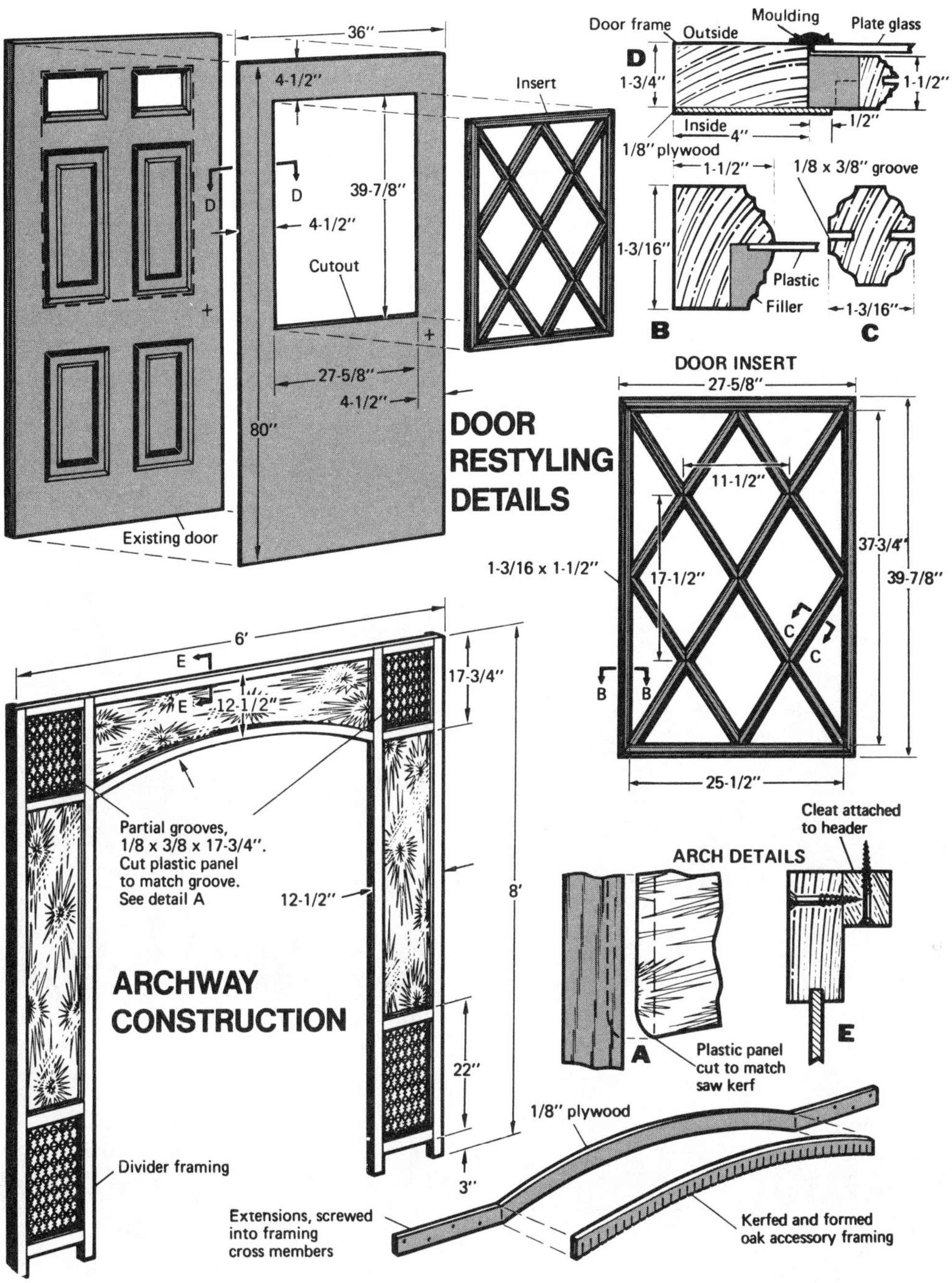

The upright sections are made as separate units, using dowels on all corners to gain extra strength. Before assembling the foyer divider, which was ultimately painted black, it proved to be advantageous to paint the inside edges and the grooves in advance. This permits you to coat the inside of the grooves, which otherwise would show up nonblack through the plastic panel.

It is not difficult to form the curved section of the arches if you follow a time-honored cabinet-making technique. The ¾ x 1½-in. oak framing is about as rigid as a piece of steel. So the only way to produce the curve is by means of kerfing—a series of saw cuts partially through the wood at close intervals. This "breaks the back" of the wood, rendering it quite flexible. The job is generally done with a circular saw which makes a rather wide kerf. Instead, I used the band saw to produce a finer cut. Make a series of cuts through the solid edge ⅜ in. apart

down to within ⅜ in. from the grooved edge.

Determine the amount of curve desired and draw the curve onto the worktable. Next, partly drive nails in positions that will hold the piece in this curved condition. Remove the piece and cover the area with wax paper to prevent the workpiece from gluing itself to the table. Make a pasty glue by mixing in some fine sawdust. Brush the mixture well into the crevices, both sides, and place the strip onto the jig bending it around the nails. Use a scraper to remove the excess before it hardens. When it's dry, clamp the piece in place over the upright sections to mark and cut off any excess at the ends.

The ⅛-in. plywood backing glued to the

TAPE A PIECE of paper to the plastic panel inserts to facilitate both marking and bandsaw cutting (left).

FOR A NEAT JOB, paint the grooves before installing plastic. Use a few drops of glue for added strength.

OAK FRAMING PIECES are cut to size on a table saw. The new tongue must be formed on the cutoff side.

DOWELS BEEF UP the corners, and a partial groove must be cut where the arched insert intersects.

OLD TRICK of running many parallel saw kerfs into oak frame for arch makes the frame easily bendable.

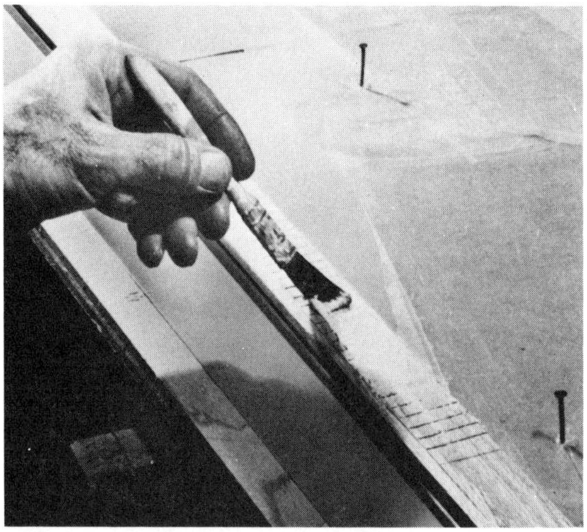

WATER-SOLUBLE GLUE, mixed with fine sawdust, is brushed into the kerfs and serves as an effective filler.

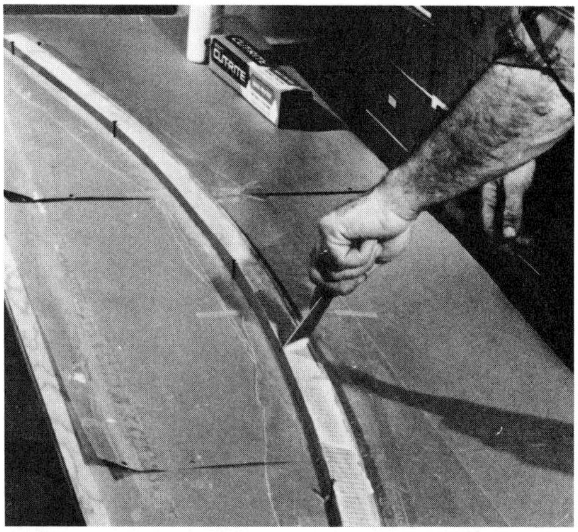

BEFORE GLUE DRIES, flex the strip to the desired arch by bridging preset nails. Scrape off excess glue.

curved piece serves two purposes: First, to reinforce it and, second, to provide a simple means for attaching to the uprights. The plywood can be glued on oversize and trimmed in place later. Leave sufficient overhang to form a "wing" on each side. The wings form built-in brackets which are screwed into the uprights.

The corresponding verticals are similarly framed but, for looks, make the inserts of hardboard filigree. Here, again, you'll speed the job if you complete all the carpentry first, mark the pieces as you cut them for easy reassembly later, and then paint the filigree outdoors where you can spray it, rather than spend unnecessary time fussing with a brush.

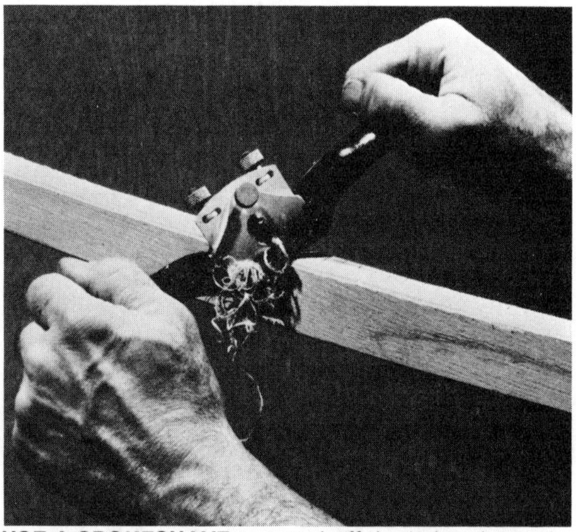

USE A SPOKESHAVE to round off the ⅛-in. plywood facing that must be added to one side of the frame.

TO MARK curved strip for an accurate joint, clamp it in place (below left). When satisfied with the fit, apply glue to the groove, force the arch into place and hold with brads well set into predrilled holes.

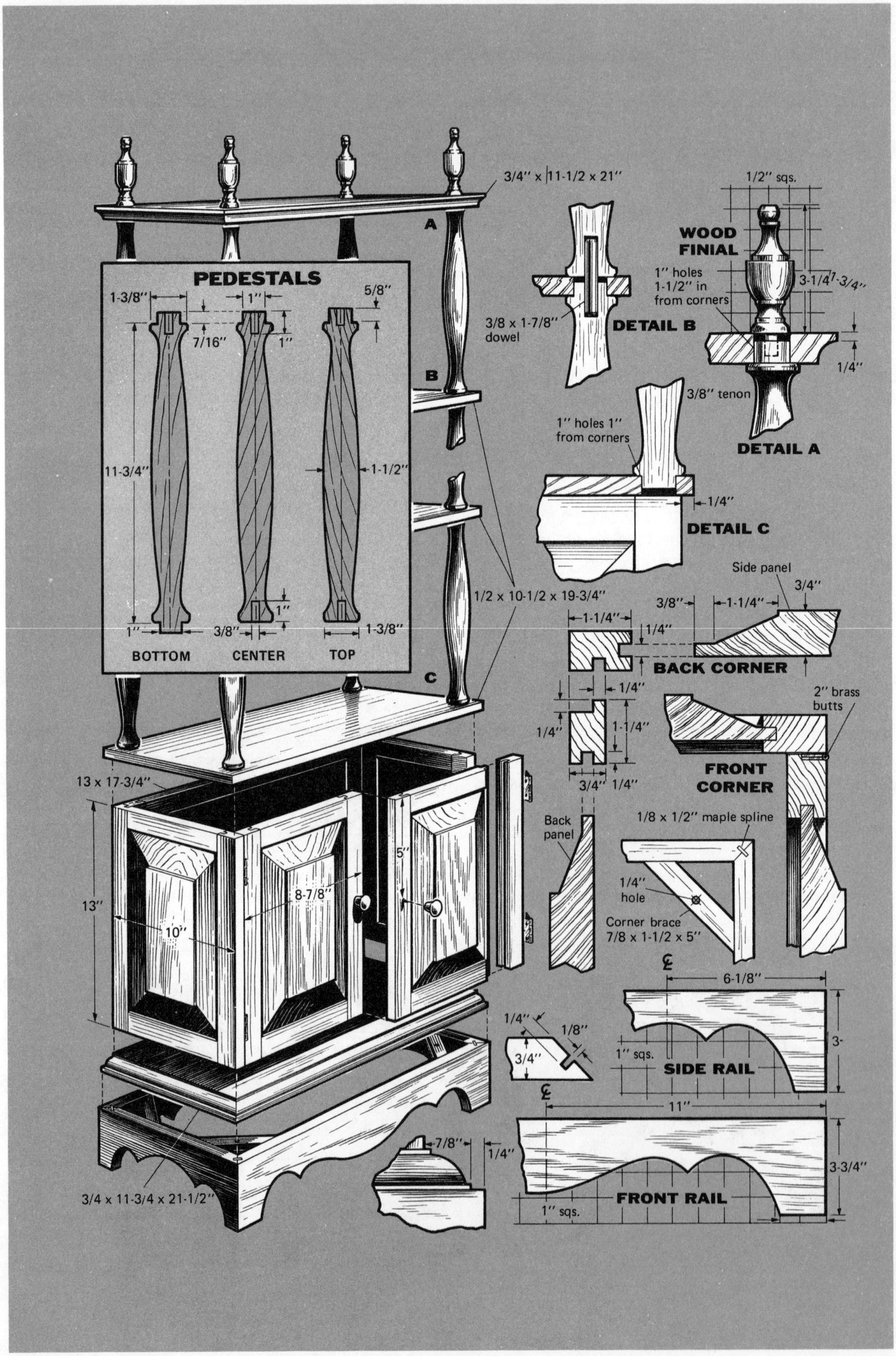

3/4" x 11-1/2 x 21"
A
PEDESTALS
1-3/8"
1"
5/8"
7/16"
1"
11-3/4"
1-1/2"
1"
1"
3/8"
1-3/8"
BOTTOM
CENTER
TOP
B
C
1/2 x 10-1/2 x 19-3/4"
13 x 17-3/4"
13"
10"
8-7/8"
5"
3/4 x 11-3/4 x 21-1/2"
1/2" sqs.
WOOD FINIAL
1" holes 1-1/2" in from corners
3-1/4"
1-3/4"
1/4"
3/8 x 1-7/8" dowel
DETAIL B
3/8" tenon
DETAIL A
1" holes 1" from corners
1/4"
DETAIL C
Side panel
3/4"
3/8"
1-1/4"
1-1/4"
1/4"
BACK CORNER
1/4"
1/4"
1-1/4"
3/4"
1/4"
2" brass butts
FRONT CORNER
Back panel
1/8 x 1/2" maple spline
1/4" hole
Corner brace 7/8 x 1-1/2 x 5"
6-1/8"
1/4"
1/8"
3/4"
1" sqs.
SIDE RAIL
11"
7/8"
1/4"
3-3/4"
FRONT RAIL
1" sqs.

Build a cabinet for your curios

By CLARE DAVIS

PERFECT FOR DISPLAYING your prized pieces of bric-a-brac, this graceful tier of open shelves and supporting storage cabinet make a handsome piece for the foyer of your home. The original, made of red oak, was finished with sealer and three coats of clear lacquer, but it will look equally as elegant in walnut or any other fine cabinet wood.

Basically, it consists of three subassemblies: a base, a cabinet and a tier of open shelves. The base, measuring 12¼ x 22 in., is made of four mitered pieces which are joined with glue and ⅛ x ½-in. hardwood splines. In the original, all four members were scroll-cut. The back member could be left plain if the unit is to be placed against a wall. You'll need to make full-size paper patterns for the scrolls for tracing on the work. These are made by ruling off 1-in. squares and drawing in the design as given in the patterns for the front and side rails.

Bandsaw the pieces, then glue and spline them together and check for squareness. Mitered braces (1½ x 5 in.) are added to the four corners after being counterbored for screws. The latter are used to attach the base to the floor of the cabinet.

The cabinet consists of five raised panels which provide the back, ends and doors. Except for overall size, all are made alike basically in that solidstock centers are set in grooved stiles and rails.

The raised panels can be formed quickly on either a radial or bench saw by tilting the blade, but you won't be able to form a tongue as shown. Such a shape actually requires a special shaper cutter. However, the tapered cut as it comes from the saw will enter the groove snugly if carefully made. To form a neat ⅛-in. shoulder at the end of the tapered cut, each panel is passed face

SEE ALSO
Bookcases . . . Cabinet furniture . . . Chests . . . Cupboards, china . . . Lowboys . . . Pier sets . . . Shelves . . . Storage walls

RAISED PANEL INSERTS of solid stock can be cut with either radial or bench saw by tilting the blade.

CLAMPS ARE USED first in gluing bottom to cabinet base, later flathead screws are driven up from below.

COMPLETED CABINET BASE is shown with scroll-cut bottom attached. Use brass butts to hinge doors.

SHELF-SUPPORTING SPINDLES rest in holes drilled in corners of shelves. Dowel pins join the spindles.

down over the saw with the blade raised a scant 1/8 in. Notice that tenons are cut on the top and bottom rails to enter the grooves in the stiles.

Use glue only on the rail tenons, not on the panels themselves. Finally, glue the ends to the back panel and clamp.

While the glue is drying, glue up solid stock for the floor of the cabinet, cut it to size and shape the edges with a cornerbead cutter in your router. Glue, plus screws driven up from below, is used to attach the floor to the assembly. If desired, the floor can be merely glued and clamped first, and the screws driven later. Here you should watch that the work doesn't shift as it's clamped. The scroll-cut base can now be attached to the floor with screws through the corner braces.

The three 1/2-in shelves of the upper assembly are identical in size and all have 1-in. holes bored 1 in. in from the corners. The thicker top shelf has similar holes drilled at the corners but 1 1/2 in. in from the edge. This leaves the turning of the twelve shelf-supporting spindles and the four finials. Basically they are alike except that the four bottom ones have a tenon turned on both ends. Dowels and glue are used to join the spindles end to end. In the case of the finials, tenons are turned to fit the holes in the spindles. Finally, the tier unit is glued to the cabinet and the doors are hinged with brass butts. Small stop blocks are placed on the inside and bullet catches used to hold the doors shut.

FOR BENCHTOP PLANING without a vise, or if your vise will not open far enough for the width board you want to plane, attach a casement-window latch to the edge of your workbench to serve as a planing stop. The latch can be simply flipped out of the way when not in use. Casement latches are sold at most hardware stores.—*Victor Lamoy, Saranac Lake, NY.*

MARRING YOUR WORK or barking your knuckles severely with the handle of a keyhole saw might easily happen even when you're cutting with care. To avoid such accidents, slip a short section of old garden hose over the blade and up against the handle of the saw.—*Howard E. Moody, Upper Jay, NY.*

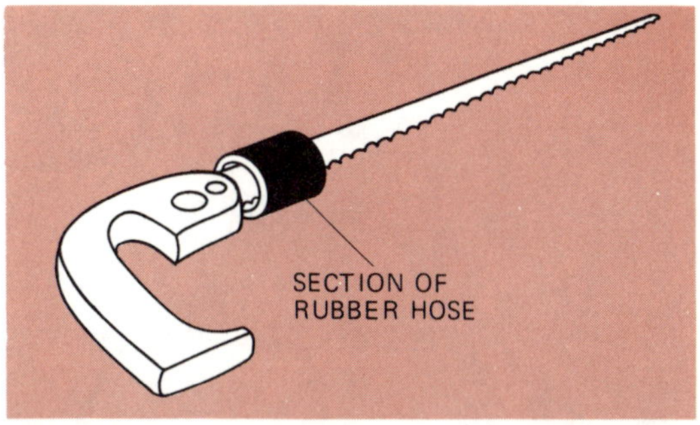

CUTTING SHALLOW SAW KERFS in the lap faces is a method I have used for preparing half-lapped joints for gluing and fastening. Kerfs provide space into which excess glue can ooze and may strengthen the finished joint. If edges of the frame will be exposed, the kerf holes can be filled and sanded smooth.—*Roger Moylan, Los Angeles.*

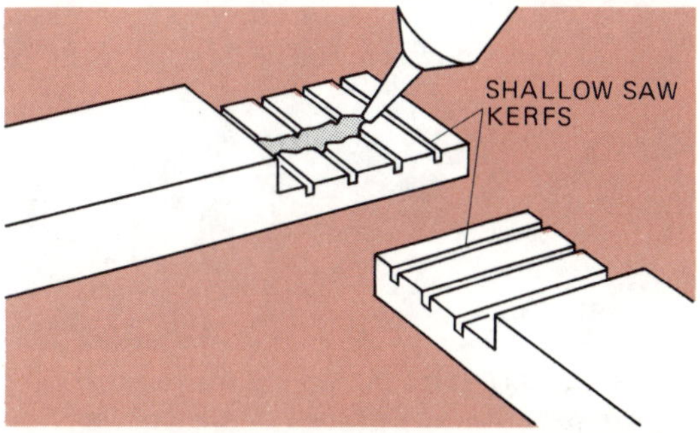

A SIMPLE HOLDER that will keep a paint can from accidentally sliding off your stepladder can be improvised from a C-clamp and a large rubber band (or strip from an inner tube). Tighten the clamp to the shelf and stretch the rubber band around both the can and the screw shank of the clamp.—*Victor Lamoy, Saranac, NY.*

SOLO TABLE-TENNIS practice is possible even without a tip-up, playback-type table. To do it, set a card table on its side, with two legs extended on your table-tennis top. Apply tape along the contact edge of the card table to protect the surface of the table-tennis top against scratches.—*Alex Jarett, St. Louis.*

How to get in shape

By JACK GALUB

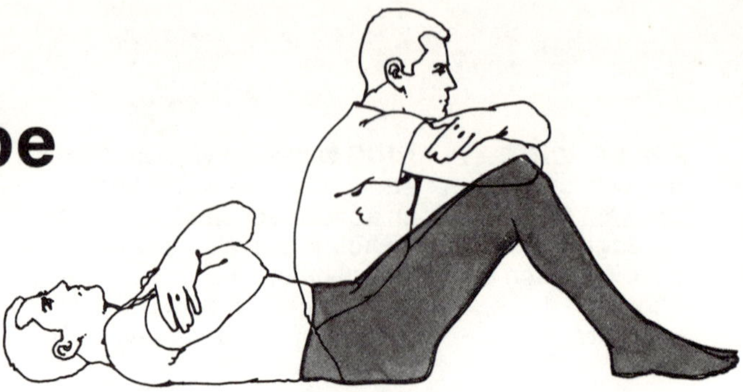

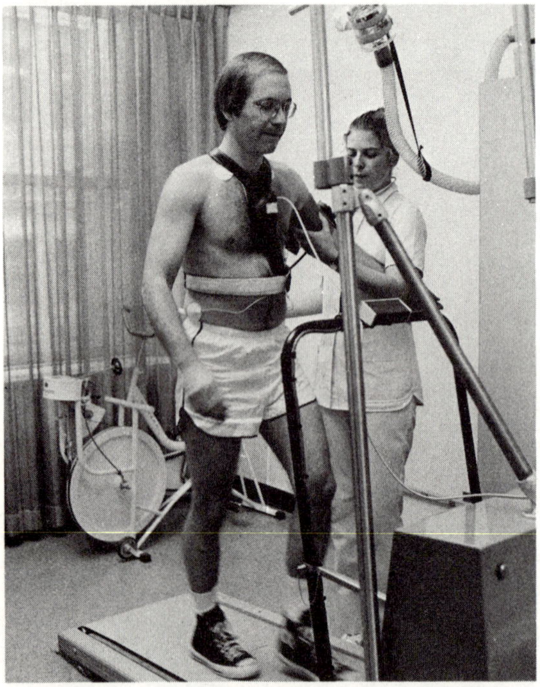

THE STRESS TEST is uphill work as the treadmill's angle is increased. Charles Perschetz, of Cardio-Metrics, demonstrates during an EKG.

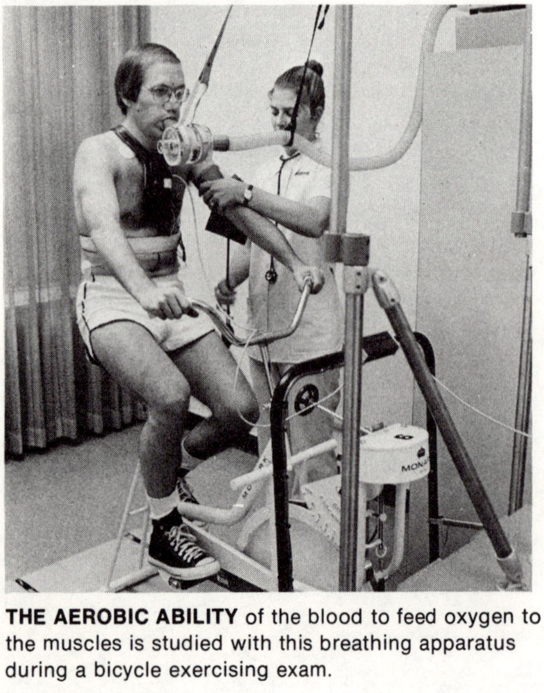

THE AEROBIC ABILITY of the blood to feed oxygen to the muscles is studied with this breathing apparatus during a bicycle exercising exam.

■ EVERY WEEKEND, OUTDOORSMEN are in here with wrenched knees, sore backs, sprained ankles," complained the emergency room nurse. "Our cardiac team keeps working overtime. If people would take time to get into shape before they go out, much of what we're doing wouldn't be necessary."

But this year can be different. By starting a training program now, you can be in good enough condition to cut down the chance of becoming another hospital statistic.

Conditioning for the field has three key targets: improved cardiovascular fitness, increased flexibility and agility, and specific muscle strength. Sounds complicated? Some 60 years of fitness medical research show that if you're now in fairly good shape you can start rounding into condition at the end of a month or so. If you've grown fat and flabby, you may need six to eight weeks.

Stamina–that ability to hike 10 miles or more without feeling completely exhausted–depends on your heart and your respiratory system's ability to supply oxygen to the more than 600 muscles in your body, particularly when you are backpacking up a hill or heading into the wind. Fortunately, the heart is an endurance muscle. The more regularly it is exercised with fast walking, jogging, bicycling or swimming, the better it works under stress. Hearts that aren't adapted to regular exercise peak out too quickly. Like a detuned car engine, they can develop an irregular rhythm. Sometimes they grind to a halt.

The most effective way to check your cardiovascular system today is the stress test. You ride a special stationary bicycle or climb an electrically driven treadmill that can be tilted into an ever-steepening hill. Your heart's reaction is recorded on electrocardiograph (EKG) tape and monitored by a cardiologist on an oscilloscope. You'll also breathe into an electronic apparatus that

**Backpacking . . . Camping . . . Canoes . . .
Conditioning, physical . . . Hunting . . .
Skin diving . . . Skis, snow . . . Sports, water . . .
Tennis**

determines your body's ability to feed oxygen to your muscles. The stress test may also detect heart problems which could cause sudden death unless treated. These tests are now given in some hospital exercise centers or by such licensed groups as Cardio-Metrics, Inc., New York City, which specialize in the testing and prescription of conditioning programs for cardiacs and noncardiacs alike.

Interval training, a sophisticated walk-jog formula, is usually prescribed to ease an outdoorsman into a conditioning program. Each session is divided into warm-up, stimulus, cool down, with the stimulus making the heart work to build up fitness. Extensive research indicates that 75 to 85 percent of your age-related maximum heart rate (see table) must be reached for a planned length of time for cardiovascular improvement. During your sessions, you monitor your pulse regularly for five seconds (and then multiply by 12 for pulse rate) to make sure you are not overworking or underworking your heart.

If there are no testing facilities near you—and an exam by your doctor assures you of a good cardiac profile—you can develop your own shaping-up program. If your profile is poor—a history of heart disease in your family, high blood pressure, overweight, too much smoking—a complete physical checkup and consultation with your doctor is essential before you start.

Begin easily—you're not out for the Olympics or your local ball club. Jogging takes a slow short stride, done from the heels forward rather than on the balls of the feet. First try jogging 50 paces and walking 50 for 10 or 15 minutes. As your wind builds up, you can walk less. You may find yourself slow-jogging a quarter mile in two weeks, half a mile in a month. With no park or track nearby, you can jog around the block or from room to room at home.

For the flexibility and agility you'll need while hiking and climbing, practice walking on the outsides of your feet and then the insides with your ankles turned in. These exercises are awkward and difficult at first, but a few minutes every other day will stretch and strengthen muscles, tendons and ligaments.

Next, imitate a basketball guard or boxer with feet apart, knees slightly bent. Bob, weave and pivot on the balls of your feet, followed by jumps several inches off the floor. For the lower back and hip joints you will use canoeing and climbing, bend your knees until you can put your palms on the floor. Then try straightening your legs while pulling in your abdominal muscles. Two or three stomach contractions held for five to 10 seconds are enough for each exercise session.

Push-ups should be added to your every-other-day routine. Starting flat on the floor, push up to full arm extension and then lower with body straight until your chest touches the floor. Most people at first aren't able to do more than one or two properly without cheating by bending the body.

MAXIMUM WORK RATE

For training to be most effective, a workout pulse rate at 75 to 85 percent of maximum efficient heartbeat is recommended. But moderation is vital: Check with your doctor and ease into training.

Age	Maximum pulse/heart rate	85%
20	200	170
22	198	168
24	196	166
26	194	164
28	192	163
30	190	161
32	189	160
34	187	158
36	186	158
38	184	156
40	182	154
45	179	152
50	175	148
55	171	145

continued

FOR BACKPACKING

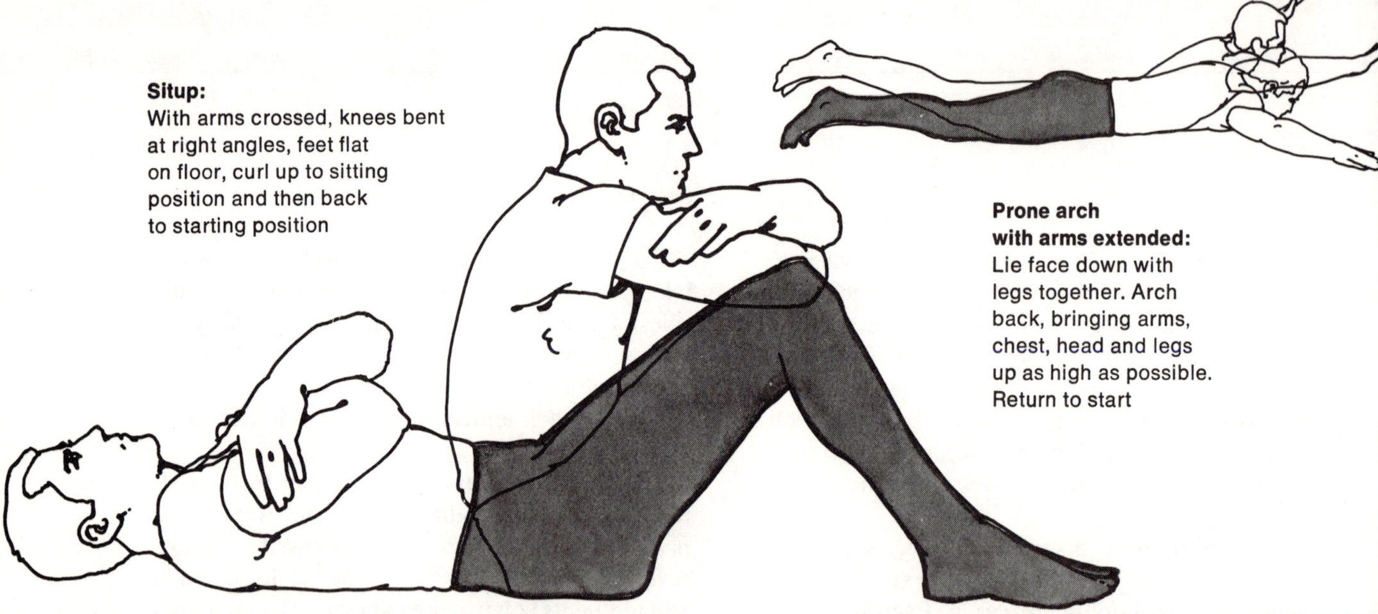

Situp:
With arms crossed, knees bent at right angles, feet flat on floor, curl up to sitting position and then back to starting position

Prone arch with arms extended:
Lie face down with legs together. Arch back, bringing arms, chest, head and legs up as high as possible. Return to start

FOR CANOEING

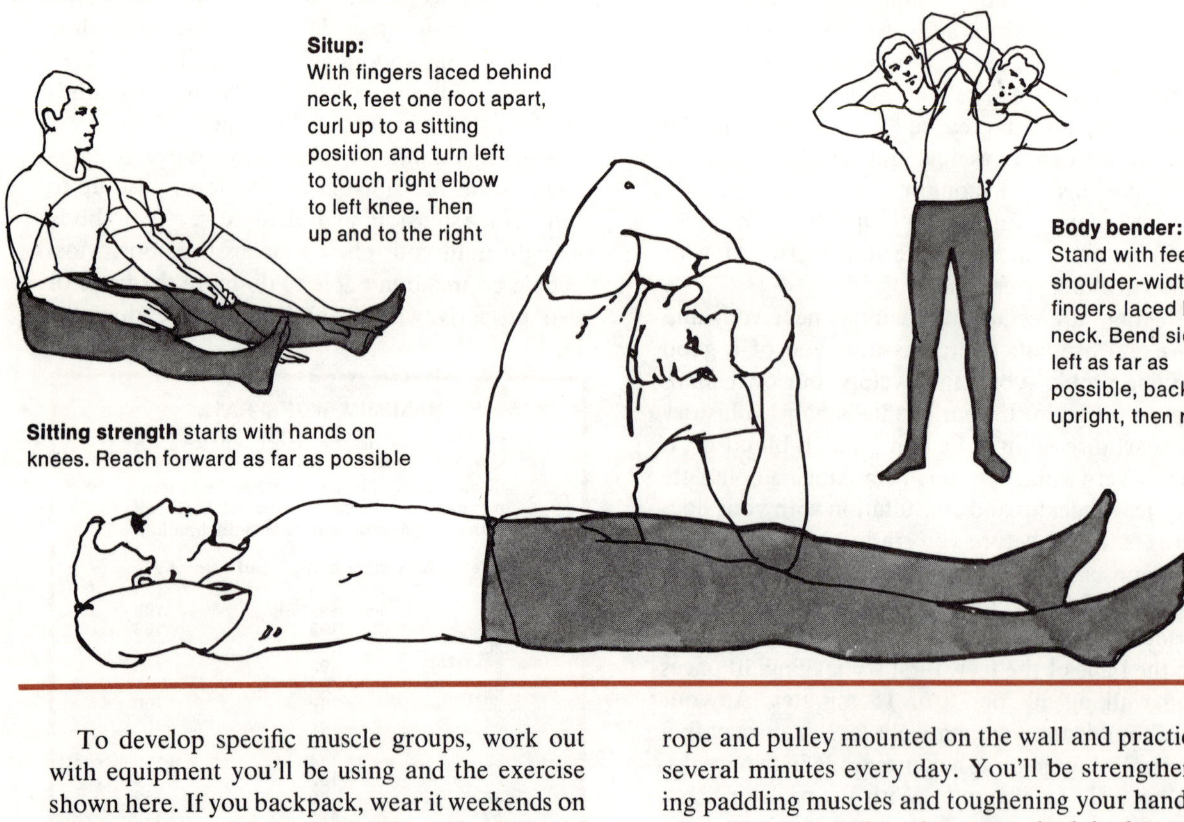

Situp:
With fingers laced behind neck, feet one foot apart, curl up to a sitting position and turn left to touch right elbow to left knee. Then up and to the right

Body bender:
Stand with feet shoulder-width apart, fingers laced behind neck. Bend sideways left as far as possible, back upright, then right

Sitting strength starts with hands on knees. Reach forward as far as possible

To develop specific muscle groups, work out with equipment you'll be using and the exercise shown here. If you backpack, wear it weekends on short fast hikes. If you usually carry 20 pounds of gear, double it to 40 for practice. Use your heavy field shoes for early hikes but not for jogging; that requires training shoes. If you want to jog with more load, wrap on ankle weights after you have completed the third or fourth week of workouts.

For canoe training, rig a paddle with weighted rope and pulley mounted on the wall and practice several minutes every day. You'll be strengthening paddling muscles and toughening your hands, as well, for those long hours on the lake later in the season.

The easiest way to strengthen the upper muscles you'll be using when rock climbing is to actually climb. A school gym, if available, usually has a vertical rope plus the horizontal ladder to swing along. For simple but effective workouts,

FOR CLIMBING

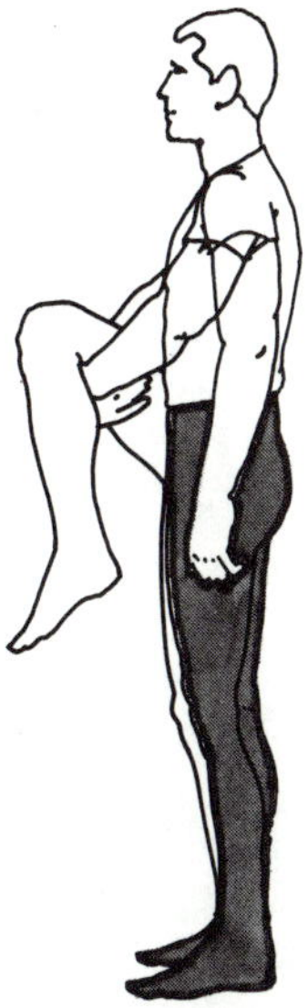

Knee lift:
Raise left knee, grasp leg and pull against body while keeping back straight. Lower, repeat, lifting right knee up to body

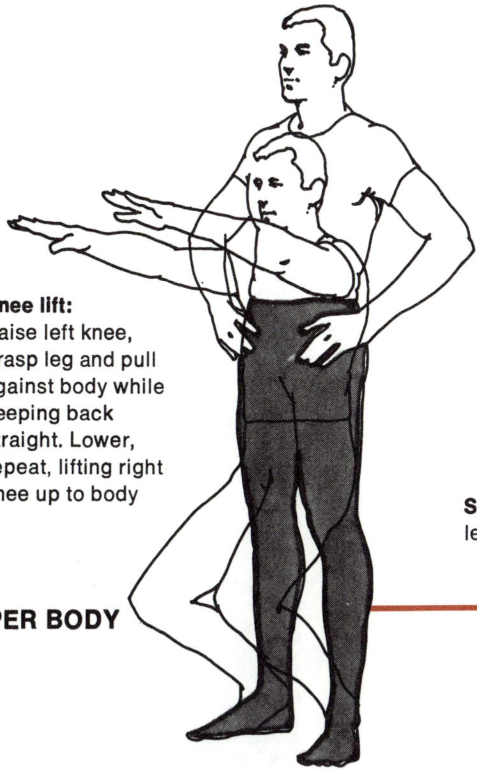

Half knee bend:
Stand erect, hands on hips. Bend knees halfway while extending arms forward, palms down. Hold. Return to standing position and repeat exercise

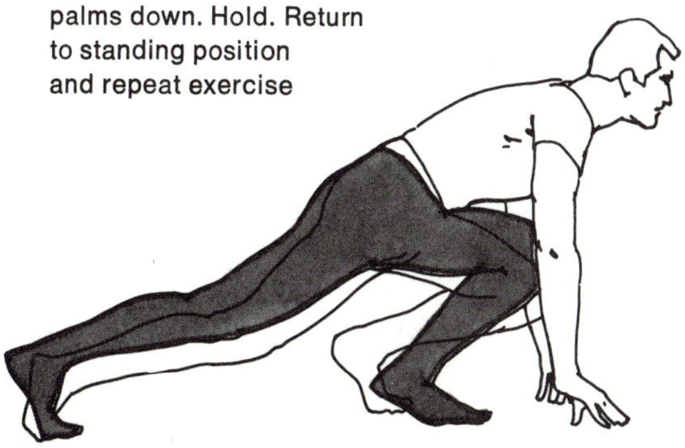

Sprinter starts with fingers forward on floor, left leg back. Reverse legs in bouncing movement

FOR ARMS AND UPPER BODY

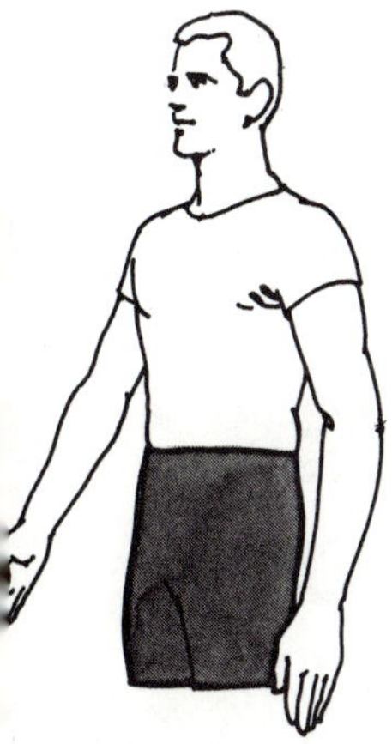

Upper body isometrics can start with push back on wall

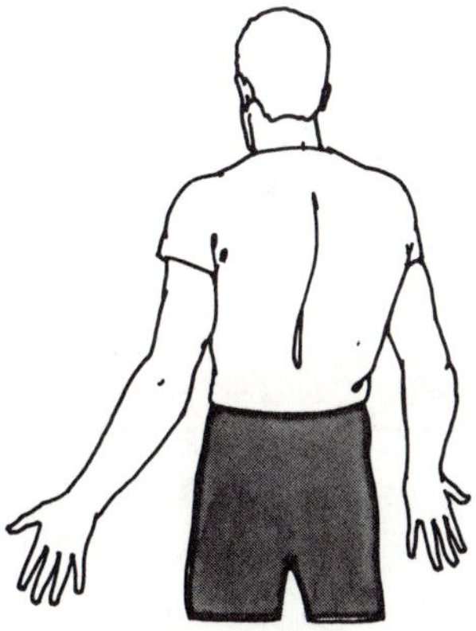

Next face wall and push, again keeping arms straight

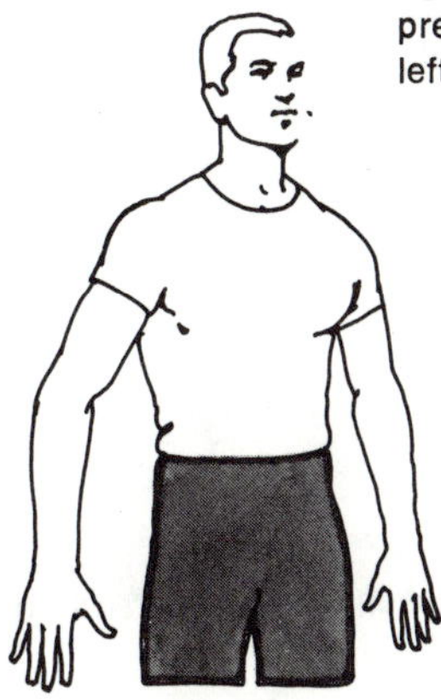

Standing in doorway, press outward with backs of hands

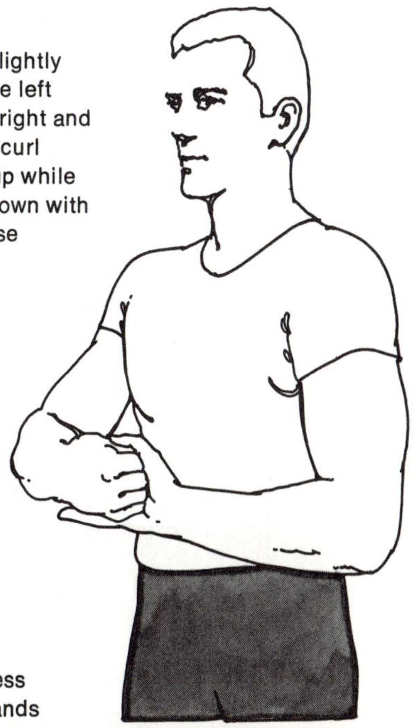

Arms:
With feet slightly apart, place left hand over right and attempt to curl right arm up while pressing down with left. Reverse

rig a store-bought chinning bar in a doorway at home and practice doing pull-ups.

The number of pull-ups you can complete should gradually grow as your strength develops.

The isotonic exercises—those in which muscles are actively flexed, compressed and stretched—and the isometric strength builders—where muscles pull or push against stationary objects or against each other—are both represented in the exercises selected here for outdoorsmen. They should be practiced as shown for best results.

When you're practicing isometrics, breathe naturally. Usually three or four contractions, held for five to 10 seconds, are needed to make the exercises work. Do not hold your breath as that tends to build up internal pressures.

Once you've learned these easy ways to get yourself in shape, go back to them, when your outdoor activities taper off. The payoff is in good health and active sport all year long.

Build a weight bench for exercise

By HARRY WICKS and JOHN CAPOTOSTO

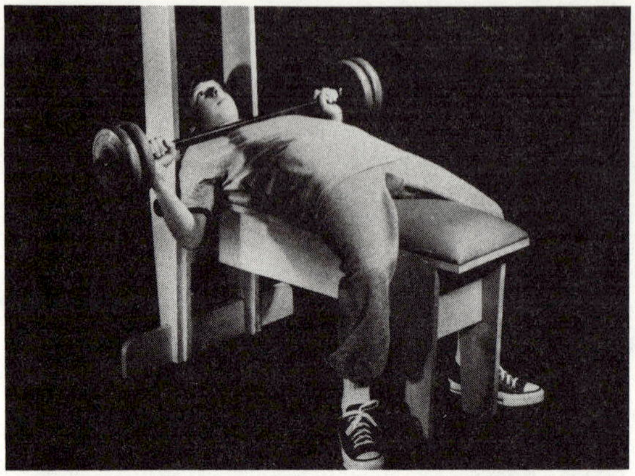

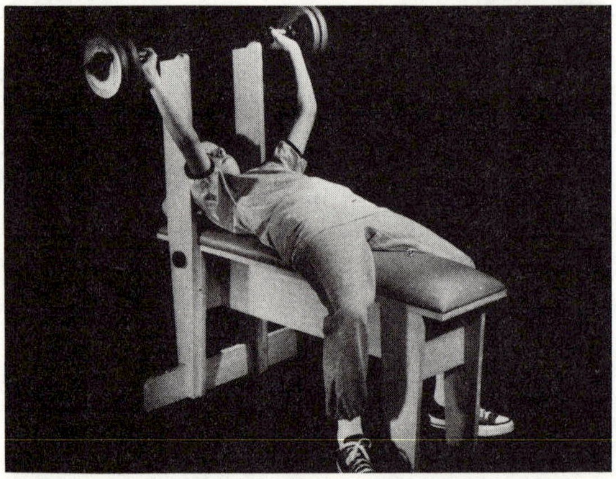

WEIGHT BENCH can be used to develop tricep and bicep muscles. For correct bench use, see facing page.

■ ONE OF THE BEST ways for an athlete to ready himself for an upcoming sports season is to follow a daily program using a weight bench and barbell. The bench shown is based on a design by high-school teacher and coach Jack Fisher of Newark, N. J. The stabilizer foot at the head end of the bench makes it as rigid as expensive commercial benches you'll find in sporting-goods stores.

The original bench was made entirely of ¾-in. fir plywood and covered with plastic laminate for durability and looks. The laminate, of course, is not necessary, but since little of it is required, it's worth considering. All four short legs are alike except that only two are notched; the two tall legs are identical. A handscrew turned into a tee nut embedded in each rear short leg is used to attach the tall legs to the bench and makes it simple to remove them when desired. Both crosspieces are the same size, but you'll notice that the rear one is notched to provide clearance for the threaded handscrews. If you have difficulty obtaining the 2-inch-thick cushion foam and hand-

SEE ALSO
Backpacking . . . Camping . . . Hunting . . .
Skin diving . . . Skis, snow . . . Snowshoes . . .

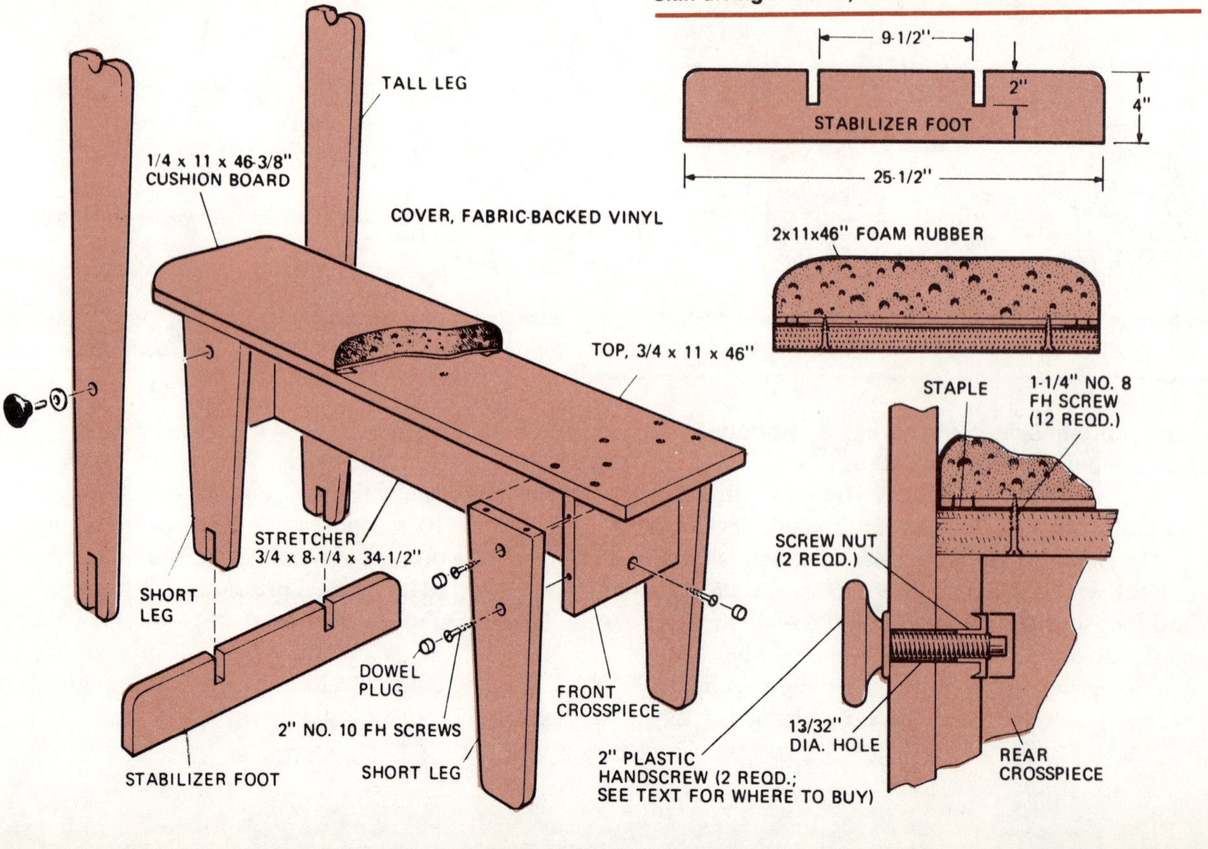

NAILS ARE USED to assemble bench temporarily, but for strength and rigidity, finish with screws and glue.

NOTCHED STABILIZER FOOT should have a snug fit with mating notches on two short, nonadjustable legs.

SCREWHEADS ARE PLUGGED if bench is to be stained or painted. For laminated bench, simply fill and sand.

AFTER BORING ½-in. clearance hole, tee nut for hand screw is driven home with a couple of hammer blows.

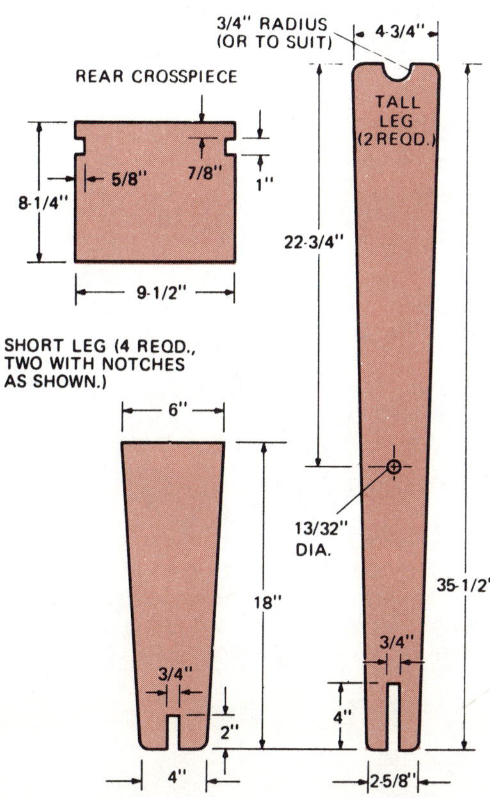

screws, Armor Co., Box 290, Deer Park, N. Y. 11729, will supply the cushion for about $4.50 and the handscrew set for about $2, both postpaid.

Once the bench is built, it is important that it be used properly. A quickie use-course is given below; serious students should consider buying a weight-lifting book.

How to use a weight bench

1. Always stretch and loosen up before lifting.
2. Position: Lie on back, feet flat on floor with eyes directly under bar. Hands in wide position to work on chest (pectoralis); hands close to work on arms (strength).
3. Straighten arms to clear bar off support, then bring bar forward over chest. Lower bar to chest while inhaling. Raise bar to full extension while exhaling. Complete desired number of repetitions and replace bar on the support.

In general. Weight to use depends upon individual strength; use weight that is heavy for you (one you can't lift more than 10 times). For strength, increase weight as your strength increases. For endurance, use weight you can lift 15 to 20 times each session.

SOLDER TWO STRAIGHT PINS (one bent) to a No. 40 or 47 bulb and you can test 9-v. transistor radio batteries from discount lots through the wrapping. Look for a bright, steady light.—*John Walker, Nanticoke, PA.*

A RUBBER ERASER produces a pleasing polish on a revolving workpiece and can be used to apply rouge. Its resilience lets it follow contours. For greater abrasion, use an ink eraser.—*Walter E. Burton, Akron, OH.*

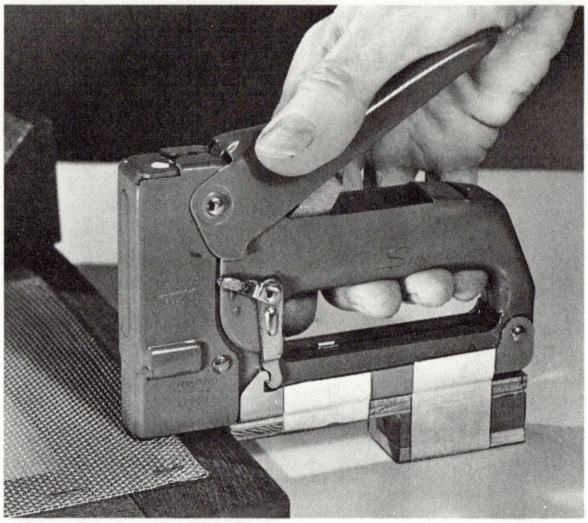

REPEATED STAPLING is easier with raiser and depth blocks taped under your staple gun. Width of blocks should be about ¾ in. for most models with height to suit work.—*John W. Lower, Chambersburg, PA.*

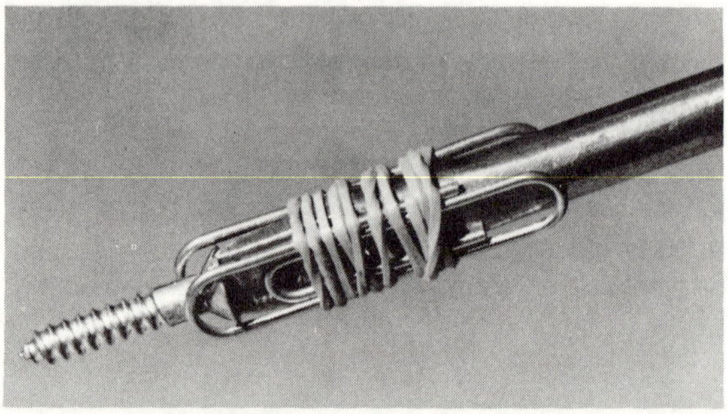

TO START A SCREW in a tight spot, hold its head between the ends of paper clips held to your screwdriver with a rubber band. The screwdriver will pull away easily afterward.—*William Swallow, Brooklyn, NY.*

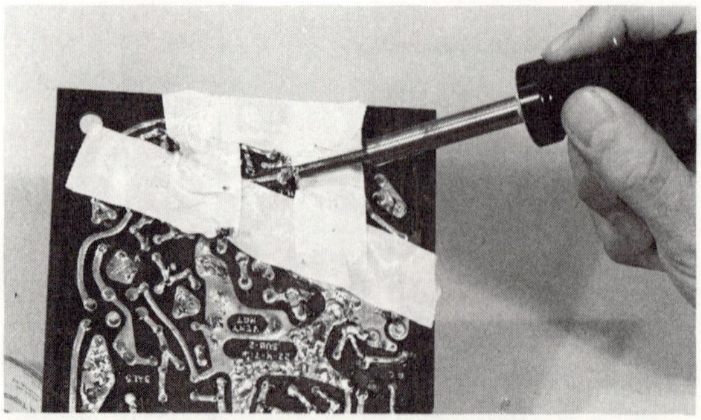

HAVING LOCATED THE FAULT in a printed circuit, I mark it off with masking tape to keep solder where it belongs—or to find the spot again later, if the repair must be delayed.—*Ken Patterson, Regina, Sask.*

Tin-can reel for an extension cord

You can avoid those annoying tangles in your extension cord with this easy-to-make windup reel

By JOHN CAPOTOSTO

SEE ALSO

Electrical wiring . . . Fluorescent lamps . . . Lighting . . . Post lamps . . . Testers, continuity . . . Wiring, electrical

■ HERE'S A PROJECT you can finish in an evening—an extension-cord reel that plays out as much line as you need, when you need it. Mounted on a swivel bearing, the cord unwinds quickly; when you're through with it, you merely crank it up.

It goes together quickly. Use two small screws through predrilled $\frac{3}{16}$-in. holes to attach the utility box to the plywood disc. Run the cord through two Romex connectors, one installed on the side of the can and the other in a knockout of the utility box. Leave about 8 in. of cord protruding from the box, then mount it using two round-head screws in the drilled holes. The disc with a rectangular cutout can now be installed with screws. Mount the swivel bearing on the upright first, then to the reel. To maintain polarity, wire the outlet as shown in the drawing.

TWO-LB. COFFEE can is the reel core.

THE CORD REEL can be assembled in one evening for pennies—the electric box and duplex will probably be your only expenses. When a job is finished, the cord is quickly cranked into the reel.

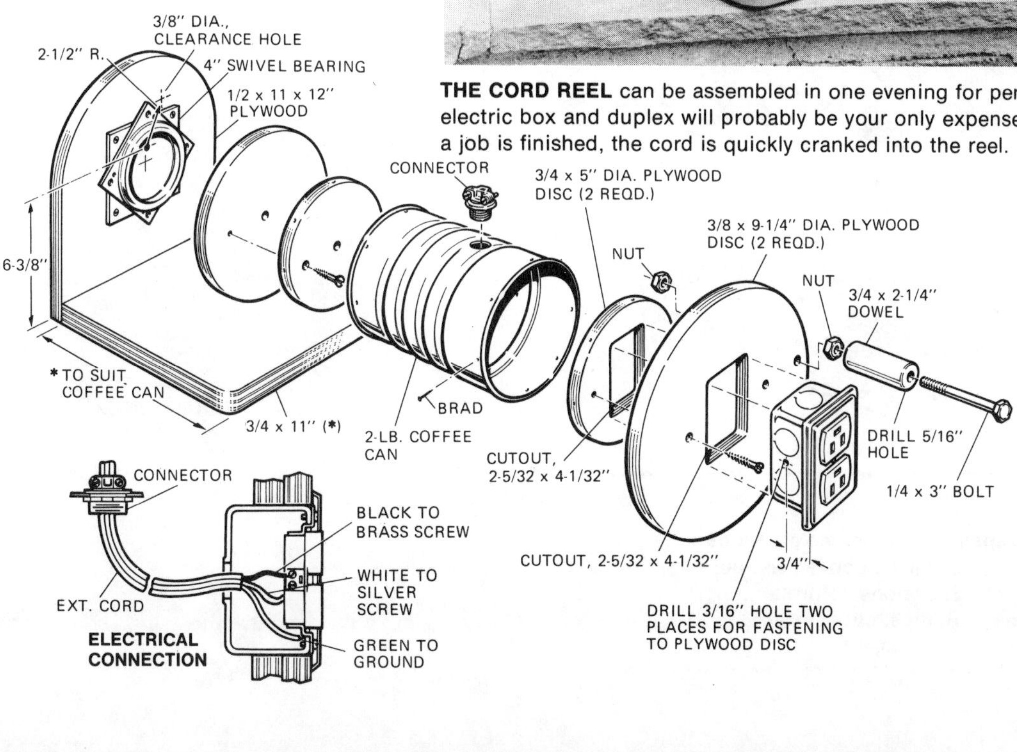

How to replace your exhaust system

By MORT SCHULTZ

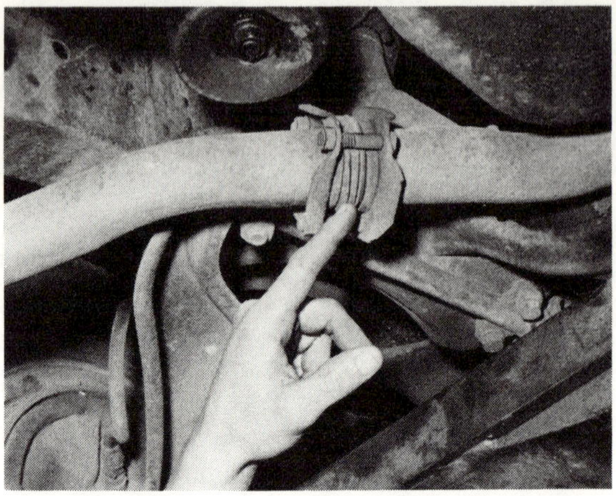

CLAMPS ARE USED to secure the components of the exhaust system. Various types are used. If rusted tight, use penetrating oil or a hacksaw to remove.

■ I PROVED it to myself: if you want to save money you should replace rotted exhaust system parts or, if necessary, the entire system *yourself.*

Using a six-cylinder Dodge Dart as an example, I surveyed a mail-order house (J.C. Whitney and Co. of Chicago), a new-car dealer and a local supplier to find out how much each would charge for parts alone. I then asked two nationally known companies (Midas and Scotti) what they would charge for installing an exhaust system.

At the time this was written, the charge for mail order parts was about $25. The local supplier wanted about $37 for the same parts. My new-car dealer was getting about $54. However, the muffler he would supply was guaranteed for as long as I owned the car.

Midas and Scotti asked $60 and $65, respectively, to install an exhaust system in the Dodge. Mufflers supplied by both are guaranteed for as long as you own your car. The tailpipe furnished by Scotti is also guaranteed.

dirty work but worth it

I can't deny that replacing an exhaust system can be a dirty, sweaty job, but I figure it's worth a little perspiration to save $35 or $40. The toughest part is usually loosening nuts and bolts that have frozen stiff over the miles.

TWO EXHAUST-SYSTEM variations are shown here. At top is a single system with crossover pipe: one branch for each side of the engine. In dual system at bottom, identical exhaust lines are separate.

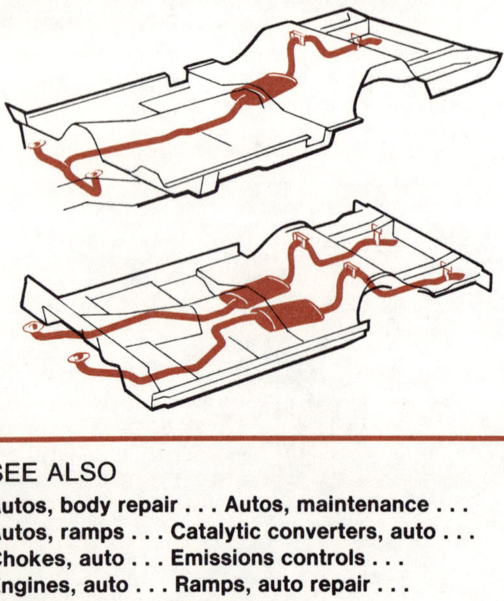

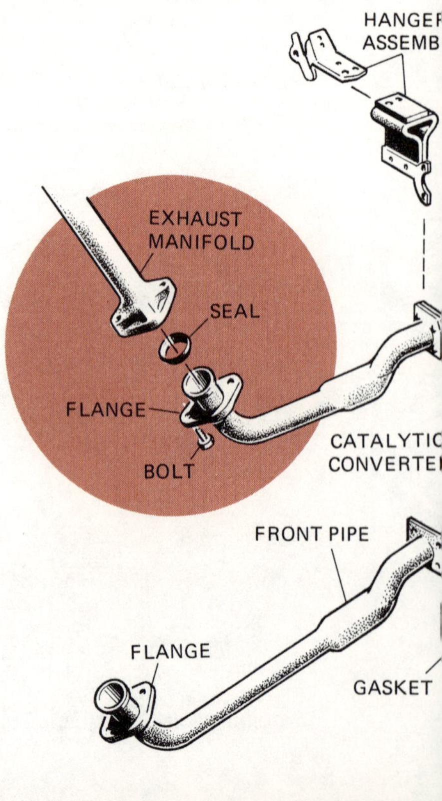

SEE ALSO

Autos, body repair . . . Autos, maintenance . . . Autos, ramps . . . Catalytic converters, auto . . . Chokes, auto . . . Emissions controls . . . Engines, auto . . . Ramps, auto repair . . . Stalling, auto . . . Tune-up, auto

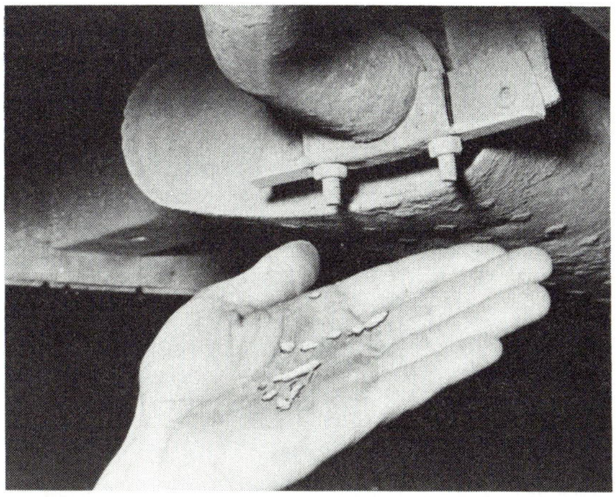

EXHAUST SYSTEM inspection should be done periodically because of danger of carbon monoxide. Flake off rust to see how deeply it has eaten into metal.

CONDITION OF MUFFLER is checked by ear: Dull thud when rapped indicates pending failure; sharp ringing, a sound muffler.

However, you have an ally in penetrating oil. Drown stubborn fasteners with oil and let set 10 to 15 minutes. The fasteners may need another shot before they loosen.

If a nut and bolt prove particularly stubborn, cut them away with a sharp chisel and hammer.

If the entire exhaust system has to be replaced, and you're not trying to salvage parts for reuse, the only fasteners you normally have to remove are at the exhaust pipe-to-exhaust manifold connection. Other parts can be cut away in a manner easiest for you. You can use a hacksaw or an exhaust and tailpipe cutter that will cost about $15.

Do not use a torch. Someone inexperienced working with flame beneath a car is playing with danger. There is always a chance of accidentally having flame get in the way of a gas line or fuel tank.

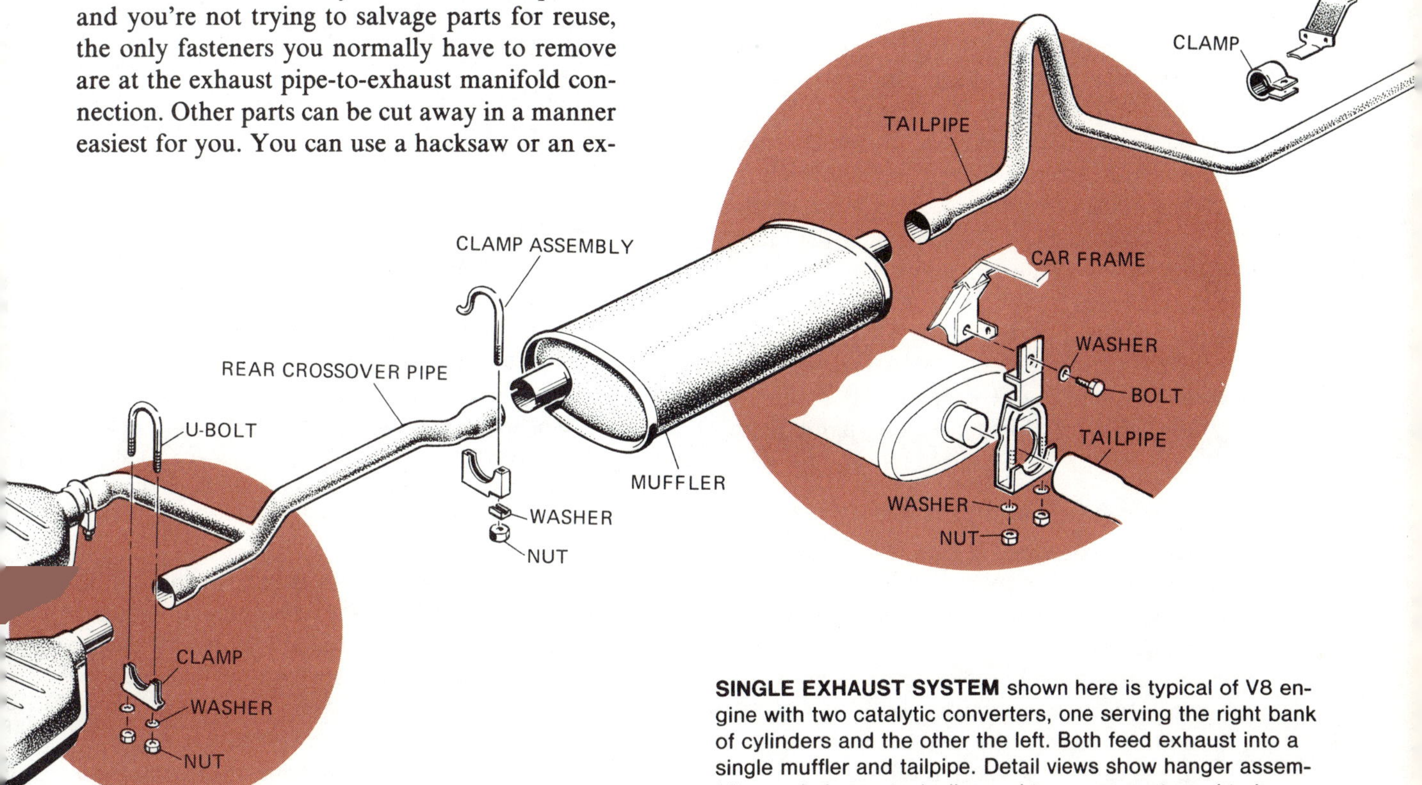

SINGLE EXHAUST SYSTEM shown here is typical of V8 engine with two catalytic converters, one serving the right bank of cylinders and the other the left. Both feed exhaust into a single muffler and tailpipe. Detail views show hanger assemblies and clamps typically used to secure parts and to hang system from car frame. Make sure you have all the parts you need before starting the job and remember that you won't be able to get close enough to these red-hot parts to start work if you've just used the car!

Round out your tool needs with socket and open-end wrenches, and a tube of exhaust-system joint sealer.

a rack simplifies job

You can tackle exhaust-system replacement lying flat on your back, if you must, but the job is made much easier by getting the car in the air. If you're friendly with a guy at a local gas station or garage, maybe he'll let you use his lift during off-hours. If not, you can place the car's four corners on jack stands. Just make sure the stands are strong enough to take the weight and are properly set.

The exhaust system should be cold when you work to avoid burns.

Every exhaust system has three common parts: exhaust (front) pipe, muffler and tailpipe. Parts are suspended from hangers which are bolted to the undercarriage, and joints where parts meet are usually secured with clamps.

Most cars have one exhaust system, but some with V8 engines have two. A dual exhaust system is nothing more than two identical (or almost identical), but separate single-exhaust systems, one serving the engine's right bank of cylinders and the other serving the left bank.

The front pipe of cars having V8 engines and single exhaust systems is a so-called crossover pipe—a single pipe having two branches.

One branch attaches to the exhaust manifold on the right side of the engine, and the other attaches to the exhaust manifold on the left side. Exhaust feeds from both branches into the common pipe and out through one system.

Many cars also have resonators, which are merely second mufflers, smaller than the main muffler, that help further reduce engine noise.

don't damage valuable parts

A catalytic converter is part of the exhaust system, but most times other exhaust parts fail much faster than a converter which is designed to last 50,000 miles.

This means that in replacing an exhaust system having a catalytic converter you have to exercise care not to damage the converter when taking it from the car and when reinstalling it.

Also watch how you handle long exhaust pipes and tailpipes that are still in usable condition when disconnecting them to replace a shot muffler. When releasing one end of the pipe and shifting to the other end to make a disconnection, support the pipe by wrapping a length of soft wire around it and tying it to a rail or cross-member. This keeps the pipe straight and stops it from bending.

After new and/or reusable parts are put back together, spread a liberal quantity of exhaust-system joint sealer around the joints before you tighten the clamps. The sealer, not the clamp, prevents the joint from leaking.

Up front where you may have to remove the exhaust pipe from the exhaust manifold, there may be a gasket. If there is, throw it away and replace with a new gasket.

If you have a torque wrench and are able to get your hands on manufacturer's tightening torques for fasteners (specs are given in service manuals), use it. However, a torque wrench isn't really necessary. But caution is.

use care in tightening

Tighten fasteners securely—that is, enough to keep parts from moving and banging against the undercarriage. But don't tighten them to a point where you'll crush pipes.

To give you guidance in replacing an exhaust system, here are directions to follow when doing the job on Valiants and Darts with six-cylinder engines and without catalytic converters; and on Granadas, Monarchs, Comets and Mavericks with eight-cylinder engines, single exhaust systems and no catalytic converters.

procedures basically similar

No matter what kind of car you own, you will find many similarities and few minor differences between the procedure you have to use and the procedures outlined here.

To replace the exhaust systems of Valiants and Darts with six-cylinder engines and without catalytic converters:

1. Disconnect the two nuts holding the exhaust pipe flange to the exhaust manifold. Discard the gasket.

2. Remove the two U-bolt nuts of the U-bolt holding the front of the exhaust pipe at its neck.

3. Inspect the exhaust pipe U-bolt and U-bolt hanger assembly, and replace it if damaged or deteriorated.

4. Turn your attention to the muffler, and note that the muffler and exhaust pipe in this car is an integral, one-piece assembly. When you have to replace one, you have to replace both.

5. At the rear of the muffler, remove the U-bolt holding the muffler and tailpipe together, and slide the muffler forward, disengaging it from the tailpipe. Lower the muffler and exhaust-pipe assembly to the ground.

6. Inspect the muffler-tailpipe U-bolt and U-bolt hanger; replace it if damaged or deteriorated.

7. Remove the bolt holding the tailpipe support to the car's frame and lower the tailpipe to the ground.

Some models have a resonator as an integral part of the tailpipe. If either has been damaged, both have to be replaced.

8. Inspect the tailpipe support, and replace it with a new one if the support is damaged or deteriorated.

9. Begin installation by attaching the exhaust pipe to its U-bolt. Engage the U-bolt nuts loosely.

Caution: If the exhaust pipe and muffler are an integrated unit, be sure to support the muffler in some way as you work on the exhaust pipe, so the muffler doesn't fall and get damaged.

10. Install a new gasket at the exhaust pipe flange and exhaust manifold connection. Engage the two connecting nuts loosely.

11. Notice the small pipe extension at the rear of the muffler. Engage it in its U-bolt hanger assembly and connect it to the tailpipe as securely as possible.

12. Secure the tailpipe to its support, engaging the bolt loosely.

13. Install the U-bolt at the muffler-tailpipe joint and engage the two U-bolt nuts loosely.

14. Coat all joints with exhaust-system sealer, and make certain the entire exhaust system is properly aligned so there is no strain on any part before tightening fasteners. If you have a torque wrench, here are the specifications to follow:

- Exhaust pipe-to-exhaust manifold nuts: 35 ft.-lb.
- Exhaust pipe U-bolt nuts: 95 in.-lb.
- Muffler-to-tailpipe U-bolt nuts: 150 in.-lb.
- Tailpipe support bolt: 200 in.-lb.

tackling 8-cylinder systems

To replace the exhaust systems of Granadas, Monarchs, Comets and Mavericks with eight-cylinder engines, single exhausts and no catalytic converters:

1. At about the middle of the crossover pipe, remove fasteners from the hanger that holds the pipe. Support the pipe to keep it from falling and being damaged as you continue your work elsewhere if the pipe can be salvaged.

2. Remove the nuts attaching the crossover pipe to the resonator inlet pipe, and remove the nuts attaching the crossover pipe flanges to the exhaust manifolds. This releases the crossover pipe, which can now be removed.

3. Notice that if this is the car's original exhaust system the resonator inlet pipe, resonator, resonator-to-muffler pipe, muffler and tailpipe are all welded together in an integrated unit. It is removed by removing the two bolts holding the resonator to its hanger assembly at the rear of the resonator.

4. At the rear of the muffler, loosen and remove the two bolts holding the muffler-tailpipe to its hanger assembly. The assembly is now free and can be removed.

5. Inspect hangers and replace any which look shot.

Important: Replacement exhaust system parts for these cars are normally provided in separate, rather than integrated pieces, which are secured together with clamps. The parts normally furnished are exhaust pipe, resonator and resonator inlet pipe, muffler-tailpipe assembly, and crossover pipe.

6. Begin reassembly by attaching the crossover pipe loosely to its hanger and connecting the crossover pipe flanges loosely to the exhaust manifolds.

7. Connect the resonator inlet pipe-resonator assembly to the rear of the crossover pipe. Coat the joint with exhaust-system sealer and attach the clamp loosely.

8. Attach resonator to hanger and secure the fasteners loosely.

9. Connect the front of the resonator-to-muffler pipe to the rear of the muffler, coat the joint with exhaust system sealer and attach the clamp loosely.

10. Attach the muffler-tailpipe assembly to its hanger and secure bolts loosely.

11. Join the rear of the resonator-to-muffler pipe to the front of the muffler, coat the joint with sealer and secure with a clamp.

12. Make sure the exhaust system is aligned straight and true so there's no strain on any point, and tighten fasteners securely. If you have a torque wrench, here are the torque values to abide by:

- Crossover pipe-to-exhaust manifold nuts: 25-35 ft.-lb.
- Crossover pipe support bracket nuts: 8-14 ft.-lb.
- Exhaust pipe-to-resonator inlet pipe flange: 20-30 ft.-lb.
- Resonator-to-resonator hanger bolts: 10-20 ft.-lb.
- Muffler-to-muffler hanger bolts: 8-14 ft.-lb.

A porch becomes a family room

By HARRY WICKS

■ THERE ARE REAL advantages in buying an older home but there are also some points on the minus side. The biggest liablility, as far as my wife and I were concerned, was a front sun porch that seemed more like a greenhouse than a room. It had nine windows and a pair of French doors. This made it just about impossible to arrange furniture sensibly and get full use of the room.

SEE ALSO
Basement remodeling . . . Ceilings . . . Garage remodeling . . . House additions . . . Railings . . . Remodeling . . . Shelves . . . Storage walls . . . Windows

The room required a lot of curtain and window-washing, plus twice-a-year storm and screen-changing chores. This—and our real need for a family room—prompted the project you see on these pages. By doing it myself, I was able to keep total construction costs to about one-third of the amount a contractor would have charged.

Windows. The project was started by closing in the windows as shown. The double-mullion window installed in front is sized to satisfy FHA requirements—5 percent of floor space for ventilation, 10 percent for light. Vinyl clad on the exterior, the windows won't need painting for at least 10 years. And the muntins are removable.

BEFORE: Over-windowed porch on front of older home was of little use—lots of work inside and out.

AFTER: Double window meets FHA minimum requirements; rebuilt room functions for everyday living.

When the glass needs washing, it's a simple four-pane job. The windows come finished on the exterior; you, of course, supply the interior trim. Notice in the drawing that the center mullion was covered with a shop-made molding.

All framing for windows and the recessed radiator was accomplished in one day with the help of a friend. I completed the balance of the job over four weekends.

Walls. The original plaster walls were left intact. In the holes created by the new framing, insulation was installed between studs and then plasterboard was applied. To bring the plasterboard flush with the existing walls, it was necessary to shim the face of the studs about ⅜-in. As shown in photos of the exterior, the holes were covered with ¾-in. sheathing, 15-lb. felt and clapboard. Finally, in the crawlspace below, insulation was installed between joists. This completed the rough construction.

The wall finish selected was Cambridge Red Antique hardboard paneling. The material was also available in four other colors, each toned to match one of the popular antiquing kits on the market. (This made it simple to finish the trim to a perfect match).

Since room height was just about 8½ ft., I left the 1x6 baseboard in place and rested the panels atop. As they were cut, scraps were carefully placed aside for use on other parts of the job. All paneling was applied using a generous amount of adhesive and color-matched nails. Any mars or nail holes were filled with Panel Touch, a Masonite product that comes in tube rather than stick form.

The ceiling. This was in terrible shape, so I added furring strips and covered it with paneling. I picked up the cheapest V-groove plywood available. After installing the panels, I sealed, primed and painted them white. The beams that cover the joints are 4x4 cedar that I "antiqued" (roughed with an adz). Beams are held in place by countersunk screws which are concealed by short lengths of doweling. To create a "half beam" look, 2x4s were used at both ends of the room.

Along both sides (length) of the room, I installed a 1x6 skirt (or apron) at the ceiling. Where it was necessary to butt two boards end-to-end, I invented a joint that would give an Early American feeling (see skirt butt joint detail, page 1143). Dowels at these joints heighten the effect. Skirts were notched for the beam ends to rest on. To make the job go faster, all materials used for beams and skirts were stained and antiqued before installation.

Entertainment center. Now the busiest corner of the house, this built-in was challenging, but fun, to build. It is built in place and permanently fastened to the wall. The counter height is a standard 36 in. The deck and shelves below give ample storage for items such as records, games and photography gear. Sliding doors were used for a practical reason; swingers would have required clearance in the room, thus restricting furniture placement. Above the deck, four 2x12s (for economy, structural grade was used) were installed vertically to create shelf space. These were placed to give three bays of equal width. At bottom, they rest on shop-made plates that were

WITH A FRIEND HELPING, author knocked out windows in one day and had the room closed in by sundown. Opening was stripped down to the wall studs before any rebuilding was started. For safety, keep work area free of debris.

ROUGH OPENING is measured for new framing (left); exterior sheathing is applied next. Small opening in background (right) is framed for windows, which go in next. Windows here were installed with one stud between them.

WINDOW INSTALLATION is simple; plastic "fins" that you insert into the side jambs are provided with holes for use in nailing to sheathing. To prevent leaks, felt is stapled over the fins. Clapboard, which follows, finishes exterior.

cut from exterior, 5/4-in. casing that was saved when the old windows were torn out. For appearance, their edges were shaped with an ogee cutter in the router. The verticals were simply toenailed at top into the ceiling, at bottom into the counter and at several points along the back edges into the wall. Before installing them, the grooves for the flush-type wall standards were routed.

ENTERTAINMENT CENTER, framed chiefly with ¾-in. plywood, is built to room width.

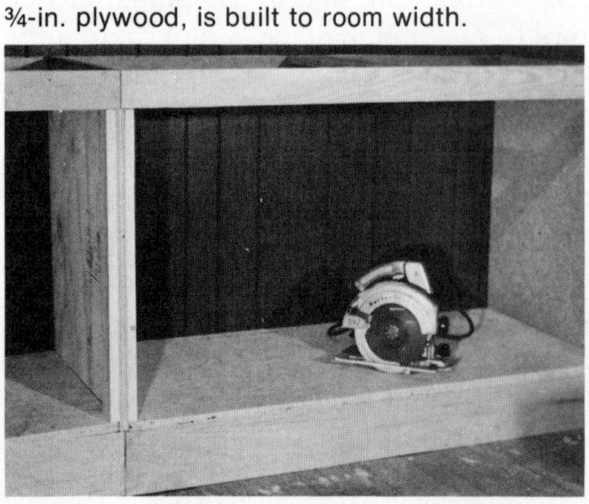

FACE OF UNIT was skinned with paneling applied with glue and brads.

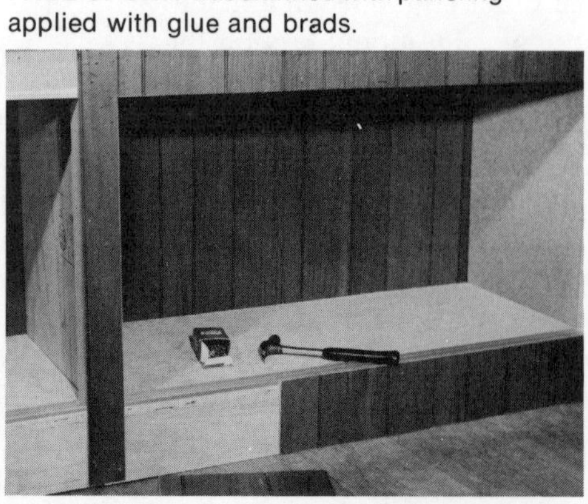

BUILT-IN ENTERTAINMENT CENTER

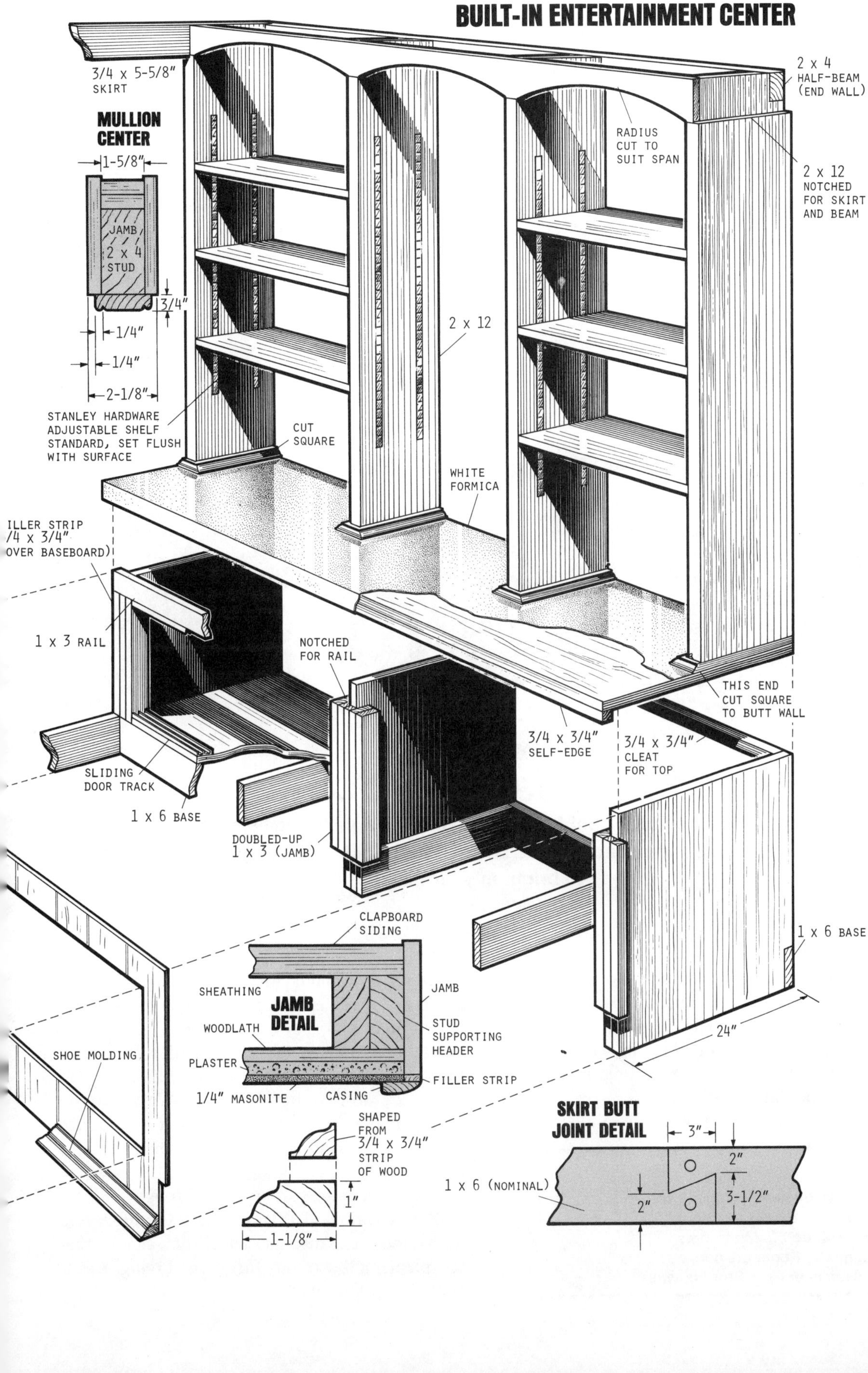

4 great ideas for family rooms

Noted interior decorator Shirley Regendahl took a plain family room and turned it into an exciting living space that is cheery and bright. You can use the same ideas to brighten your house

■ WITH SOME imagination and flair you can turn the drabbest family room into one that is functional and inviting. The bright and cheery room above is the kind of place in which you might like to spend an evening reading, listening to music or entertaining friends.

The project was co-sponsored by Pittsburgh Paints and Popular Mechanics magazine. We asked designer Regendahl to create a room that is fun to be in and easy to maintain. The four elements that make this a particularly exciting room—from cubed planters to sparkling painted floor—are do-it-yourself projects. We show you how to make the cubes, mirror shelf and lounge as well as how to apply that low-maintenance floor.

To complete the garden-room-brought-indoors look, one wall is clad with a paste-on brick and the window expanse has matchstick shades that complement the rattan furniture. Living greens add the garden touch.

SEE ALSO

Basement remodeling . . . Game tables . . .
Hi-fi centers . . . House additions . . .
Modular furniture . . . Mudrooms . . .
Remodeling . . . Room dividers . . .
Sliding glass doors . . . Storage walls

1 PLYWOOD PLANTERS

Elegant simplicity is the word for these contemporary plant stands. Fashioned of ¾-in. A-D plywood and then painted, both could be built in a single Saturday workshop session.

Construction has been made simple by keeping the sides identical. Thus you can cut and assemble parts production-style. Use a portable circular saw with a clamped-on guide to make the cuts, or do the cutting on your table saw. Make sure cutting is done with the good side up to avoid splintering along exposed edges. A veneer blade, or masking tape along the cutting line on the side where blade breaks through also reduces splintering. When parts are cut, assemble for a test fit. If cube doesn't have square corners, use a saw or block plane to true them up.

Disassemble parts and reassemble with glue, screws and nails as indicated. A flowerpot cutout at top, sized to suit, is optional. Sand and dust box, apply shellac or primer. Finish with Pittsburgh Paints high-gloss, alkyd-oil quick-dry enamel. Masking tape will assure straight lines when painting on triangles.

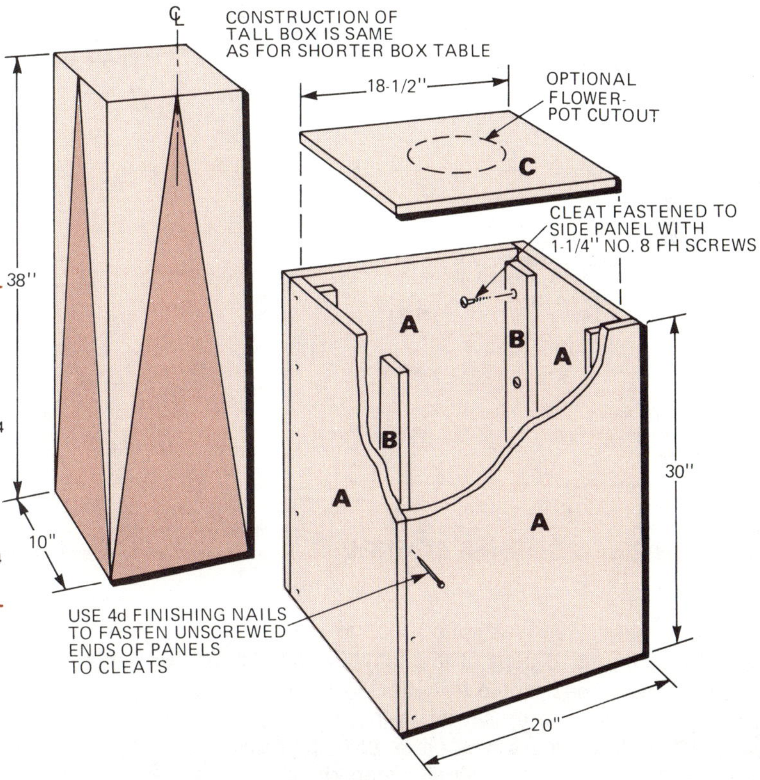

MATERIALS LIST

Key	Pcs.	Size and discription (use)
Short cube		
A	4	¾ x 19¼ x 30″ A-D plywood (sides)
B	4	¾ x 2½ x 29¼″, pine (corner cleats)
C	1	¾ x 18½ x 18½″, A-D plywood (top)

Misc.: White glue, 1¼″ No. 8 fh screws, 4d finishing nails, 4 furniture glides (optional) shellac or primer, paint.

Key	Pcs.	Size and discription (use)
Tall cube		
	4	¾ x 9¼ x 38″ A-D plywood (sides)
	4	¾ x 2½ x 37¼″, pine (corner cleats)
	1	¾ x 8½ x 8½″, plywood (top)

Misc.: White glue, 1¼″ No. 8 fh screws, 4d finishing nails, 4 furniture glides (optional) shellac or primer, paint.

2 PAINTED WALL SHELF

This handsome shelf, ideal for displaying plants beneath a mirror, is a lot easier to build than its looks might suggest.

Start by cutting all parts to size, as shown, and take the time to sand all surfaces smooth before assembly. Begin assembly by fastening ¾x1in. stock (B, D and E) to bottom piece (A) using glue and screws. Locate the support brackets (F) on the bottom piece and mark location for three screws per bracket. Bore screw clearance holes in A and transfer the marks to the brackets. Bore pilot holes in brackets and fasten brackets to the bottom using glue and 1¼-in. No. 8 fh screws.

With pilot holes bored, you can install the unit on the wall using lagscrews and washers as shown. Add part C at the front using glue and screws, then install the top piece, A, with glue and 4d finishing nails. To avoid excessive hammering, which could damage the wall, bore pilot holes for the nails, and set nailheads below the surface. Fill the resulting holes with wood plastic filler.

To finish, seal all wood parts—especially the end grains on the filler strips—with water-white shellac. Next day, sand lightly, dust and apply primer. When primer is dry, apply Pittsburgh Paints No. 54-352 white high-gloss, alkyd-oil quick-dry enamel following the instructions on the label.

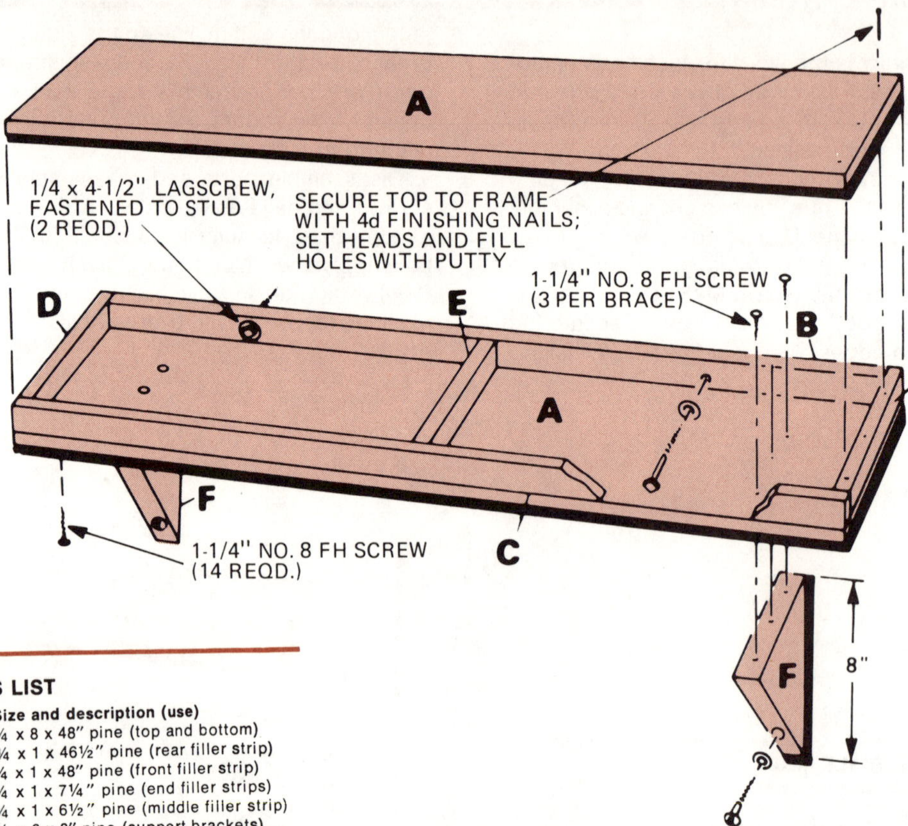

MATERIALS LIST

Key	Pcs.	Size and description (use)
A	2	¾ x 8 x 48" pine (top and bottom)
B	1	¾ x 1 x 46½" pine (rear filler strip)
C	1	¾ x 1 x 48" pine (front filler strip)
D	2	¾ x 1 x 7¼" pine (end filler strips)
E	1	¾ x 1 x 6½" pine (middle filler strip)
F	2	¾ x 6 x 8" pine (support brackets)

Misc.: White glue, 20 1¼" No. 8 fh screws, 1½" finishing nails, wood plastic filler, 120-grit sandpaper, pigmented shellac, two ¼ x 4½" lagscrews with washers.

3 CUSHIONED CORNER LOUNGE

The functional, foam-cushioned lounge really defines the shape and uses of this family room. The basic frame is constructed from one-by pine stock and then skinned with sturdy ¾-in. A-D fir plywood. The drawers are also made of fir plywood. You'll need about two and a half sheets of plywood to construct this sofa lounge.

Start by cutting frame members to size and notch them as indicated. Assemble dry to test fit pieces. When satisfied, proceed to assemble them with white glue and 4d finishing nails. Use bar or pipe clamps to keep the unit square as you work. Allow the assembled frame to dry overnight.

During your next session, cut plywood, along with backrest cap (G) to cover the frame. Note that the backrest (C) should be cut with the saw set for a 15° bevel on the top and bottom edges. Check to be sure that each piece of plywood will fit properly before making your cuts.

To conserve plywood, cut the drawer fronts (O and S) right from the sofa back (D). To do so, lay out drawers in pencil and drill a series of 6 or 7 1/16-in.-dia. holes, touching one another, on each line of cut. In the slots thus formed, insert the blade of a sabre saw and proceed to drop out

MATERIALS LIST—LOUNGE

Key	Pcs.	Size and description
A	2	¾ x 27¼ x 30" fir plywood
B	1	¾ x 14 x 96" fir plywood
C	1	¾ x 16½ x 96" fir plywood
D	1	¾ x 30 x 96" fir plywood
E	4	¾ x 2½ x 94½" pine
F	4	¾ x 2½ x 30" pine
G	1	¾ x 3½ x 96" pine
H	6	¾ x 2½ x 14" pine
I	1	¾ x 27¼ x 96" fir plywood
J	10	¾ x 2½ x 25¾" pine
K	8	¾ x 1½ x 27¼" pine
L	2	¾ x 15¼ x 8" fir plywood
M	4	¾ x 8½ x 18" fir plywood
N	2	¼ x 18 x 18⅞" fir plywood
O	2	¾ x 8⅞ x 23⅞" fir plywood
P	2	¾ x 7¾ x 18⅜" fir plywood
Q	2	¾ x 3 x 18⅜" fir plywood
R	2	¼ x 18 x 18⅞" fir plywood
S	2	¾ x 3⅞ x 23⅞" fir plywood
T	4	¾ x 3 x 18" fir plywood

Misc.: White glue, foam cushions, washable fabric to cover cushions, zippers and cord for welting (optional), 4 drawer pulls; 4d finishing nails and 1½" No. 6 fh screws as required; 120-grit sandpaper; paint; water-white shellac, primer paint.

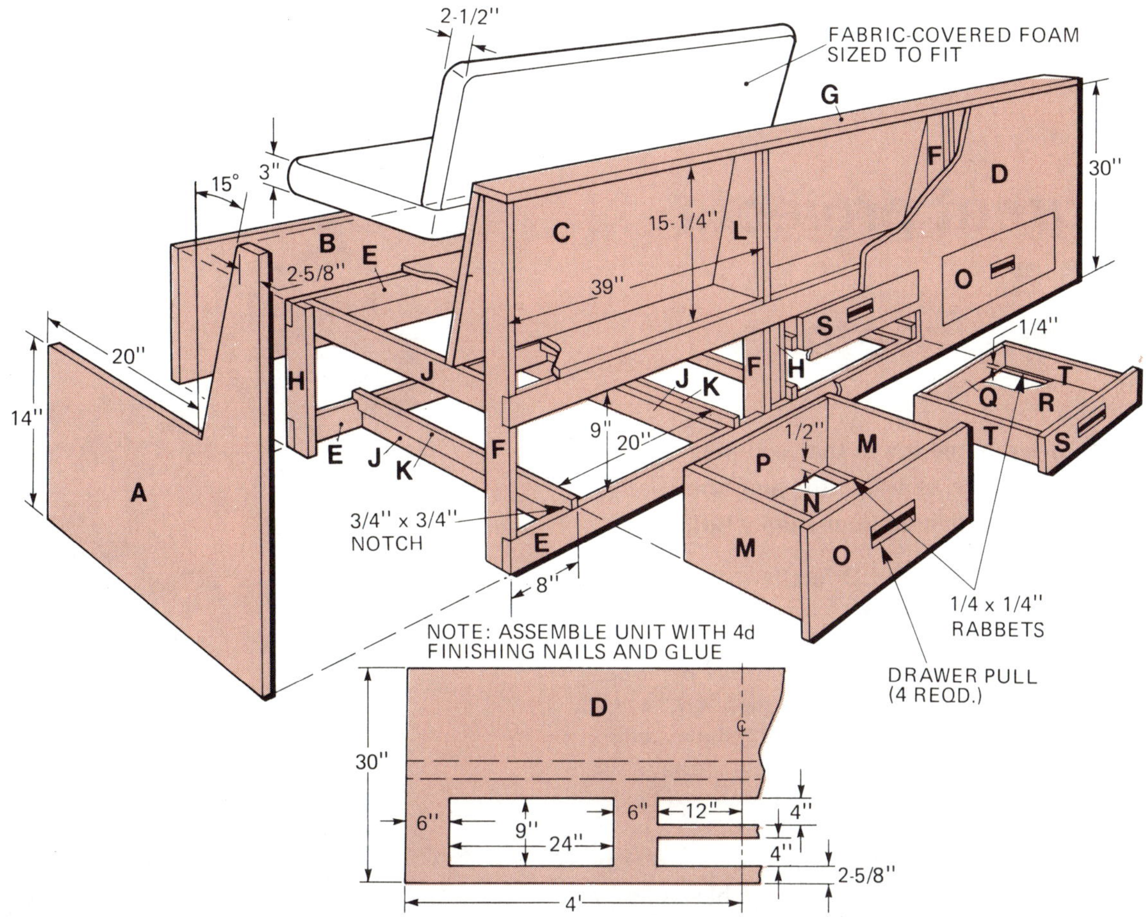

drawer fronts. The proper clearance is automatically provided for.

Next, nail and glue plywood to the pine frame, rechecking for square as you go. Set all the nail heads and fill the holes with wood plastic filler.

Cut remaining parts to drawers along with grooves in sides M and T. Install drawer pulls and assemble pieces with glue. Use screws, which will provide better holding power, at the drawer joints. This is especially important on joints where front and sides meet.

Sand all exposed surfaces and edges smooth and seal with water-white shellac. After priming, the same paint used on the walls, Pittsburgh Paints Blossom white, No. P2537, can be used as the finish coat.

4 FLOOR GRAPHICS

The bouncy color scheme of the floor sets off the neutral wicker motif and plant collection to produce a cheerful vibrancy. Before painting on the floor graphics, clean floor thoroughly. Use turpentine to wash away accumulations of wax and sand glossy areas with 320-grit sandpaper. Pick up all dust with a tack cloth, prime and then lay out the pattern with masking tape. We used Pittsburgh Paints Brilliant Yellow, No. 54-302; Black, No. 54-309 and White, No. 54352. All of these are durable, washable, high-gloss, alkyd-oil, quick-drying enamels.

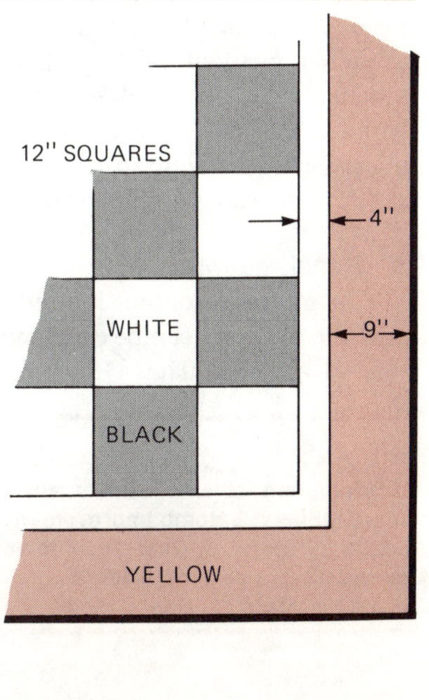

5 great projects for a family room

Here are some ideas that will help you create a room to serve as a hub for just about any indoor activities your family enjoys

■ A WELL-DESIGNED family room provides the setting for a variety of activities. The room shown here features a breakfast/snack counter that readily converts to a refreshment bar when friends come to visit. A contemporary, wraparound sofa with cushions and pillows offers plenty of seating. The center of attraction is the fireplace wall. These ideas were developed by designer Shirley Regendahl for PPG Industries.

The key to any multipurpose room is to keep the plan simple—and furniture durable and easy to clean. Route traffic around (not through) the area used for relaxing, to prevent it from seeming unsettled and hectic.

Coherent visual impact, also helps make the user feel good about the room. For example, it would be disorienting to have the snack counter visually intrude upon the lounging area. In this instance, the designer used graphics painted on the floor to distinguish the two areas.

An area with several zones of activity also needs to be visually unified. To achieve this, the unpretentious look of rough-textured wood was specified. To obtain this textured-wood effect without the expense of rough-sawn wall and ceiling panels, 8-in.-wide strips were ripped from ¼-in.-thick sheets of C-D plywood.

1. Snack counter

This multiuse counter is sized for eating from one side only, but can be extended on the kitchen side to accommodate a four-place setting. For durable service, the surface can be covered and edged with plastic laminate.

The bar surface may also be painted as shown in photo. Low-gloss, ebony enamel was used because it stands up to heavy-duty use and is easy to wipe clean.

Begin construction by cutting notches in legs. Test-fit all joints and then assemble frame with 1¼-in. brads and glue. Clamp overnight. Use ¾-in. plywood for shelves and countertop.

2. Painted floor

To paint runner design on floor, use a latex-based, urethane enamel to resist wear from heavy traffic. It cleans easily with a wet sponge and mild detergent. Our design has a white background with Black Pearl stripes, Gray Wisp diamonds and Fleet Gray triangles. Use paper pattern when marking triangular and

SEE ALSO

Backgammon tables . . . Basement remodeling . . . Game tables . . . Home improvement . . . Mobile furniture . . . Occasional tables . . . Remodeling . . . Room dividers . . . Sewing centers . . . Snack tables

YOU'LL FIND that this 16 x 16-ft. area can be recycled over and over, beginning the day as a place for breakfast, and ending the day as a fine spot for the family to get together with a favorite table game.

diamond-shaped areas. Masking tape applied to borders before painting will assure straight, clean outlines.

3. Wrap-around seating

This sofa will stand up to continuous use. Pillow coverings should be removable and made from washable fabric for easy cleaning. To build, cut out as many frames from ½-in. C-D plywood as required and notch for plates and cleats as shown. Seats and seatbacks should be made from ¾-in. A-C plywood. The sofa back should be solid ¼-in. A-C plywood. Panel the front to match the wall or use solid ¼-in. A-C plywood.

When joining benches at a right angle, butt bench frames, then cut sheathing to fit. The seat and seatback will have to extend beyond the end of one section. Use 1½-in. No. 6 fh wood screws to secure the butt joint where seatbacks meet.

4. Fireplace wall

This wall may be thought of as an assemblage of three-dimensional and one-dimensional shapes. If the log bin and artificial fireplace with electric logs don't suit you, you might build book compartments and display shelves in their places.

Plan the openings you desire and build frames (as shown in log bin plans) to support a five-sided box, sized to suit. The only difference between constructing the 33 x 46½-in. fireplace box and the log bin is that a larger header is required at the front of the firebox opening to support the weight of the stud, nailers and paneling above. Use doubled 2 x 4s nailed with wide face flush to the new wall surface. Trim all openings with ¼ x 1⅛-in. lattice.

Construct wall of 2 x 4s, 24-in. O.C. The paneling is cut from ¼-in. C-D plywood into 8-in.-wide strips. Apply stain before cutting plywood. Cut edges may have to be retouched later. Nail strips to wall at sole and top plates. Bridging halfway up the wall, also serves as a nailer.

5. Raised hearth

The hearth/bench is easy to construct. A 2 x 4 ledger strip nailed to the studs in the fireplace wall supports the back of the hearth. The front and ends are really a small wall, paneled and stained to match the fireplace wall. Use a 1 x 12 for the top, and stain to match seating and trim.

SNACK COUNTER

1

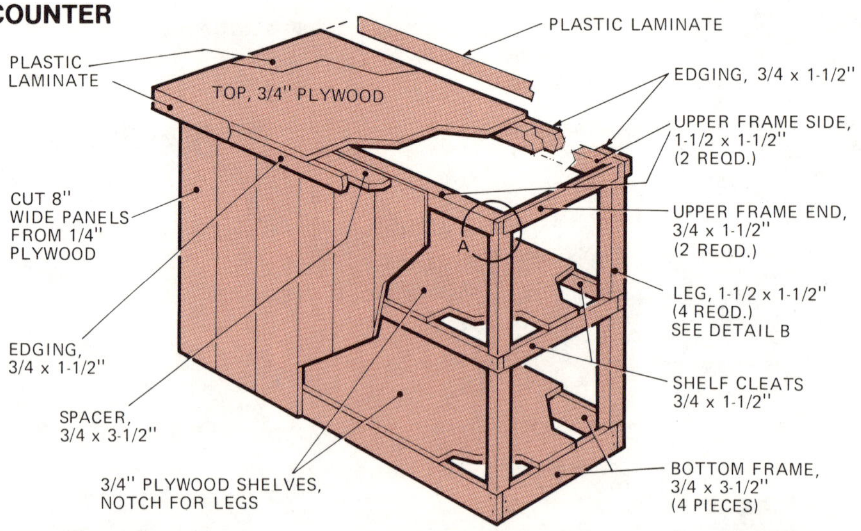

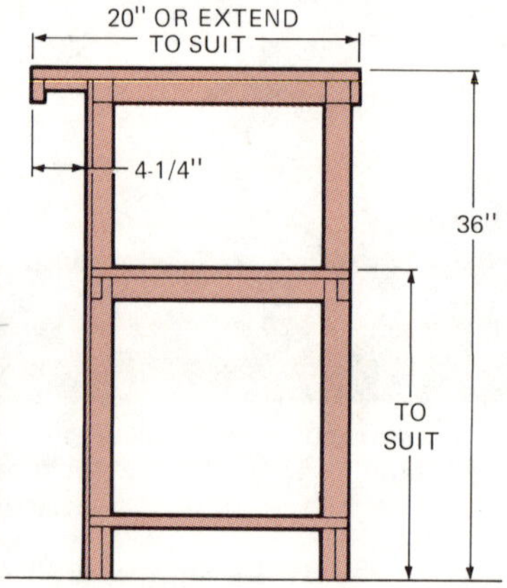

CROSS-SECTION VIEW

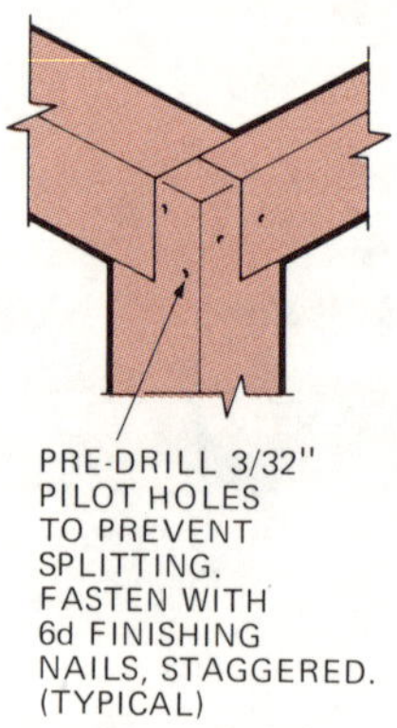

DETAIL A

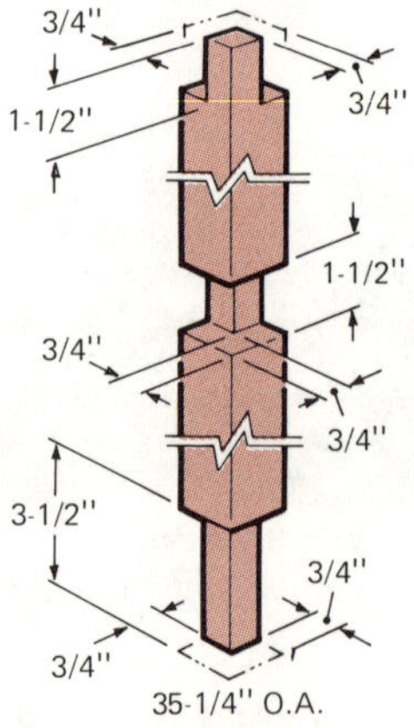

DETAIL B

2

PAINTED FLOOR

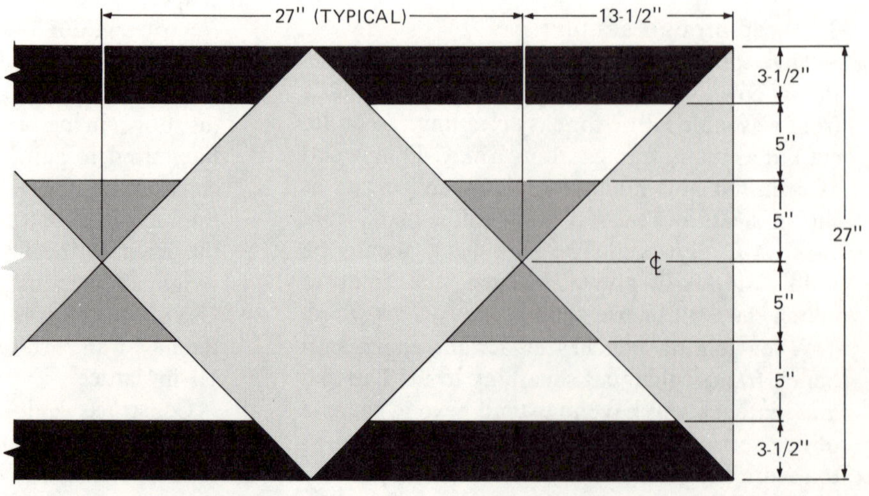

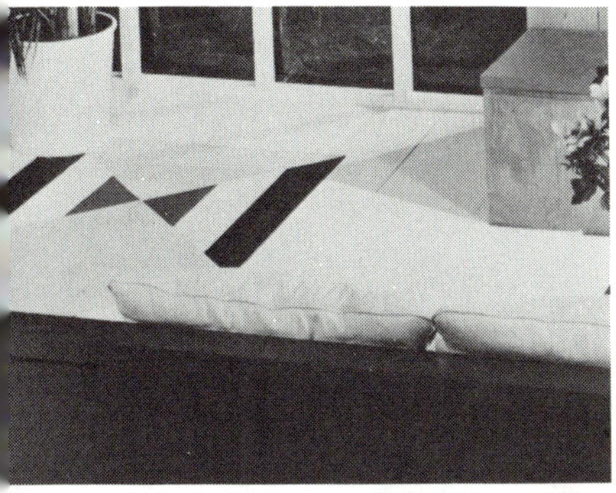

3

4

5

WRAP-AROUND SEATING

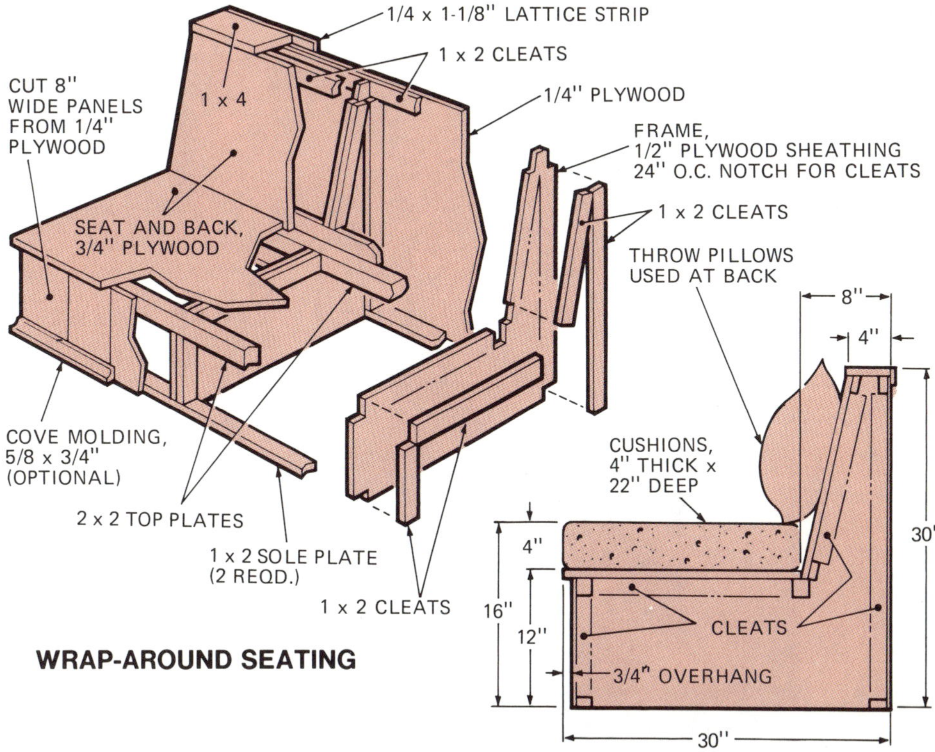

RAISED HEARTH

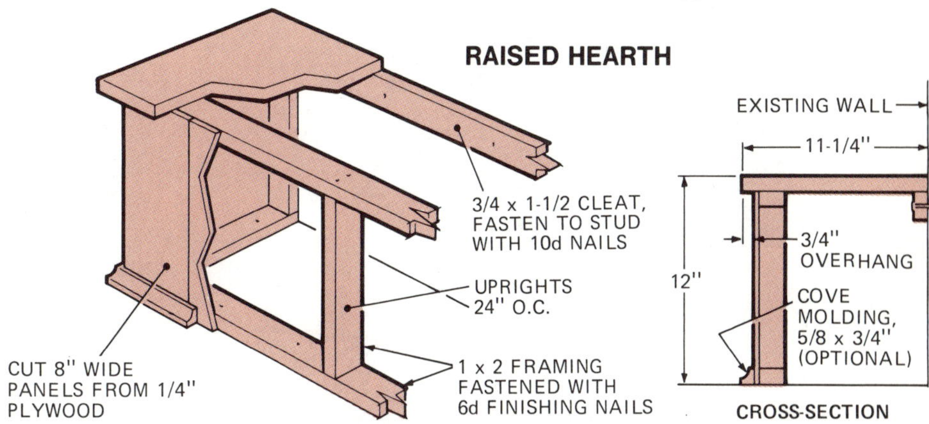

LOG BIN

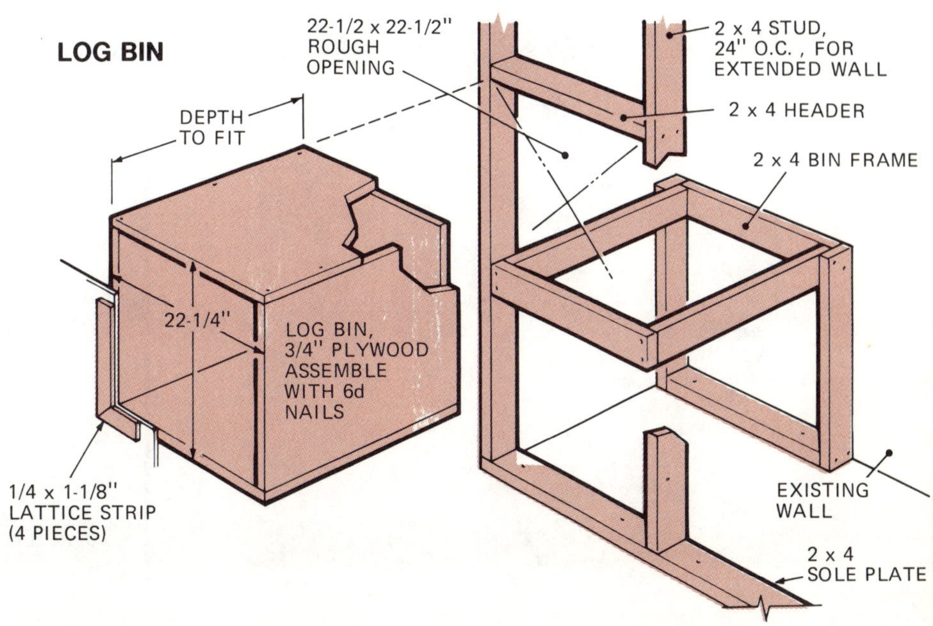

THIS FAMILY ROOM gave the homeowner a playroom with storage space to spare. Bold splashes of color and zebra-striped closet doors add to the visual impact.

A FLOOR PLAN was laid out carefully to provide three distinct and separate areas for adults, youngsters and dining. A built-in sofa offers additional storage.

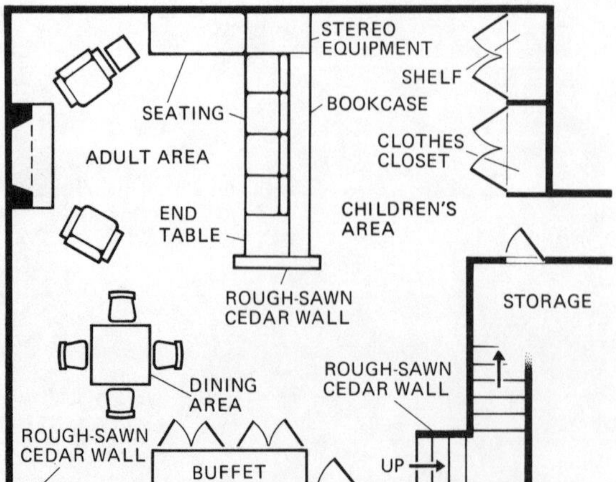

Bold patterns for family rooms

By HARRY WICKS

By using new materials and being a little daring, you can build a family room with a personality all its own

■ THERE'S NO RULE that says you can't simply frame and panel a basement to convert it into a usable family room. But why let such conventional thinking limit your creative imagination? With some foresight and planning, you can add splashes of color, use "different" materials and design a basement family room with a personality of its own.

The three basement family rooms on these pages, for example, reflect individual family preferences in decorating and room usage. And all ideas shown are valid and easy to duplicate if you want something in your basement family room other than the customary paneled-wall look.

As can be seen in the floor plan on the facing page, the owner wanted to gain three distinct uses from his family room. First, he wanted an area—with adequate storage—for the youngsters to play in; second, an adult room for parties and get-togethers; and finally, a generous-size dining area for family gatherings. Careful planning guaranteed these uses to make it an area for the whole family to enjoy.

A little daring, such as the use of zebra-stripe, "wet-look" wallpaper kept the room's appearance

A COLONIAL TAVERN look (top, left) wanted by owner Ted McLaren, was created by using weathered siding on walls. The contemporary mood (left) is heightened by the dramatic effect of a split-level bar.

SEE ALSO

**Bars . . . Basement remodeling . . .
Basement waterproofing . . . Fireplaces . . .
Game tables . . . Home improvement . . .
Remodeling . . . Storage ideas . . . Storage walls . . .
Wallpaper**

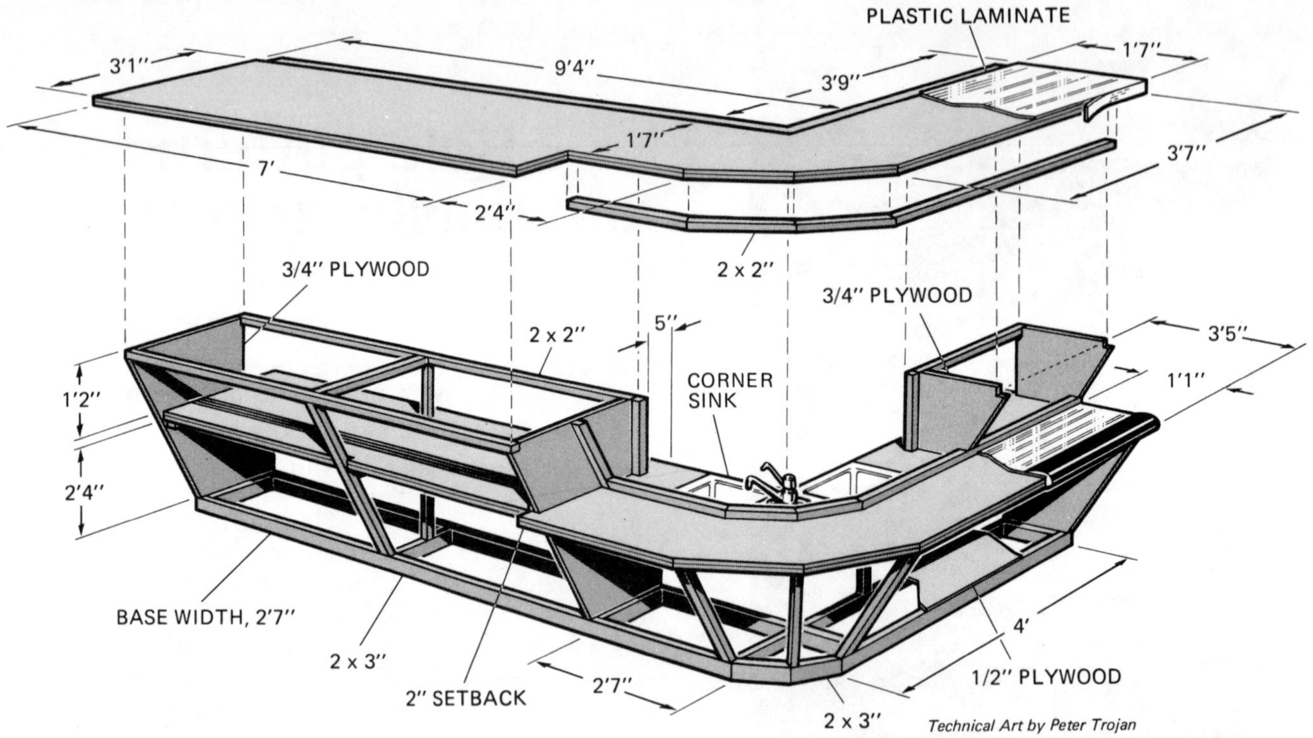

Technical Art by Peter Trojan

consistent with the rest of the home.

The same approach is true of the split-level bar shown on these pages. The clever design is further enhanced by the canopy and decorative valance. Notice that the lower "level" has a bumper along the outside edge. This is simply Naugahyde-covered foam rubber.

The bar and the wall opposite (shown below) are in the Jack Laboe home in Golden Valley, Minn. The remodeling was a do-it-yourself project. Jack simply covered the lower half of the walls with prefinished birch plywood. Above the dado he applied striped wallpaper over plasterboard for pattern and color.

The seating arrangement along wall opposite the bar has built-in storage and plastic-laminated armrests

To achieve the warmth that typical American inns offered weary travelers a century ago Ted McLaren (Minneapolis) utilized materials salvaged from old farm buildings. Aside from adding great authenticity, the old boards kept overall costs down. The owner claims that by doing the basement himself, total cash outlay was under $500—including that factory-built fireplace. The stones were gathered by the McLaren clan and Ted was his own mason.

When planning your basement, there are other points to keep in mind besides color and cost. First, it pays to lay out the room in scale on graph paper. Done this way, the room can be designed for maximum efficiency before you ever lift a hammer. Second, after you have decided upon decor, spend several Saturdays visiting well-stocked lumberyards to learn what materials are now available. If you haven't investigated in this area lately, you'll be pleasantly surprised to find how much stone, brick, weathered siding and "wallpaper" comes in 4 x 8-ft. panels to make do-it-yourself installations a snap for just about any home handyman. Finally, do the work, then sit back and watch the family enjoy the new family room.

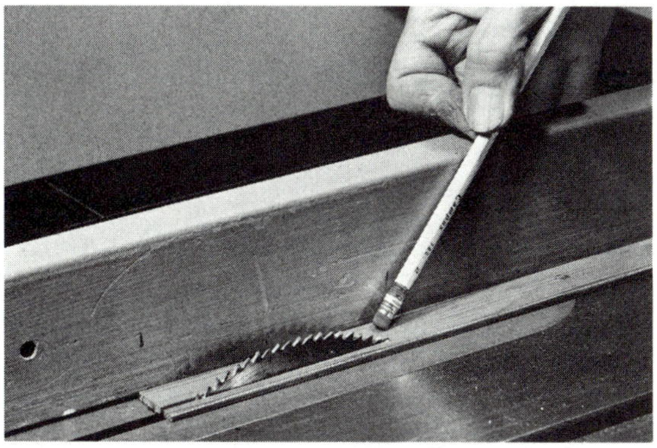

NEW PENCIL with soft eraser makes a good push stick when you rip thin stock on a bench saw.—*Victor H. Lamoy, Upper Jay, NY.*

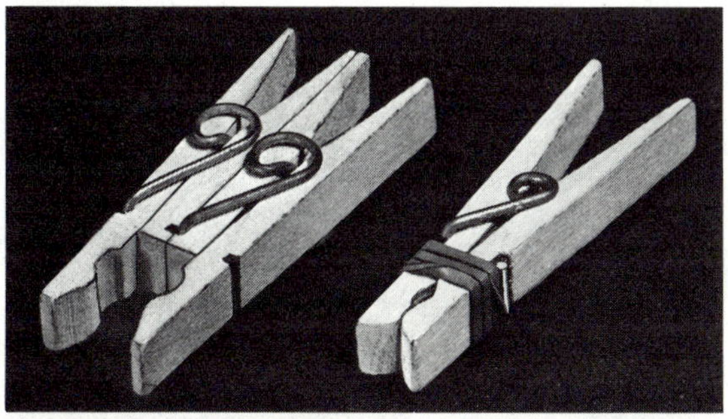

INCREASE JAW WIDTH by cutting one jaw off each of two clothespins and gluing them together. Add gripping power by wrapping them with a rubber band.—*John Krill, North Lima, OH.*

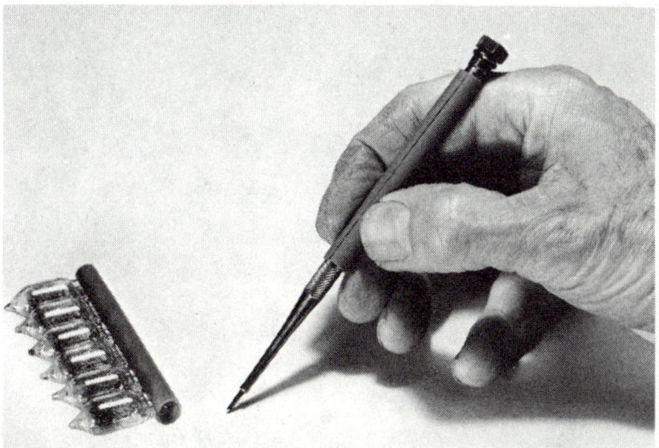

FOR A SMOOTH GRIP, I covered my scriber with a plastic tube which is used to protect the bases of A-G (all-glass) flash bulbs.—*Walter Burton, Akron, OH.*

SOAKING A PAINTBRUSH in paint thinner without the bristles touching bottom of container and fanning out helps save the brush. One method is to attach an adhesive-backed plastic picture hanger to the brush handle. Place metal hook upside down and clip over the edge of the container.—*Bernt G. Halverson, Gainesville, FL.*

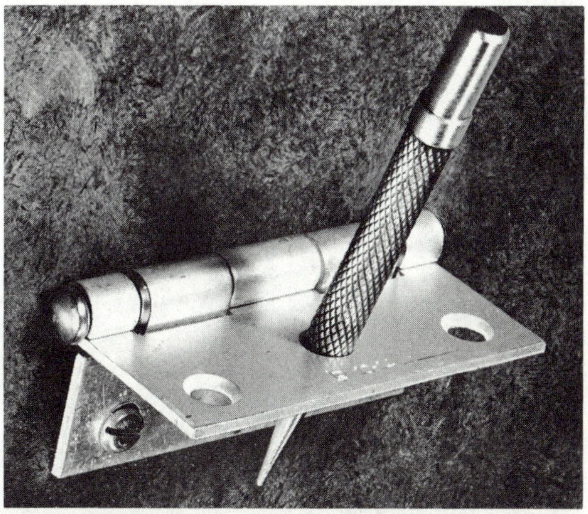

AN OLD HINGE turned backward for rigidity and screwed to the wall over your workbench—where you can't brush against it—makes an excellent holder for punches or nailsets.—*Ralph O. Fritts, Amsterdam, MO.*

Quick ways to spruce up the basement

Hide furnace, workshop, washer and dryer with quick-change walls and screeens; add some quick-made accessories, and that 'impossible' basement will take on a party look with minimum effort and money. Then all you have to do is provide the entertainment

SEE ALSO
Bars . . . Basement remodeling . . .
Basement stairwells . . .
Basement waterproofing . . . Bridge tables . . .
Dining tables . . . Game tables . . .
Hobby centers . . . Pool tables . . . Remodeling . . .
Room dividers

PARTY FURNITURE that you can make yourself from inexpensive plywood can include these two clever card tables. The one above is a simple box with playing-card designs added to sides; table below is supported by a Lally column.

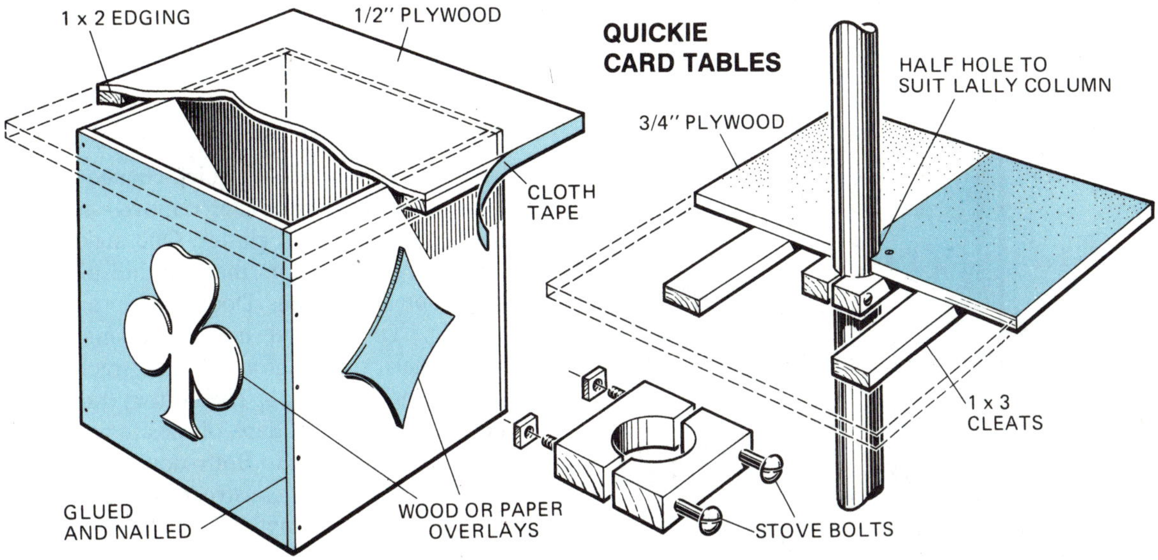

■ YOU'VE BEEN THINKING it would be fun to have a party—perhaps a big gang of 10 or more couples. But where will put them all? Your wife suggests the basement, if you fix it up a bit. But you shudder at the thought of trying to make it presentable without spending a bundle or a month of Sundays. You'll be surprised at what improvements you can accomplish for a few dollars and a minimum of effort.

Mostly, it's a case of "cover up"—hiding the furnace, oil tank, water heater; screening a washer and dryer from view, concealing your workshop or just covering up general basement clutter. Concealment alone covers a multitude of sins in sprucing up the most impossible basement.

There are other things you can do to give a party atmosphere to a dingy area. You can put Lally columns (the steel posts that support the floor above) to work supporting home-built tables. You can slap a coat of quick-drying latex paint on drab concrete walls to brighten things up. You can solve a problem floor with a roll of gaily-striped indoor-outdoor carpeting. You can round up travel posters and photo blowups to help cover up and add a festive touch. And if you don't have the right kind of furniture, you can make it.

A typical small-home basement is shown below, and on this and the following four pages you'll find instructions for making the various cover-ups and accessories suggested.

LEGEND

1. Quickie card tables
2. Folding screen
3. Quick-change wall
4. Dummy louvered window
5. Game divider and screen
6. Decorative divider
7. Cube stools
8. Buffet table
9. Fuel-tank screen
10. Indoor-outdoor carpet

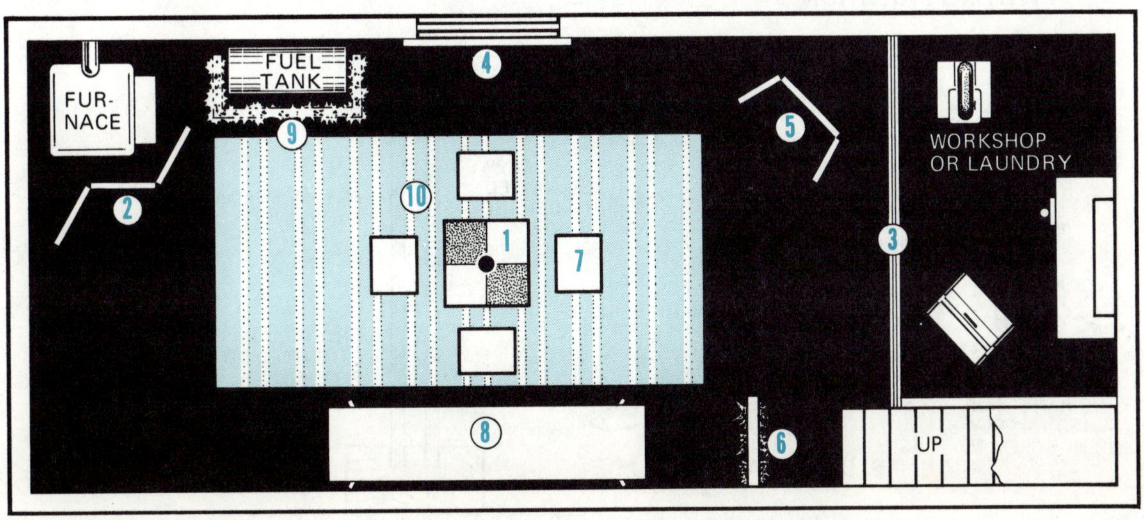

basement spruce-up, continued

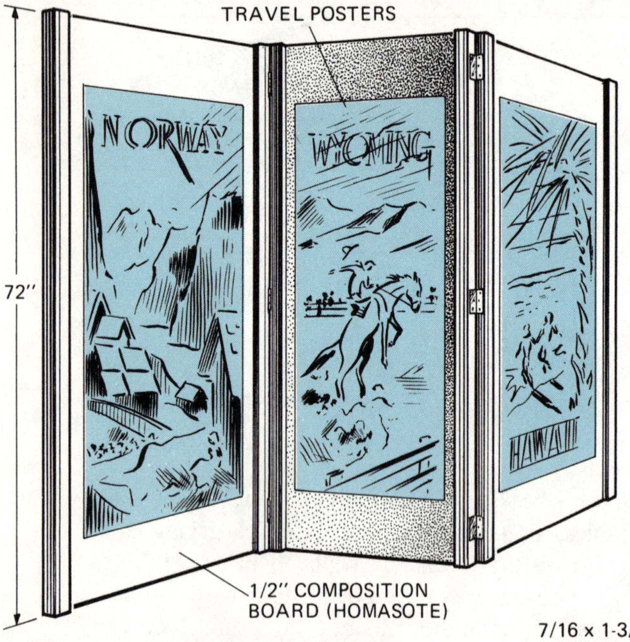

FOLDING LAUNDRY OR FURNACE SCREEN

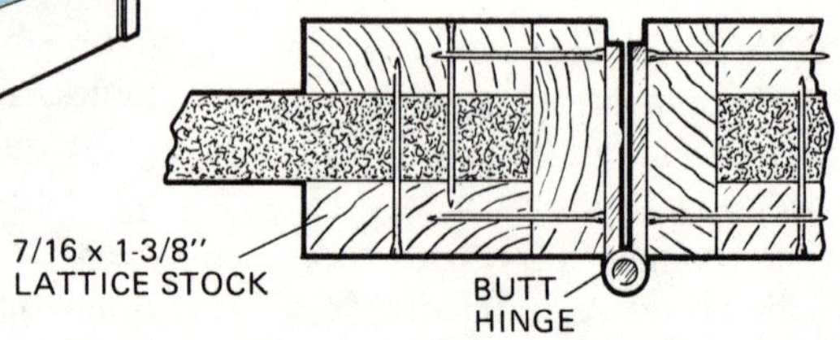

Quick-change walls

There are two kinds of quick-change partitions you can build—and later remove—to hide a workshop or basement clutter. One makes use of inexpensive flush doors that lap and pivot in holes in floor and ceiling. Doors lift up and out for storing. The second uses bypassing, prefinished panels set in grooved 2x4 tracks anchored to floor and ceiling. The bottom track can be anchored with small dabs of mastic so it can be taken up and stored. Both doors are convenient, not difficult to construct and are a fine way to hide just about anything.

PIVOTING PARTITION

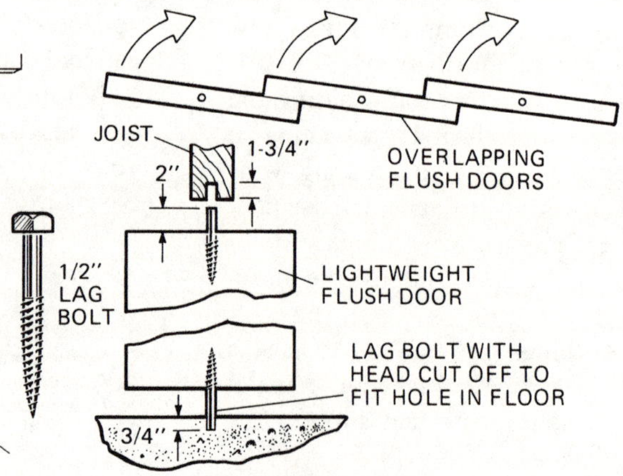

SLIDING PARTITION

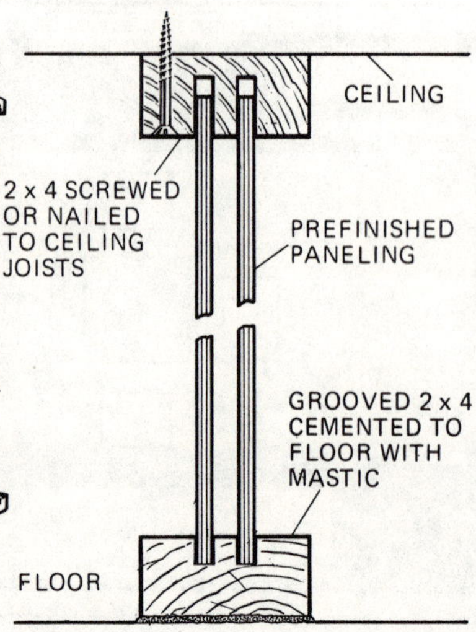

Dummy windows

For basement windows, curtains are the easy way out, but a more novel treatment uses narrow-louver shutters installed in dummy full-window frames. Attached to the wall, they take away the "basement look." If the upper shutters are hinged, the windows can be opened for ventilation.

Game dividers and screens

Folding game dividers such as a dartboard add fun to a party while hiding a washer and dryer or water heater. Legs grooved to fit plywood or hardboard are hinged to fold flat.

A conversation screen (lower right) also adds to an evening's fun when covered with humorous cartoons and pictures or posters. Its shelves provide handy places for those guests who always seem to need somewhere to set a drink or ashtray.

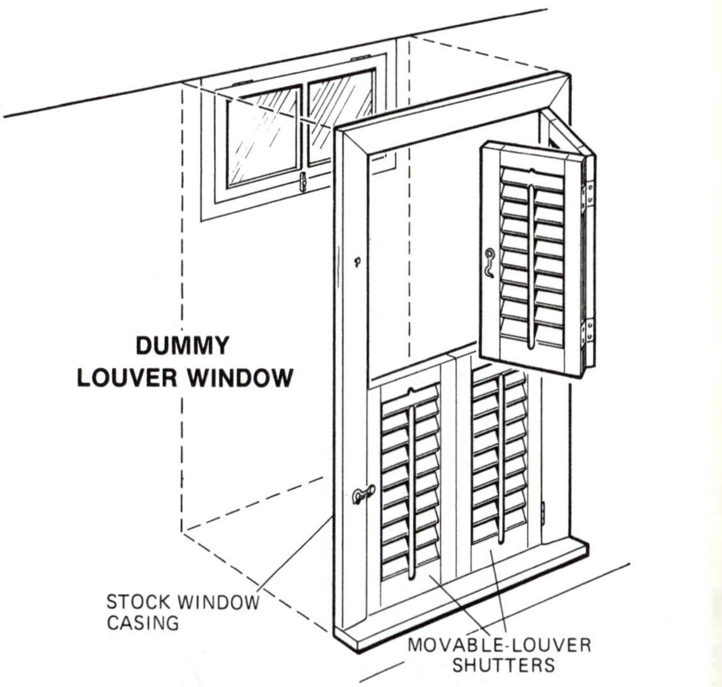

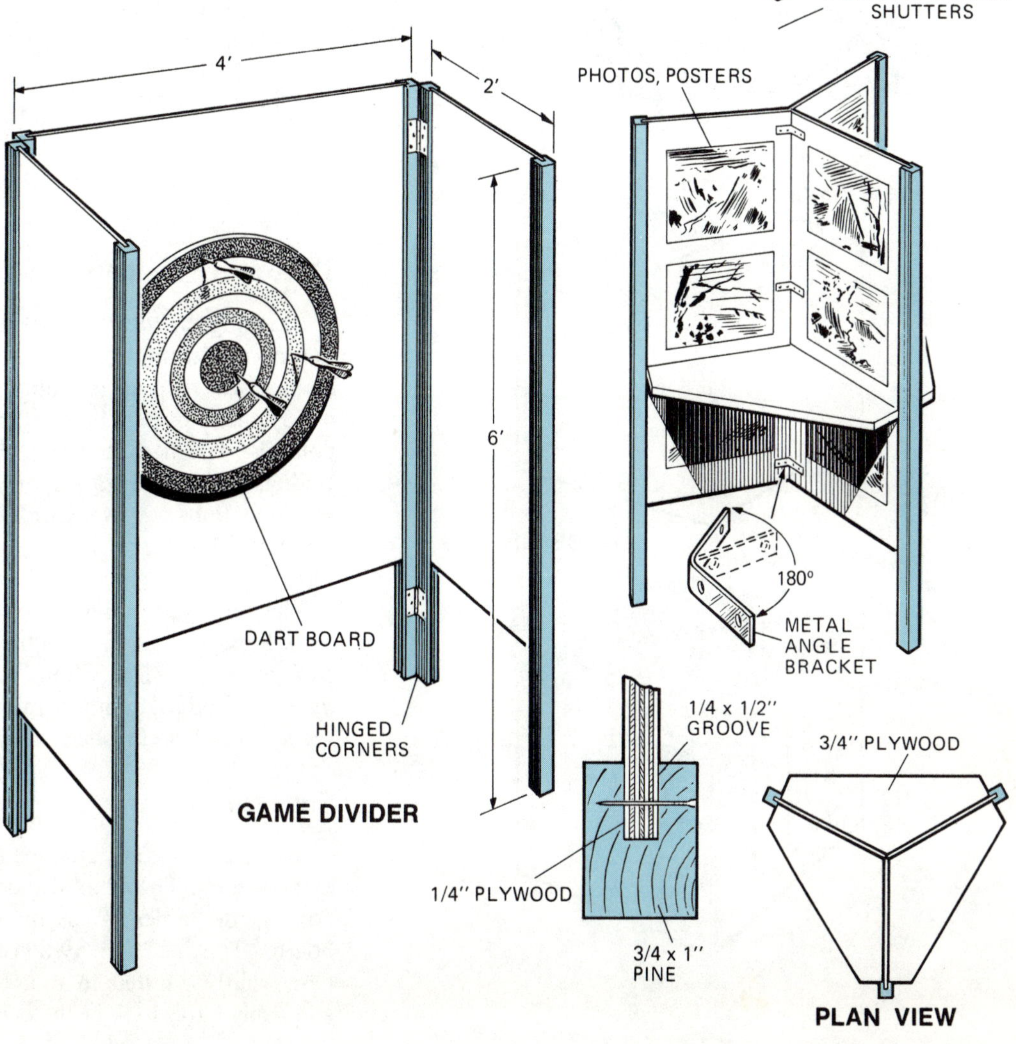

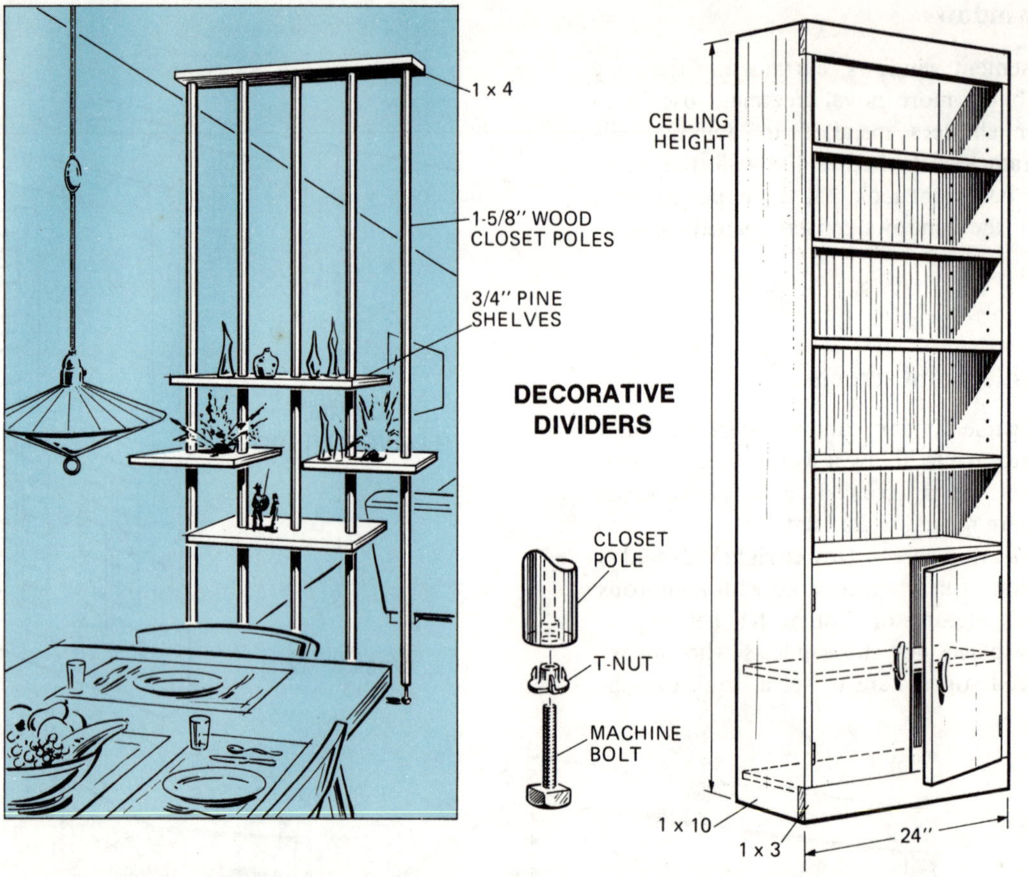

DECORATIVE DIVIDERS

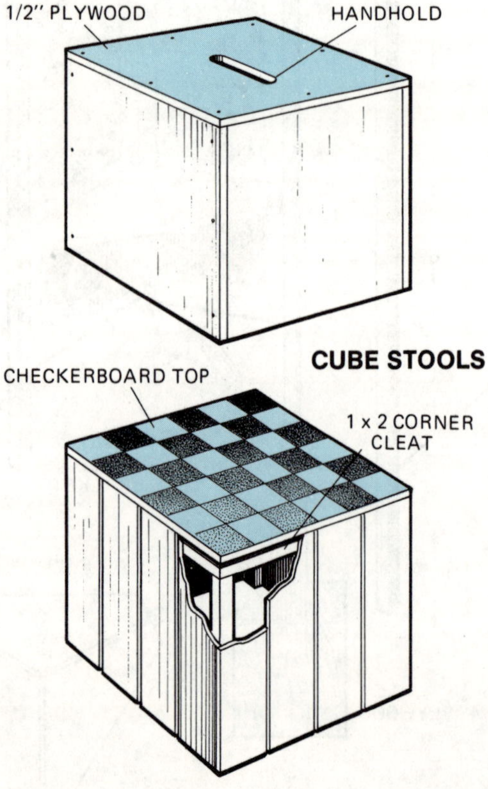

CUBE STOOLS

Decorative dividers

Blocking the view of basement stairs or partitioning off an unwanted area with a ceiling-high divider will help spruce up a room and provide handy shelf space. The see-through one of closet poles is designed to wedge between floor and ceiling. Ends of poles are drilled for T-nuts and machine bolts. A wedging action is the result when the bolts are backed out to bear against the floor.

The bookcase divider offers shelves for a record player and hi-fi equipment, with album storage below. The whole thing is made from pine in standard lumberyard sizes, the back being a piece of prefinished paneling.

Cube stools

When chairs run out, cube stools help provide extra seating. They can also double as sit-on-the-floor game tables when the tops are checkerboards. They're just plywood boxes, for the most part, wildly painted in red, blue and yellow to add a gay party look to the occasion.

KNOCKDOWN BUFFET TABLE

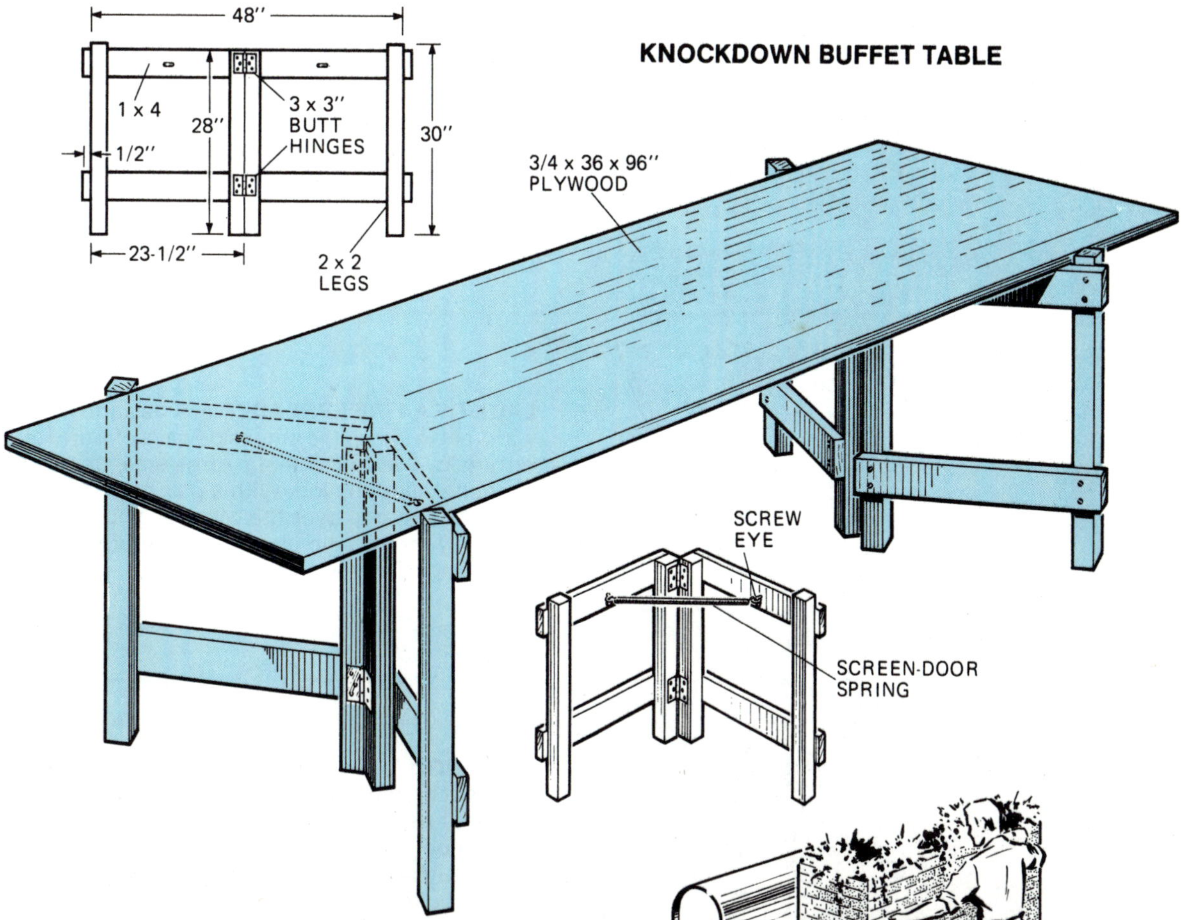

Knockdown buffet table

The easiest way to serve your guests is buffet-style and this is where you need a long, "help-yourself" table that can be taken apart and stored easily when the party is over.

This buffet table fills the bill perfectly. The top is a 3x8-ft. piece of plywood, and each pair of hinged legs is assembled from 2x2 and 1x4 material. Screen-door springs make the legs hug the top when they are spread apart.

Fuel-tank screen

No one would suspect that this attractive "brick" planter is actually hiding an ugly fuel-oil tank; you may want to leave it in place long after the party.

The rough framework consists of 2x2s covered with Celotex and then faced with simulated white brick, such as Decro-Wall, glued or stapled in place. Casters may be added, after which some artificial greenery is stuck in the holes around the top to create the planter effect.

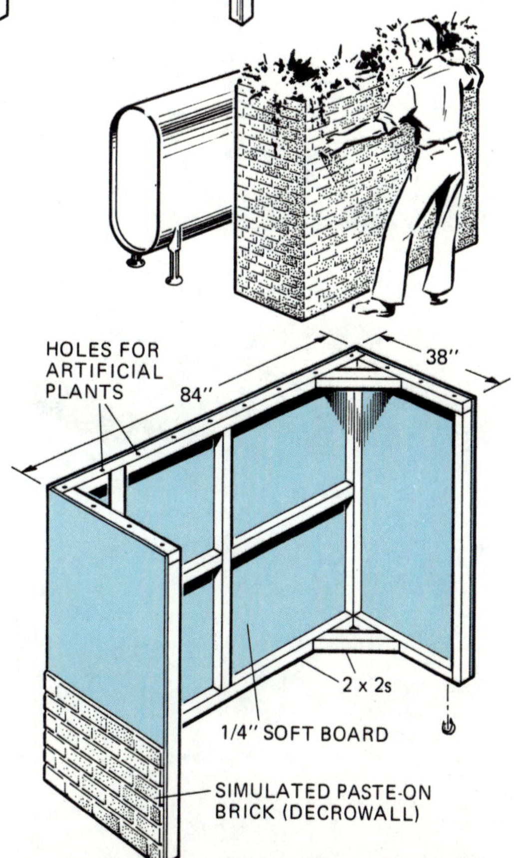

FUEL-TANK SCREEN

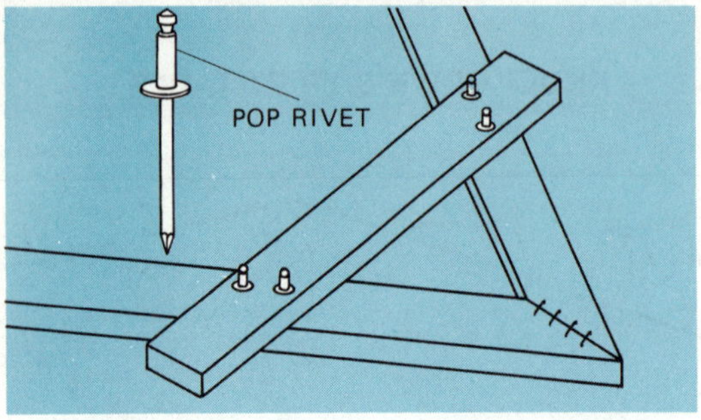

POP RIVETS make a fine substitute for double-head (scaffold) nails when needed for temporary bracing, I discovered. If driven and extracted carefully, they can be used more than once, as well as for their original purpose.—*Andrew Vena, Philadelphia.*

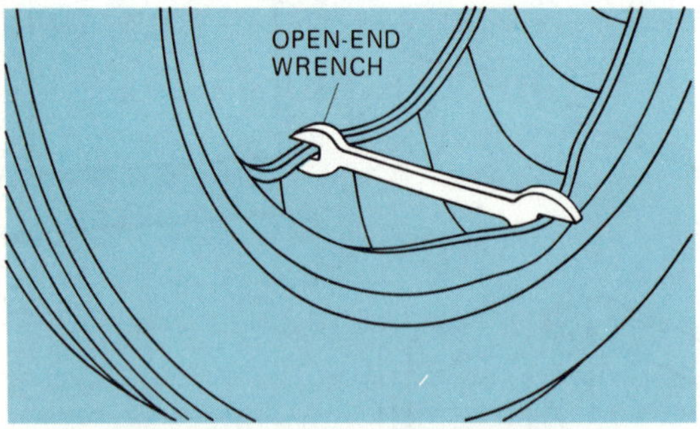

LACK OF A TIRE SPREADER can be annoying when you want to check the inner sidewalls of a tire for cuts or breaks. I've found that a large-size, open-end wrench will do the job. With a pair of wrenches, you can leapfrog one over the other as you work your way around the circumference of the tire.—*Roger Moylan, Los Angeles.*

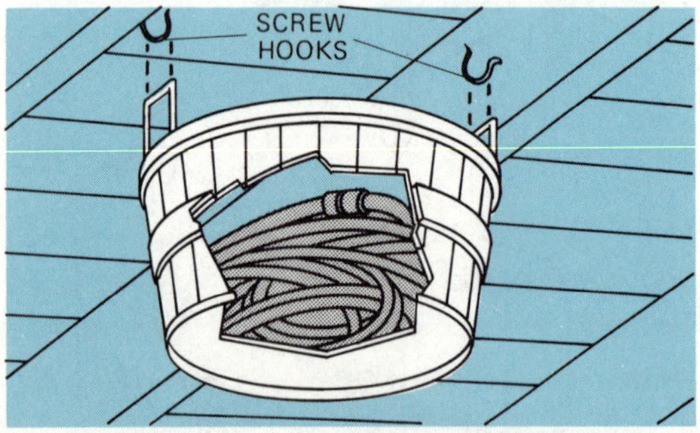

A METHOD for winter storage of a garden hose I've used successfully is coiling the hose neatly into a bushel basket and then hanging the basket with screw hooks from the basement joists. If your basement has a finished ceiling, locate a spot on your garage collar beams.—*Victor Lamoy, Saranac Lake, NY.*

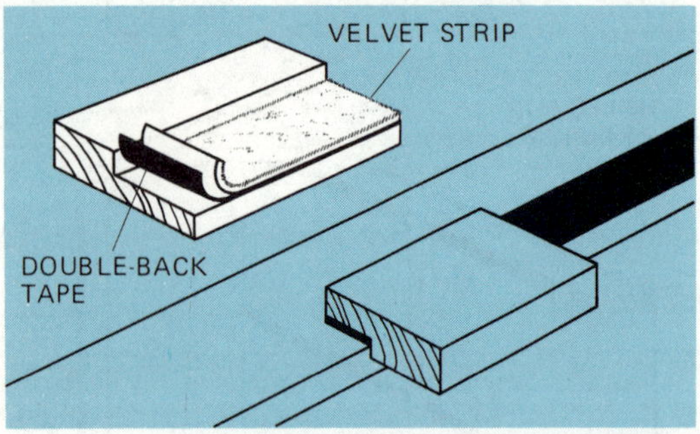

STRAIGHT (SQUARE-EDGED) BORDERS—around picture frames, for example—can be painted without the fuss of masking tape by using this simple device. Make it from a wood block, strip of velvet, and two-face carpet tape. Paint sparingly and apply very little pressure to keep paint from beading at the edge of the border.—*Richard Sturgeon, Kitchener, Ont.*

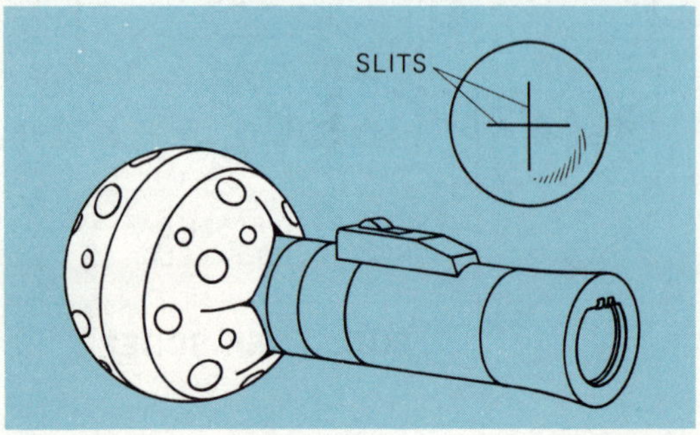

WHEN CARRYING A FLASHLIGHT in a toolbox, a glass lens is likely to be shattered and a plastic one badly scarred. Protect the lens by cutting intersecting slits crosswise into a hollow rubber ball of appropriate size, and then pushing the front end of the flashlight through the slits.—*John Krill, North Lima, OH.*

Hang anything on any wall

Whether you're mounting a pin-up lamp or a suspended bar—on a frame wall or on solid masonry—you must choose the type and size of fastener that fits the job

By ALFRED W. LEES

■ MORE AND MORE, the walls of our homes are being put to work. Today we hang dozens of things *from* walls—including buffets—and new fasteners have been developed for specific jobs.

Yet many homeowners aren't even familiar with the old standbys, such as toggle and "Molly" bolts. A comprehensive "selector chart" is needed on all wall fasteners, old and new, and on the next five pages you'll find just that.

The first thing to consider, in choosing a fastener, is the type of wall it's going into. In most homes, this will be a hollow wall above grade and a poured or block wall in the basement. In hollow walls you want a fastener that passes through the plaster or drywall face (or the wall of cinder block or hollow tile) and spreads out to anchor against the back. In solid walls, you want a fastener that holds by expanding against the sides of the hole you sink it into, whether in concrete, brick or stone.

Two additional considerations determine your choice of fastener: the weight of the fixture you're hanging, and the type of load it presents. A *light* load is under 10 lbs. (picture frames, pin-up lamps, metal soap dishes) while a load of 25 lbs. or more is *heavy*. A *shear* load is one which exerts a straight-down pull (such close-to-the-wall items as mirrors or wall clocks) while *combination* loads exert an outward pull, as well (shelves, cabinets), and require stronger anchorage. *Dead* loads, where the pull is constant, need less anchorage than *shock* loads which must withstand sudden impact or increased weight, and *vibration* loads (such as air conditioners) call for special treatment—usually a fastener that can be retightened.

We've listed those "Load in Concrete" figures only to provide a comparison between types of fasteners; as quoted by the manufacturers, these figures represent test loads in "first-quality" concrete—not safe working loads. The latter are usually calculated at one-fourth test load. When in doubt, use more fasteners or a heavier-duty type. Over-fastening can't hurt.

Except for a couple of driven types listed, fasteners must be set into a drilled hole. A carbide-tipped masonry bit in an electric drill (particularly a variable-speed type) makes fast work of this in plaster, ceramic tile, brick and concrete. Large-diameter masonry anchors, however, call for hand-hammering with a star drill.

To select the right length hollow-wall fastener, you must know the thickness of the surface wall. You can determine this by drilling a small trial hole at the mounting location and inserting a crochet hook or sturdy wire with a hook bent at one end. Catch the hook against the back of the wall and jamb your thumb against the face of the wall. Back the hook out and measure between its lip and your thumbnail. This is the thickness the fastener must penetrate before its anchoring device can function. Where the fastener must pass through the mounting plate you must add that thickness, too.

SEE ALSO

Bolts . . . Drapery rods . . . Frames, picture . . . Hinges . . . Nails . . . Screws . . . Shelves

"ALL-PURPOSE" FASTENERS

PLASTIC ANCHOR

NYLON EXPANSION (NYCAM)

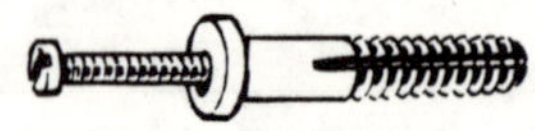

NYLON DRIVE ANCHOR

SIZE RANGE AND LOAD CAPACITY

Screw† Size	Anchor # & Length	Holding Power
4, 6, 8	#1, 7/8″	650
10, 12	#2, 1″	850
14, 16	#3, 1½″	1075

†Although most brands come in three sizes, the recommended screw ranges differ. Where screws are not packaged with the anchors, use size recommended on package. Jordan offers a 2½″ length for ⅜″ lag screws.

One size (about 1″ long, requiring a ⅜″ hole) serves all applications, comes with 1⅛″ self-tapping screw.

Shear load tests: 280 lbs. in cement block, 50 in ⅜″ plasterboard.

Dia.	Lengths
¼″	¾, 1, 1½″
3/16″	1, 1½″

Both Tap-It (U.S. Expansion Bolt) and Jif-Eze (Jordan) come in choice of head style (round, flat, mushroom) and not all lengths avbl. in all head styles.

Shear tests: 800 lbs. in solid wall, 365 in hollow.

INSTALLATION PROCEDURES

Except for larger sizes, anchors are molded in strips; break one off and force into hole of size recommended on card; insert screw through fixture and drive into anchor.

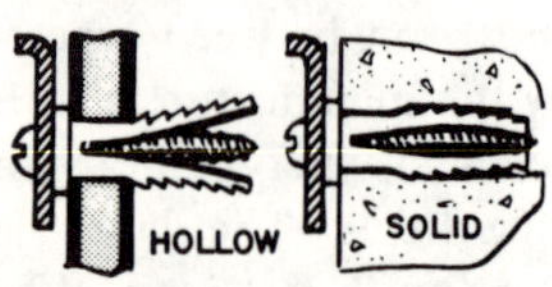

Drill hole at least 1½″ deep, pinch anchor between fingers and tap in place with hammer. Insert screw through fixture and tighten.

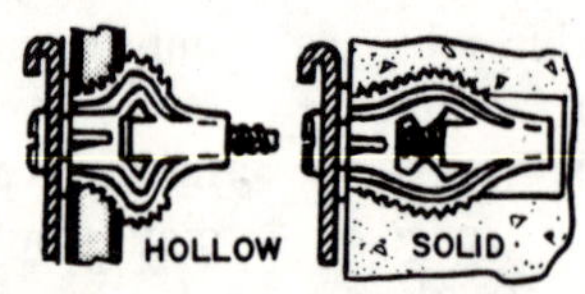

Insert fastener through fixture's mounting hole and push into wall hole. Tap nail until its head seats against fastener's.

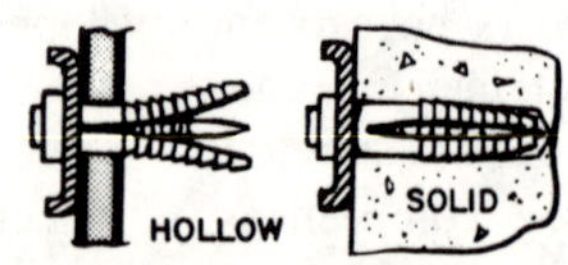

RECOMMENDED USES

Mounting any item normally held with wood screws—large pictures, mirrors, shelf brackets, drapery hardware, kitchen and bath accessories, awnings, mailboxes, Peg-Board hang-up panels . . . on concrete, tile, brick and hollow plaster walls.

Mounting any item such as drapery hardware, brackets and fixtures to any type wall: plaster, drywall, brick, marble, concrete, cinder block, stone, or even wood.

Drapery hardware, shelf brackets, mirrors, pipe straps, outlet boxes—anything with mounting hole that will pass anchor — to plaster, brick, stone, tile, concrete, composition or hardboard.

ADVANTAGES OVER OTHER TYPE

Since anchor is rustproof, it's fine for bathroom fixtures, outdoor installations. Small hole means little wall damage. Strips keep supply handy for quick use. Screw can be removed and reinserted.

One type and size of fastener for all light hanging needs. very thin lip lets you mount flush to wall. 1-pc. nylon construction.

Average installation time: 12 seconds, compared with 25 for the simplest wood-screw anchor. Comes with nail ready for tapping.

DISADVANTAGES

Hole size is critical—anchor must fit snug, and is only as good as the wall material. For light shear loads only. Won't hold against much horizontal pull, especially in crumbly masonry.

Fairly large hole required; not satisfactory in hollow wall more than ⅜″ thick, so won't expand behind most plaster walls.

Fixture can't be removed without withdrawing entire anchor, as well. Mounting hole in fixture must be at least 3/16″ in dia. White nylon head shows around nail. More expensive than plain plastic anchor.

FOR HOLLOW WALLS ONLY

NEOPRENE SLEEVE (WELL-NUT)

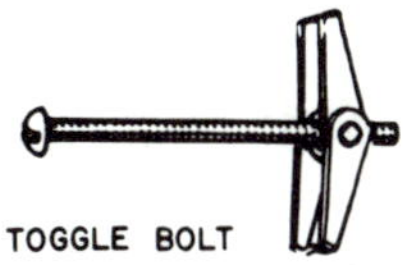

TOGGLE BOLT

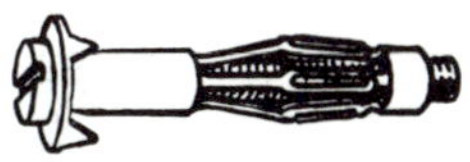

EXPANSION BOLT

SIZE RANGE AND LOAD CAPACITY

Neoprene sleeve (Well-Nut)

One standard size: shank dia. is ¼″; length 15/16″.

Load in concrete: 370; in brick: 440; in cinder block: 470.

Over a dozen other dia.-length combinations avbl. on special order (without screws).

Toggle bolt

Bolt Length	Dia.	Load (lbs.)
2,3,4″	⅛″	200
2,3,4,5,6″ †	3/16″	450
3,4,5,6″ †	¼″	925
3,4,5,6″	5/16″	1150
3,4,5,6″	⅜″	1500
4,6,8″	½″	1800

†Some makes have 2½, 3½ & 4½″ as well

Expansion bolt

Size*	Overall Length	For Wall Thickness	Load
XS	¾-7/8″	0 to ¼″	200
MS	1-1½″	1/16 to ½″	to
S	1½-2¼″	⅛″ to ¾″	500
L	2-2¾″	⅝″ to 1¼″	Difs.
XL	2½-3½″	1¼″ to 1¾″	with make

*There is no industry standard so these are compromise listings. Some brands have each length in several diameters

INSTALLATION PROCEDURES

Neoprene sleeve (Well-Nut)

Drill hole same diameter as neoprene shank (in solid wall, drill just deeper than length of screw); push Well-Nut in, up to flange, hold fixture against it while tightening screw through mounting hole. Shank bulges as nut draws up, forms rivethead against back of hollow wall or pressure fit in solid wall.

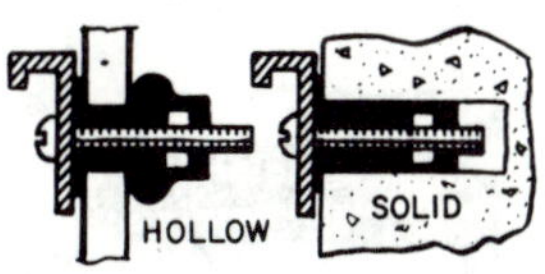

Toggle bolt

Insert bolt through fixture and spin the toggle head on several turns. Fold wings and push them through proper size hole in wall. Tighten bolt to draw wings snug against back of wall.

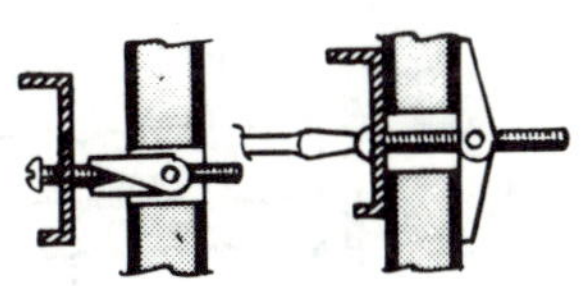

Expansion bolt

Insert unit in drilled hole, tap to embed cap teeth in wall surface, turn screw to draw split sleeve into "spider" against back of wall; remove screw and reinsert after passing through mounting hole of fixture.

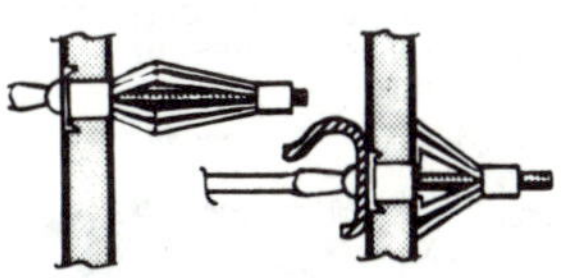

RECOMMENDED USES

Neoprene sleeve (Well-Nut): Coat hooks, drapery hardware, shelf brackets, bathroom fixtures, electrical equipment, auto accessories and trim, hi-fi speakers on dry wall, tile, glass, marble, masonry, plaster, metal, or wood.

Toggle bolt: Large hanging cabinets, heavy-duty shelf standards, wall radiators or vent fans, bathroom grip bars.

Expansion bolt: Mirrors, wall cabinets, lamps and clocks, adjustable shelf brackets, window cornices, shades and blinds, coat hooks.

ADVANTAGES OVER OTHER TYPE

Neoprene sleeve (Well-Nut): Ideal for mounting hi-fi speakers, window fans, other installations where vibration should be dampened. Creates watertight seal, will plug leaks; insulating quality in electrical installations. Neoprene stays flexible so fastener is removable, reusable.

Toggle bolt: Simple, immediate-action installation, great strength for combination loads. Alignment of mounting holes with wall holes isn't critical.

Expansion bolt: Requires smaller hole than toggle, centers bolt precisely. Remains in place for reuse if fixture is removed. Bolt is easily inserted through fixture *after* positioning on wall.

DISADVANTAGES

Neoprene sleeve (Well-Nut): Standard size not suitable to all situations (hollow walls can only be ⅜ to 9/16″ thick). Over-tightening ruins fastener.

Toggle bolt: Requires large insert hole to pass wings, so bolt "floats", does not position fixture precisely. Mounting plate must be big enough to hide hole. If fixture is removed, wings drop off, are lost in wall (See Variations). Installation awkward where fixture requires several bolts, since all must be inserted through fixture before positioning.

Expansion bolt: Slower installation (unless special tool is used). Less strength, since smaller bolt and thinner anchor metal is involved. Mounting holes must exactly align with fastener—tricky where several are involved.

MASONRY WALL FASTENERS

FIBER ANCHOR (LEAD CORE)

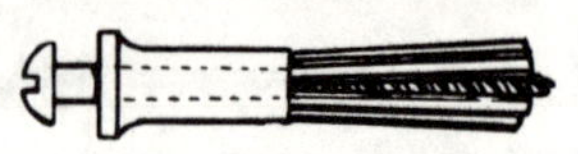

LEAD SCREW ANCHOR

LAG SCREW SHIELD

SIZE RANGE AND LOAD CAPACITY

Fiber Anchor (Lead Core)

Screw Size	Anchor Lengths	Load in Concrete
5-6	⅝, ¾, 1	550
7-8	⅝, ¾, 1, 1¼, 1½, 2	885
9-10	¾, 1, 1¼, 1½, 2	1150
11-12	¾, 1, 1¼, 1½, 2	1525
14	1, 1¼, 1½, 2	1590
16	1, 1½, 2	2150
20	1, 1½, 2	2830
22	2	3500

Lead Screw Anchor

Screw Size	Anchor Lengths	Load in Concrete
6-8	¾, 1, 1½	to 400
10-12-14	1, 1½	to 900
16-18	1, 1½	to 3000
20-22-24	1¾ or 2	1600 up

Lag Screw Shield

Screw Size	Shield Lengths	Load in Concrete
¼	1, 1½	450, 600
5/16	1¼, 1¾	800, 1200
⅜	1¾, 2½	1200, 2000
7/16	2¼ only	1650
½	2, 3	2000, 3000
⅝	2 or 2½,* 3½	2500, 3500
¾	2 or 2½, 3½ or 3¾*	3000, 4000

*Long Standard Sizes differ with brands

INSTALLATION PROCEDURES

Fiber Anchor: Use drill, plug and screw of same size. Clean hole of loose particles. Insert plug just below surface, drive screw through fixture into lead core. Only threaded section should enter plug, so use proper-length plug, recess in deeper hole if necessary.

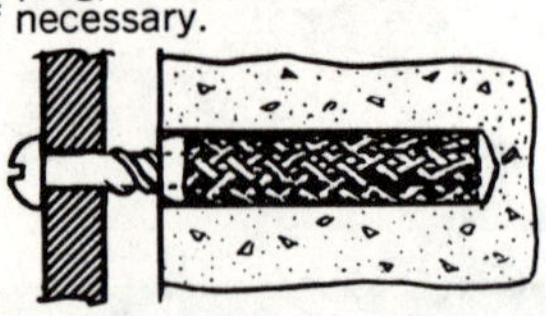

Lead Screw Anchor: Screw length = thickness of mounting plate + length of anchor + ¼″. Drill hole ¼″ deeper than anchor, set it flush with wall surface, drive screw through fixture.

Lag Screw Shield: Drill hole same size as outside dia. of shield. Set in shield flush with or slightly below surface, insert screw through fixture and into shield, which expands as screw enters.

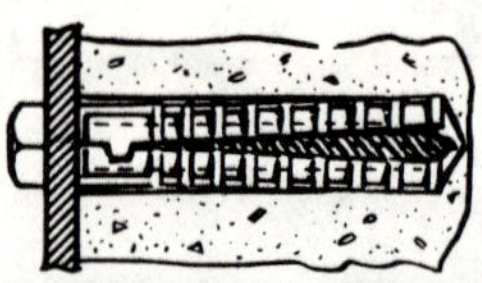

RECOMMENDED USES

Fiber Anchor: Mounting any item you'd normally attach with wood, sheet metal or lag screws (for latter, there are larger sizes than listed)—outlet and fuse boxes, mirrors, bathroom fixtures, fireplace tools, awnings, etc.

Lead Screw Anchor: Same as fiber anchor.

Lag Screw Shield: Mounting any item too heavy for plain screws—especially to a brick wall where hole can be drilled into mortar joint without marring brick.

ADVANTAGES OVER OTHER TYPE

Fiber Anchor: Easy, inexpensive, versatile. Screw may be removed and replaced without affecting anchorage. Once screw is in, plug grips wall firmly.

Lead Screw Anchor: Flared end prevents loss of fixture through drilled hole in concrete block, etc. also makes it easier to start screw.

Lag Screw Shield: Heavy ribs assure powerful gripping action. Choice of long or short for each screw dia. lets you minimize drilling in hard masonry, or use long size for more strength in weak masonry and brick.

DISADVANTAGES

Fiber Anchor: Hole size is more critical than with most fasteners. Holding power depends on strength of wall material; poor in crumbly concrete, plaster.

Lead Screw Anchor: Size for size, less holding power than fiber anchor; hole in wall must be exact fit.

Lag Screw Shield: Requires fairly large masonry bit, greater installation time since screw must be driven with wrench.

MACHINE SCREW ANCHOR

Screw Size	Dia. Hole (Inches)	Min. Depth (Inches)	Load in Concrete (Pounds)
6-32	¼	⅜	625
8-32	5/16	½	950
10-24	⅜	⅝	1100
12-24	7/16	¾	1750
¼-20	½	7/8	2275
5/16-18	⅝	1	2850
⅜-16	¾	1¼	3670
7/16-14	7/8	1½	5500
½-13	7/8	1½	7200
⅝-11	1⅛	2	7800
¾-10	1¼	2¼	8300
7/8-9	1½	2¾	10000
1-8	1¾	3½	12000

Drill indicated hole (in weak or soft masonry, go deep enough to set anchor just below surface); push anchor into hole, nut first, then "calk" with special tool. Pass screw through fixture and tighten into nut.

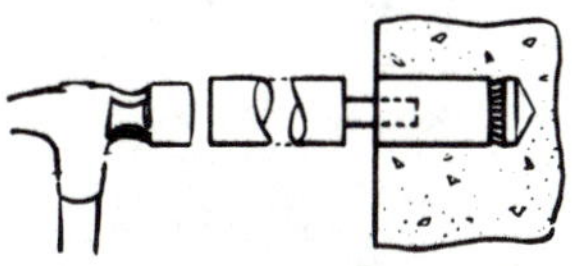

Heavy jobs such as construction (anchoring coal-bin wall stud—or floor plate to foundation when adding room).

Sleeve is precision-cast lead alloy—soft enough to press itself into the rough sides of the hole, but hard enough to give great holding power. Hard-alloy nut-cone prevents thread-stripping. Cannot be installed incorrectly; the heavier the load the stronger the grip.

Though free calking tool is included in each *box* of anchors, you must buy one separately if you need less than a box (50 or 100 anchors), and you need a different tool for each size anchor. Length of screw critical.

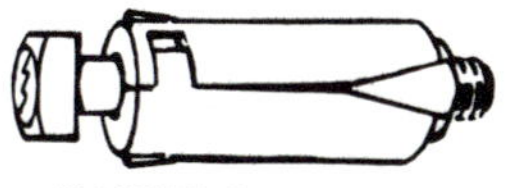

MACHINE BOLT SHIELD

Bolt Size (Inches)	Shield Lengths* (Inches)	Dia. Hole* (Inches)	Working Loads (Up to:)
¼	1½	½	500
5/16	1½-2	⅝	800
⅜	1½-2⅜	¾	1000
7/16	2-2½	7/8	1000
½	2-2 7/8	7/8	1500
⅝	2½-3¼	1-1⅛	2000
¾	3½-4	1¼-1⅜	2000
7/8	4-4¼	1⅜-1½	2300
1	4¼-4½	1⅜-1¾	2400
1¼	5½-6	2⅛	2500

Insert shield in snug, press-fit hole, its top flush with surface. Pass bolt through fixture's mounting hole and turn into shield. As bolt is tightened, it draws nut (usually wedge-shaped) forward, expanding split sleeve.

For any heavy fixture to be bolted fast—cabinets, hanging shelves, ducts, hand rails—on solid masonry. *Some brands come in Short or Long sizes in same dia.; use long size for softer masonry.

Sure, heavy-duty anchorage; shields are tough, rustproof alloy casting. Wide choice of types, including closed-end (to protect threads from drill dust) and double-expansion types (with wedge-nut at both ends) for heaviest loads.

Large, deep hole and wrench-tightening mean slower installation, and shields are relatively expensive, so use only where strong anchor is needed. Can loosen under vibration, so for that type of load, choose type that can be retightened.

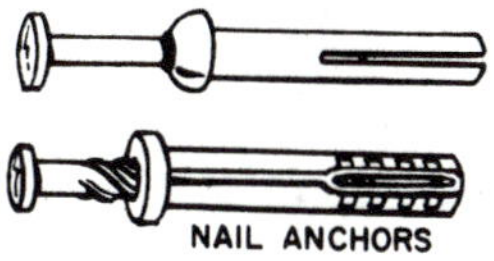

NAIL ANCHORS

Shield Dia. (Inches)	Shield Length (Inches)	Working Load (Pounds)
3/16	7/8	375
	1¼	110
¼	1	200
	1¼	240
	1½	325
5/16	1¼	300
	1¾	350
	2¼	375
	2¾	375
⅜	2	450
	3¼	485
½	2¼	525
	3½	625

Drill hole same dia. as shield, insert anchor through fixture's mounting hole and into wall. When flange is seated firm against fixture, drive nail home with a couple blows.

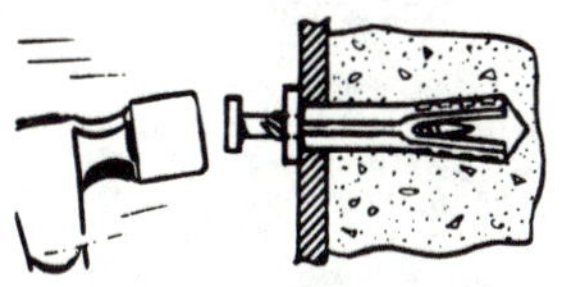

Light, dead loads: furring strips, pipe, metal window frames, downspouts, outlet boxes—to concrete block, brick, mortar, stone.

Fast—small hole means quicker drilling—and economical. Choose aluminum type for outdoor jobs, spiral-nail type for vibrating loads.

Limited holding power; fixture can't be removed once nail is set. Mounting hole must be large enough to pass shield. Except for one type with spiral nail, poor resistance to vibration or jarring.

MASONRY (CONCLUDED)

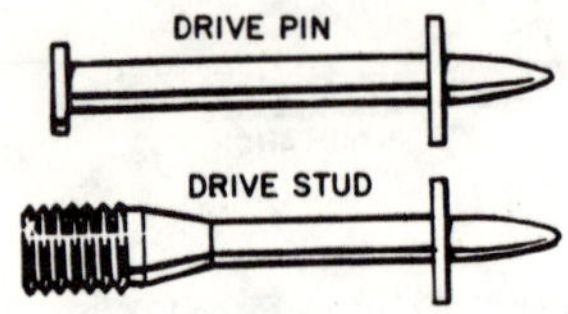

SIZE RANGE

Not completely standard from brand to brand, but pin shanks range in dia. from 1/8" (in shorter lengths) to 3/16" and include following lengths: 1/2, 3/4, 1, 1 1/4, 1 1/2, 2, 2 1/2, 3". Studs are available in some brands in 8-32, 10-24 and 1/4"-20 threads in overall lengths of 1 3/8, 1 5/8 and 2".

INSTALLATION

Choose length to let pin penetrate 1/2-1" in concrete, 3/4-1 1/4" in masonry block or mortar joint. (If pin bends, try next shorter length.) Pull drive rod out, press pin into anvil end, tap protruding point to seat pin in anvil, set point on installation spot and drive pin home with 2 or 3 lb. hammer. Washer holds fastener in tool, then slips up shank to provide support at point and keep material from pulling away between blows.

RECOMMENDED USES

Fastening pipe straps, brackets, junction boxes, mail boxes, furring strips, 2x4s or plywood, to concrete or masonry block.

ADVANTAGES

Eliminates all drilling, making for quickest possible masonry anchoring. Each fastener specially heat-treated for extreme hardness. Studs permit removal of fixture.

DISADVANTAGES

All fasteners must be installed with drive tool (retailing from $2.50 up, depending on make), can be used only in good-quality concrete (not usually recommended for brittle materials like stone, brick or tile), are limited to relatively thin fixtures (brackets, furring) where a number of fasteners can be driven.

VARIATIONS AND IMPROVEMENTS

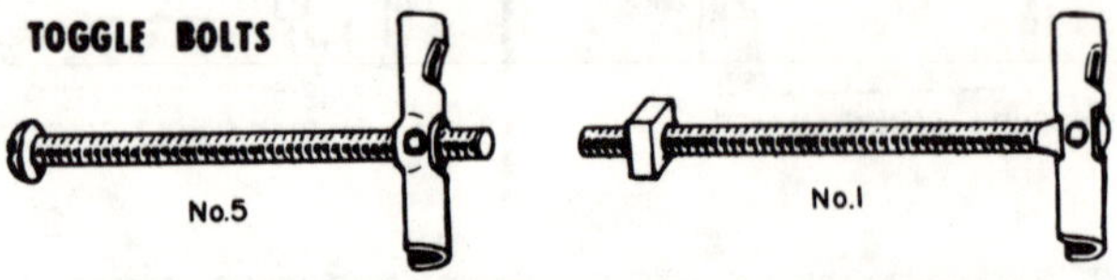

Not all standard types have spring-loaded wings. Gravity types shown above have "tumble" heads, pivoted off-center, creating strong, one-piece bearing bar. No. 5 is otherwise identical to a spring-wing, but type No. 1 has head riveted directly to stud

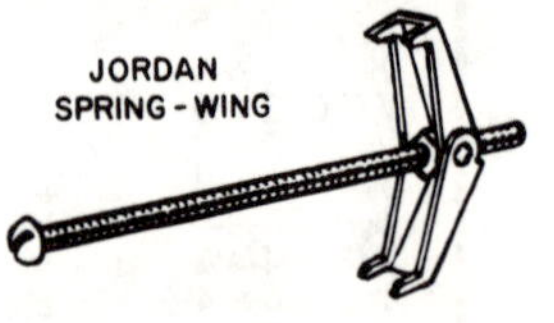

Recent innovations in toggle design include spring-wing with teeth (left) that bite into back of wall to keep nut positioned so bolt can be removed and replaced. Simplified tumbler, below, is lowest-price toggle, with S-head in constant tension so bolt never loosens up

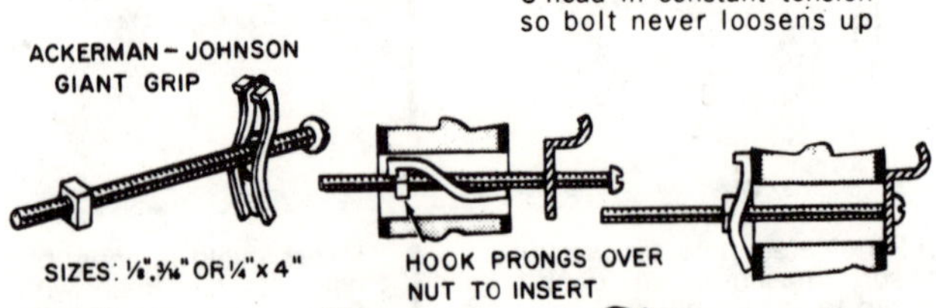

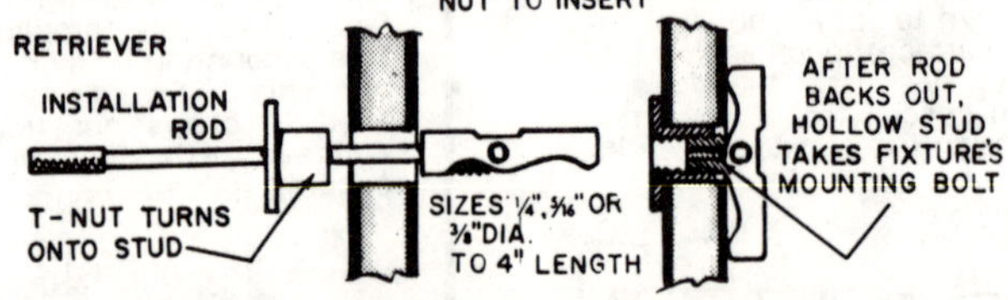

As name implies, here's a toggle that stays locked in wall like an expansion anchor when fixture is removed, yet can be retrieved for reuse by reinserting installation rod. Rod makes long bolt unnecessary. Also comes with longer stud to project from wall for nut

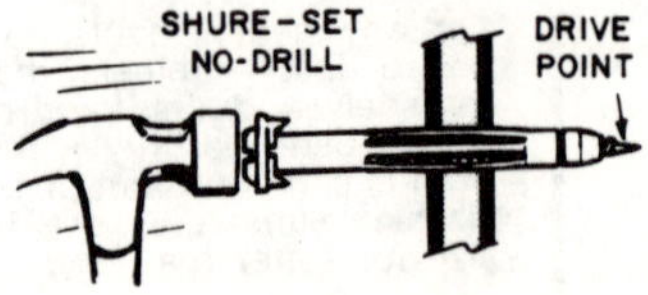

Pointed expansion anchor eliminates drilling step. Just drive it through wall till flange teeth embed, then turn screw to expand sleeve as with standard type. Ideal for softboard, other drywall

New addition to plastic anchor line has 3/8-in.-thick flange for mounting perforated storage panels. When shoulder seats against wall, flange automatically—without separate spacers—creates proper clearance for insertion of hanging hooks

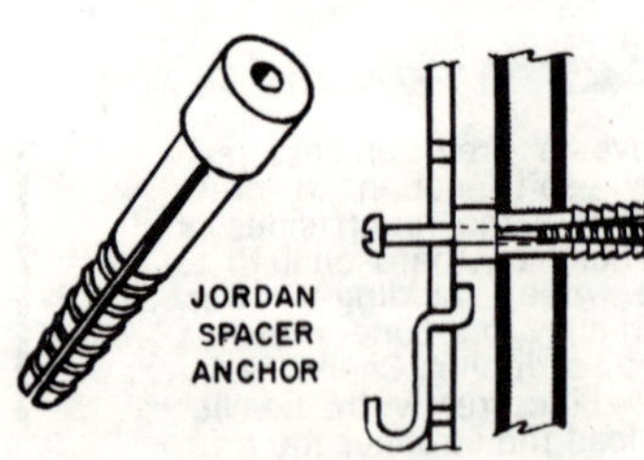

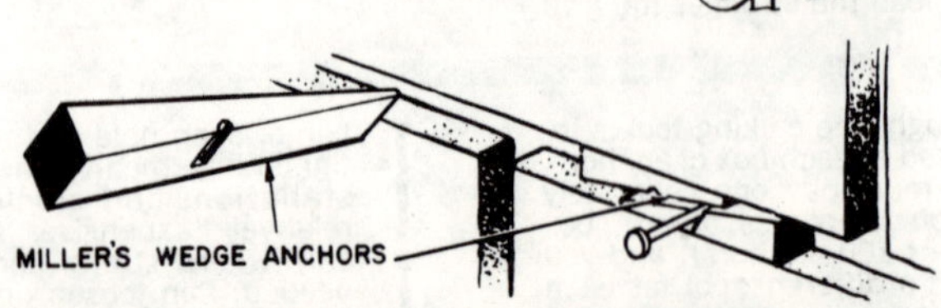

For any laid masonry with recessed mortar lines. Two (or more) lead tapers are wedged between bricks or stones, nail driven into best edge-notch for positioning fixture. No damage to masonry, and anchors can be removed without a trace by withdrawing nail

Build storage into a fence

THE LEFT STALL opens from the end to accommodate a large mower which can poke into adjacent stall.

If you dislike 'sore-thumb' toolsheds, you will like this one which becomes part of the backyard fence. It's handsome and practical

IF BOTH A FENCE and a toolhouse are on your list of projects to be built this summer, you'll kill two birds with one stone by following this unique plan. It incorporates them in a single project and, what's more, eliminates the objection of having a lonesome toolhouse in the middle of nowhere. Designed as part of a property-line fence, the toolhouse blends in so perfectly with the fence itself, the neighbors will have to look twice to see it.

You start out by erecting the fence first, using standard western-wood boards and framing lumber. Here you set 4x4 posts every 6 ft. and nail 2x8s to them with ¾-in. spaces between. The toolhouse floor, shown in the drawing below, consists of 1x4s spaced and nailed to two 4x6s treated with a wood preservative and placed in a scooped-out area to bring them slightly above ground level.

After you chink the fence openings with 1x2s for 15 ft., six 2x2 studs are nailed to the face of the fence every 36 in. Then six 2x6 mullions, aligned with the 2x2s, are toenailed to the floor across the front. A 2x6 fascia joins the mullions at the top and a 2x2 is set behind it as a ledge for pitched roof boards. A 2x4 offers a ledge for the boards at the rear.

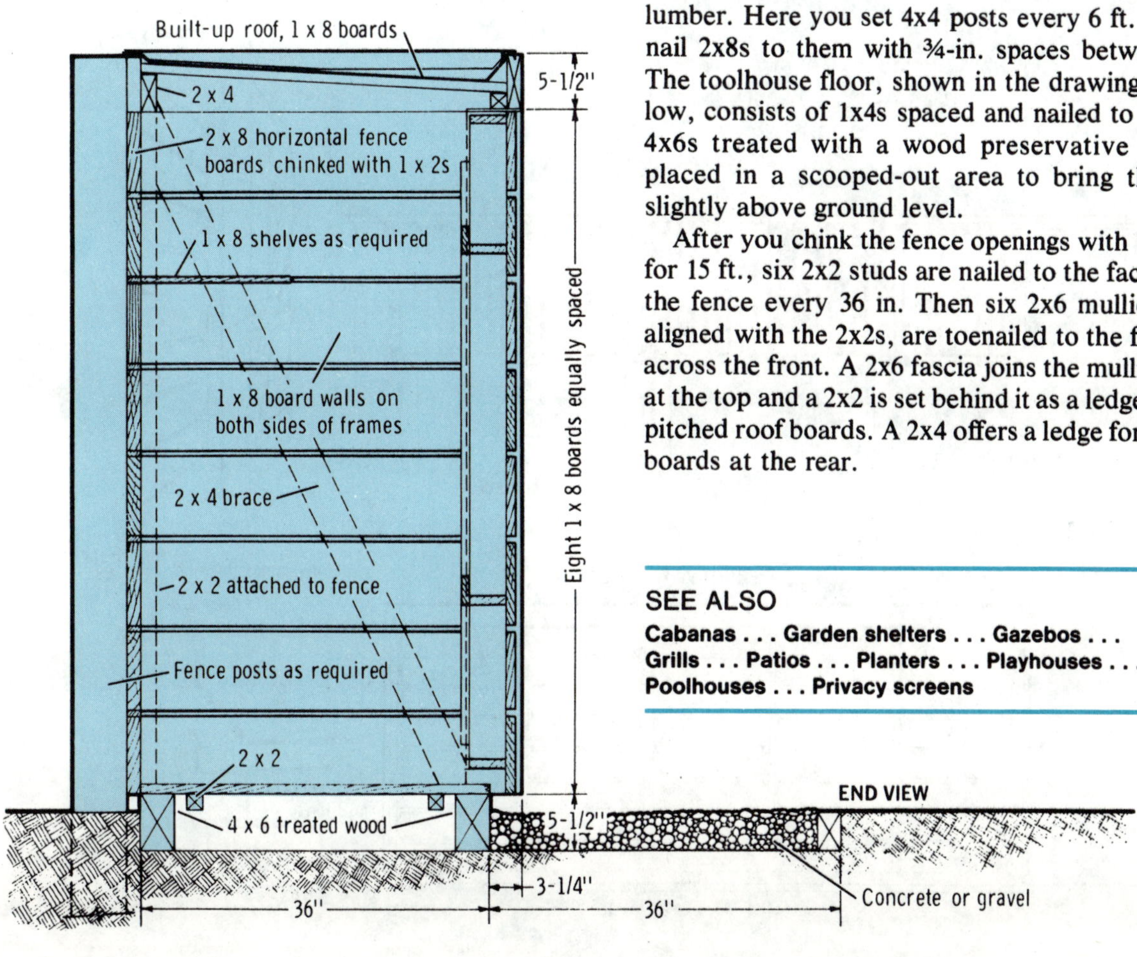

END VIEW

SEE ALSO

Cabanas . . . Garden shelters . . . Gazebos . . . Grills . . . Patios . . . Planters . . . Playhouses . . . Poolhouses . . . Privacy screens

STORAGE DOORS swing wide open to provide walk-in convenience when stowing power equipment.

Note in the roof detail that a saw kerf is run in the edge of the fascia board to accommodate a metal flashing. Standard 1x8 boards are used for the roof, and covered with roofing paper and tar after the flashing is installed.

Five stalls are made by nailing 1x8s horizontally to the studs and mullions and spacing ¾ in. apart. The three bottom boards in the partition between the first and second stalls are omitted to provide mower clearance.

The door in the left-hand stall opens from the end; other stall doors open at the front. All five doors are made alike and fitted with shelves. The 1x8s nailed to the fronts are spaced ¾ in. to match the fence. To keep rain and snow from blowing through the cracks, clear sheet plastic is tacked across the box frames of the doors before the 1x8s are nailed to them. Note that the doors are made with a lip along one side only, and that 2x2s are nailed to the mullions to provide stops for the door lips. Standard 1x2s are nailed to the mullions along the hinge side of the doors and the hinges are attached to them.

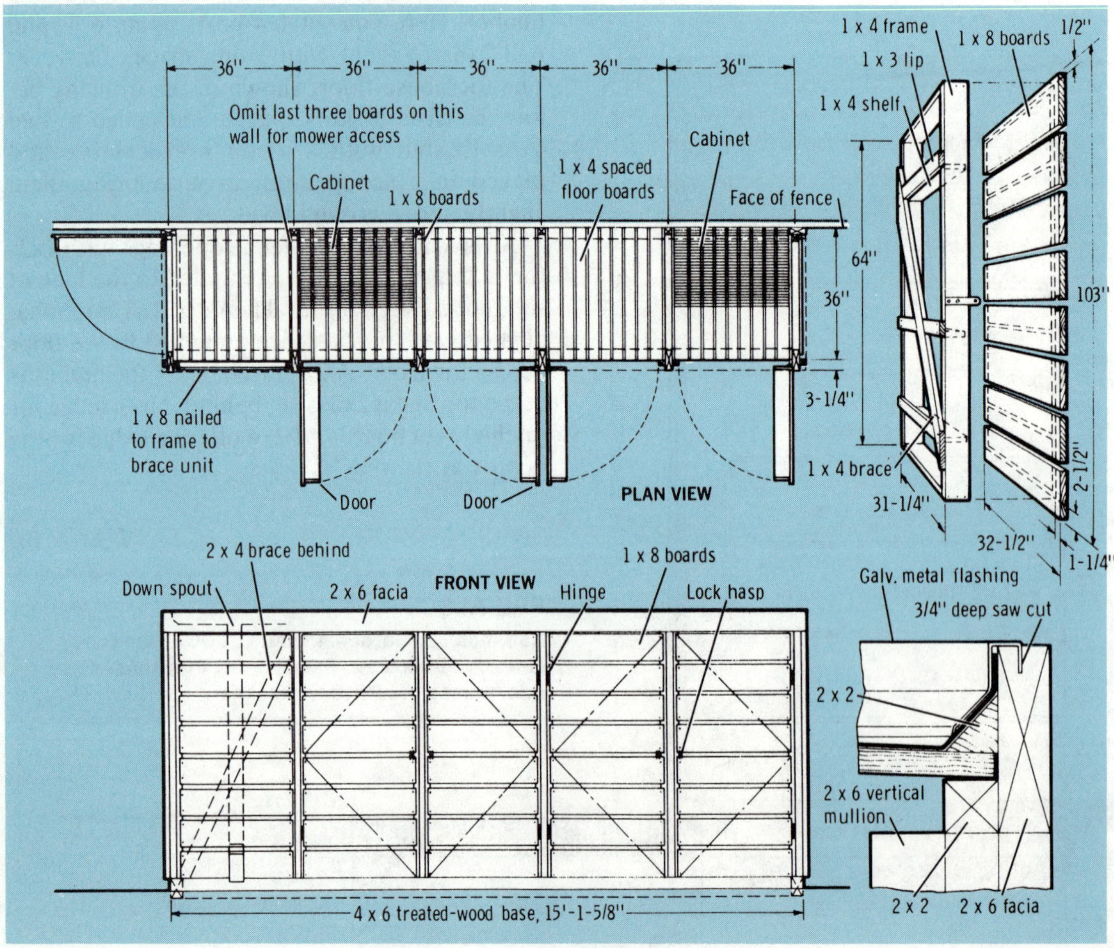

Good fences do make good neighbors. Careful plans and fence-building facts will get you off to the right start

Eight easy-to-build fence designs

THE MOST IMPORTANT step in planning a fence is deciding what you want it to do. For example, a fence can admit sunlight and allow air to circulate or it can block them out. It can furnish varying degrees of privacy.

A fence can protect your garden from neighborhood wildlife and childlife, or it can keep your youngsters and pets in so you know where they are. You can use a fence as a space divider, to define an outdoor living area or to screen a service yard. A fence can be a handsome backdrop for plantings.

The hardest part of building a fence is setting the posts. You'll do best to rent a posthole digger

SEE ALSO
Benches, deck . . . Decks . . . Gardening . . . Gazebos . . . Joinery . . . Patios . . . Planters . . . Privacy screens

How to set fenceposts

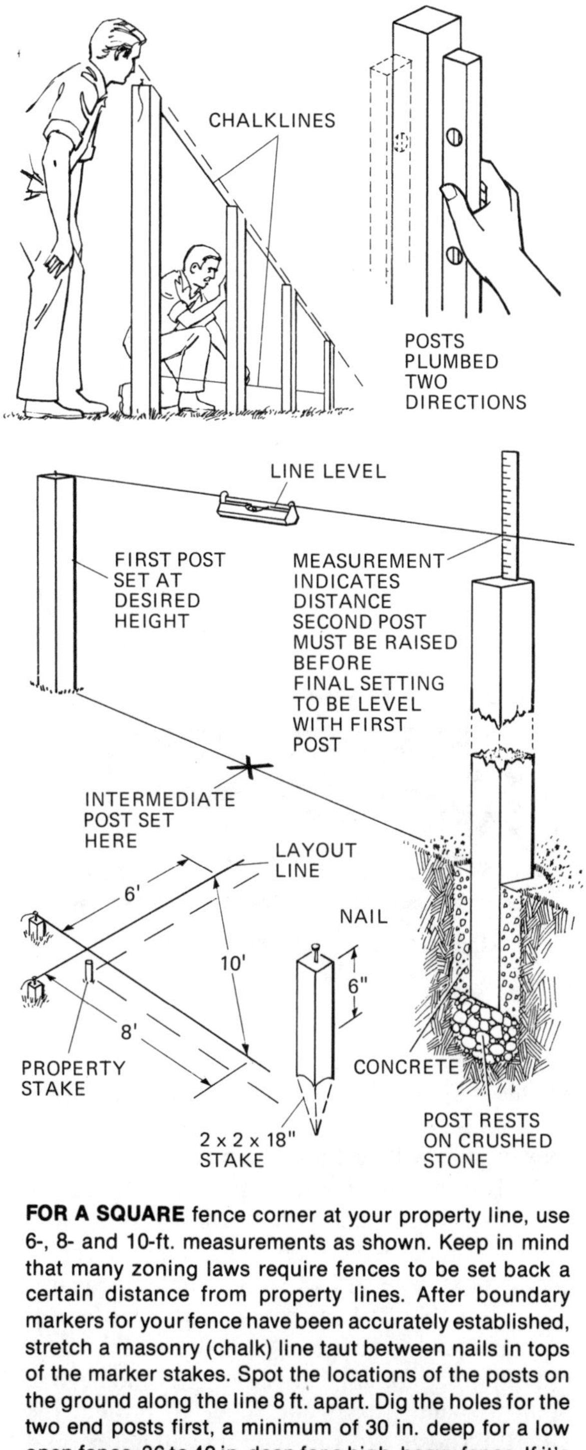

FOR A SQUARE fence corner at your property line, use 6-, 8- and 10-ft. measurements as shown. Keep in mind that many zoning laws require fences to be set back a certain distance from property lines. After boundary markers for your fence have been accurately established, stretch a masonry (chalk) line taut between nails in tops of the marker stakes. Spot the locations of the posts on the ground along the line 8 ft. apart. Dig the holes for the two end posts first, a minimum of 30 in. deep for a low open fence, 36 to 42 in. deep for a high, heavy fence. If it's a long fence, dig the hole for the second post no more than 50 ft. from the first. Set one end post to establish the fence height, plumb both planes and attach a line to the top of the post. Stretch the line to the opposite end post, hang the line level on it, and, with a helper, raise or lower the far post until the line level reads level. Set the post accordingly by digging the hole deeper or filling, then set it permanently in concrete. The post should rest on crushed stone so water will drain freely and not promote decay of the wood.

High fences

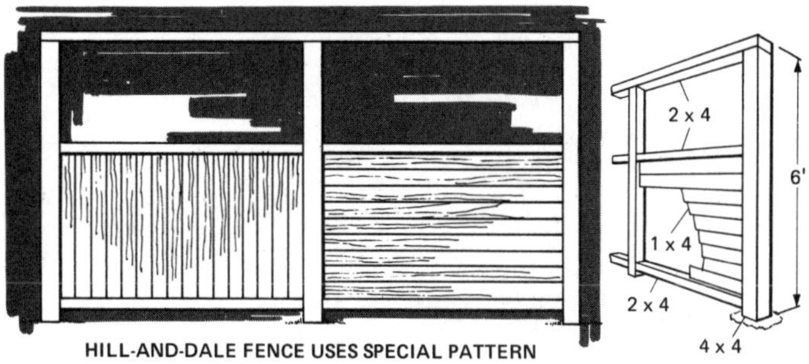

HILL-AND-DALE FENCE USES SPECIAL PATTERN

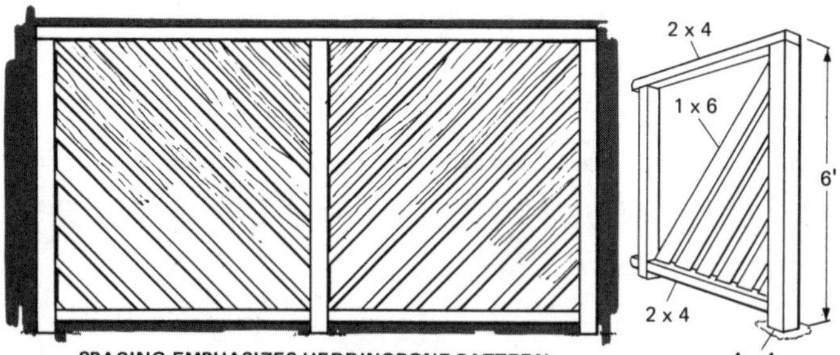

SPACING EMPHASIZES HERRINGBONE PATTERN

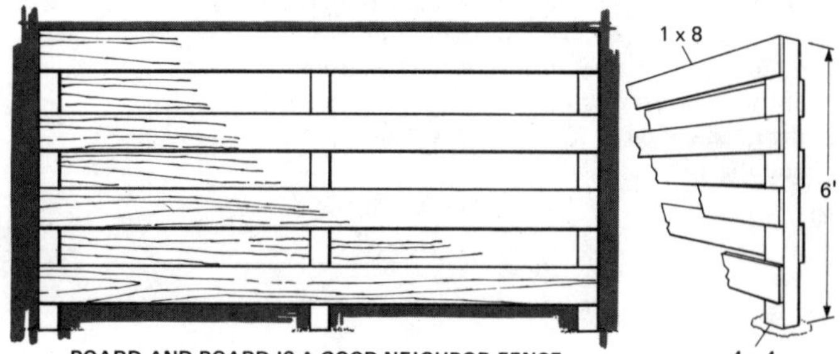

BOARD AND BOARD IS A GOOD NEIGHBOR FENCE

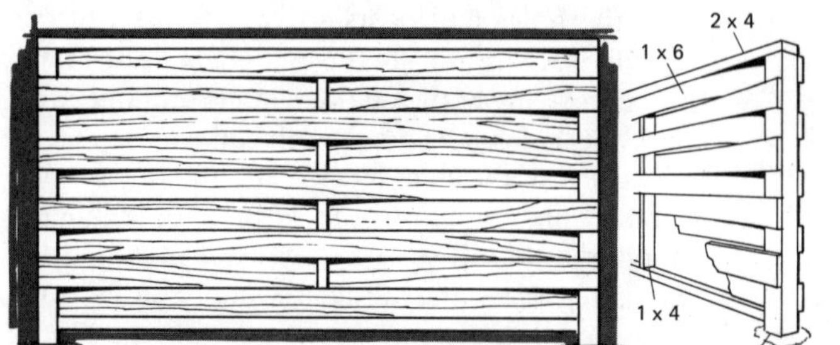

BASKET WEAVE PRODUCES BOLD SHADOW PATTERNS

ANGLE OF LOUVERS SETS DEGREE OF PRIVACY

MOST LIKELY you will have height limitations for your fence along property lines, as local building codes impose restrictions. The three low fences shown here are of minimum height and are often built to meet local requirements. All are "good neighbor" fences since they look good from either side.

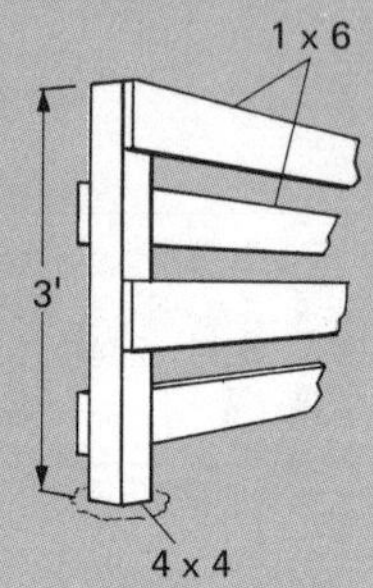

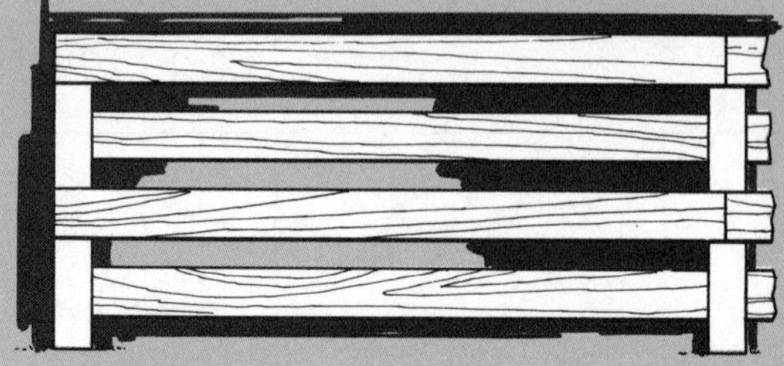

HORIZONTAL BOARD ON BOARD IS INFORMAL

ALTERNATE WIDTHS ON ALTERNATE SIDES

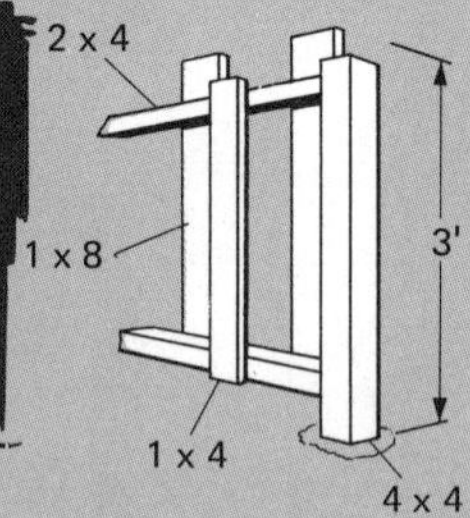

THE CALIFORNIA Redwood Assn. suggests the application of a water repellent on redwood fences. This is best done before starting your fence; coat all surfaces, edges and ends. Water repellent retards natural weathering, reduces the effects of moisture, protects wood from dirt and grime and serves as a finish itself.

MOST FENCES are built of 4x4 posts, 2x4 stringers and 1-in. boards (usually 8 or 10 in. wide). Redwood makes the best fence; unseasoned grade shrinks less than other softwoods. Your lumber dealer will help select the grade of redwood best suited for the fence you plan to build.

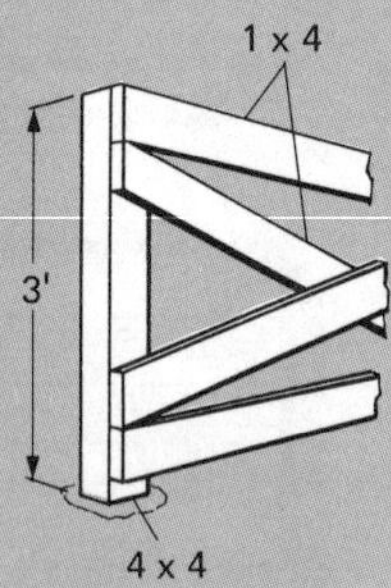

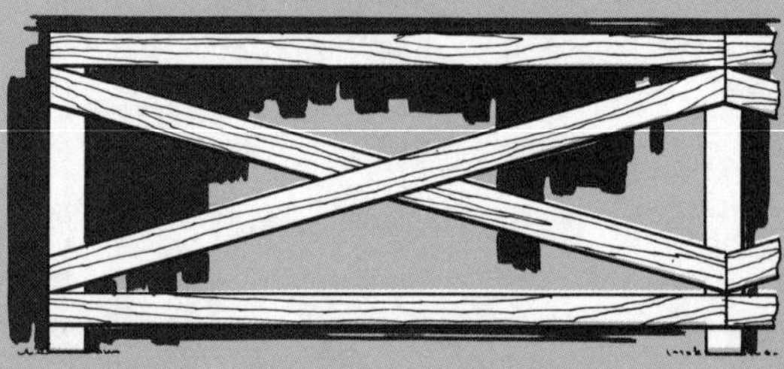

POST AND RAIL SUITS RANCH-STYLE HOMES

if you have a lot of holes to dig. The best way to align the holes and posts so your fence will be straight is to dig and set the end posts first. Then stretch a string between them at ground line and mark the holes 8 ft. apart with stakes.

The most durable fences are made of redwood, which requires the least maintenance. Lumberyards sell several grades of redwood in two categories: the all-heartwood grades and those that may contain sapwood. All-heart redwood should always be used for posts and other members of a fence that will come in contact with the ground; it contains natural extractives that protect the wood from termites and decay. The more economical sapwood grades are okay for other fence members above ground.

Drawings on p. 1205 show different ways the top and bottom rails can be joined to the posts. Toenailed butt joints are the simplest, but also weakest. The top rails should be mitered or lapped at the corner posts.

It is important that you use aluminum-alloy, stainless-steel or hot-dipped galvanized nails in your redwood fence. Common nails won't hold as well and will rust and stain wood.

Redwood fence boards come in 3, 4, 6, 8, 10 and 12-in. widths and various thicknesses. Both nominal and dressed sizes are given in the chart on the next page. A 2x4, for example, measures approximately 2x4 in. rough. After surfacing, the same 2x4 measures 1⁵/₁₆ x 3½ in.

Other than for appearance, there is no need to stain or paint a redwood fence to protect the wood. Exposure to sun and rain will not harm it but will change its color. After a few months, the wood will develop dark streaks, but these will disappear in time and the wood ultimately will weather-bleach to a pleasing driftwood gray. However, a clear water-repellent finish is highly recommended. Easy to apply, it stabilizes wood color, retards weathering and reduces moisture effects.

Post and rail joints

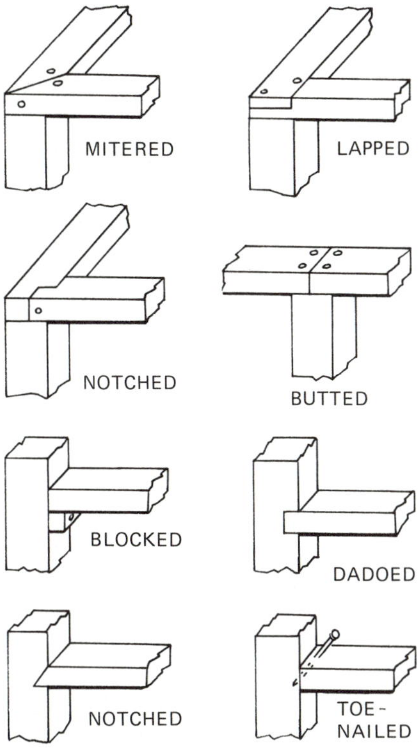

KILN-DRIED FINISH LUMBER

THICKNESSES						
Nominal	½	¾	1	1¼	1½	2
Dressed	7/16	11/16	¾	1 1/16	1 5/16	1⅝

WIDTHS						
Nominal	3	4	6	8	10	12
Dressed	2½	3½	5½	7¼	9¼	11¼

UNSEASONED BOARDS, STRIPS, DIMENSION

THICKNESSES								
Nominal	¾	1	1¼	1½	2	3	4	6
Dressed	11/16	25/32*	1 1/16	1 5/16	1⅝	2 9/16	3 9/16	5⅝

WIDTHS						
Rough (nominal)	3	4	6	8	10	12
Dressed grade	2 9/16	3 9/16	5⅝	7½	9½	11½

TAKE GOOD CARE of your redwood lumber between the time it is delivered and actually put to use. Store it under cover and off the ground. Store it where the wood will not be walked on, dented or otherwise marred, and store it flat. Lumber that is not stored on a flat surface may warp and retain a permanent bow which will show up in your finished fence.

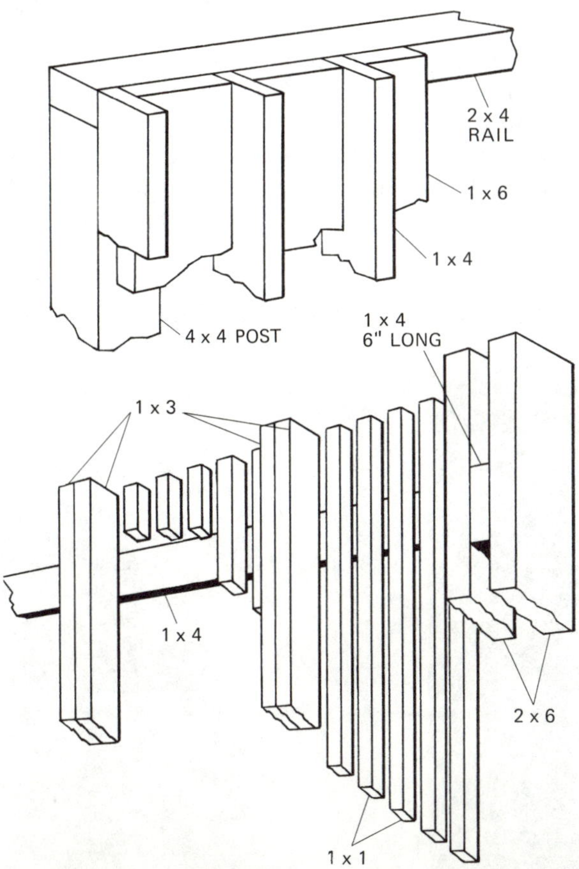

WHEN YOU combine several different sizes and shapes of standard redwood lumber, as shown here, there's no end to the attractive fences you can design and build.

THIS DECK wind screen with built-in benches and shrubbery niches provides solid-wall privacy.

AN OPEN SCREEN design effectively separates spaces without visually walling them off.

PHOTO AT LEFT was taken without a filter, the one at right with a polarizing filter. Note how the washed-out effect, caused by reflected light, is brought under control.

Better photos the easy way—with filters

By BILL WRENN

DO THE PEOPLE in your photographs sometimes have horrible gray faces even when they aren't ill? Do your pictures occasionally come back looking like they were shot underwater?

Sometimes the camera doesn't record exactly what the eye perceives.

While it's impossible to reproduce on photographic paper the brightness range our eyes can handle easily, we should be able to capture the range of detail accurately. And, with black and white film, we should be able to convert the whole spectrum of colors into a comparable spectrum of whites to blacks.

One way to do this is with photographic filters. They allow you to capture the scene the way you saw it. Or, if you wish, they allow you to change the scene to suit your imagination.

Filters come in many different shapes, sizes and prices. But they all alter the way in which your camera "sees" light.

The most common filters are glass discs with metal frames that screw onto the front of a lens housing. They are available for most types of cameras.

SEE ALSO

Camera accessories . . . Camera care . . .
Cartridges, film . . . Darkrooms . . .
Developing, photo . . . Dryers, photo . . .
Mountings, photo . . . Photography . . .
Prints, photo . . . Slides, photo

STAR FILTER changes Christmas tree bulbs at left into radiant individual stars. It can dramatically alter the lights of a city taken from a distance.

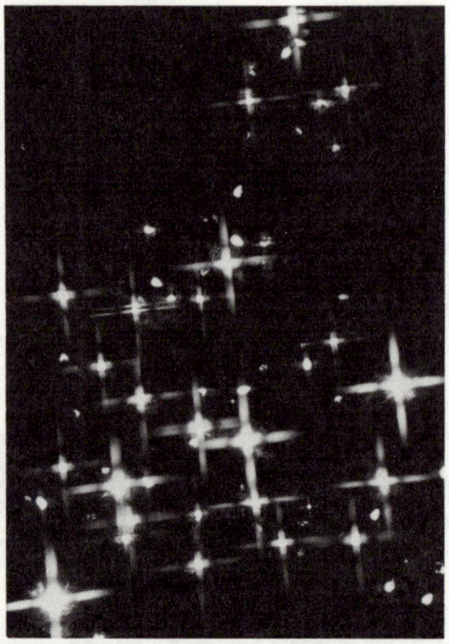

MOUNTAIN VIEW of icicles is a dramatic shot lacking something. What?

Filters have been used in black and white (b&w) photography for many years. Filters used in b&w don't actually do anything for colors, of course, but they definitely can improve tonal rendition and image definition.

Unless you are shooting frequently under unusual circumstances, you may opt for only three filters in your b&w photography: a yellow (No. 8 or 9), a green (No. 11, 13 or 15) and a red (No. 25 or 29). The higher the number the darker the hue. Thus a red No. 29 is darker than a red No. 25.

Here's the rule to remember: Each filter allows only that part of the visible spectrum *corresponding to its own color* to reach the film, and it absorbs virtually all of its complementary color.

The three additive primary colors of light are green, blue and red. Therefore a yellow filter used with b&w film causes blue areas to go darker because blue (which is the complement of yellow) has been absorbed. Thus a blue sky is darkened by a yellow filter, giving greater contrast and more prominent clouds. And a red filter, because it absorbs even more blue than a yellow filter, goes reality one better to give sumptuous sculptured clouds.

What about a green filter? It absorbs red and blue, and is particularly helpful in photographing foliage. *Without* a filter, green areas frequently come out darker in a picture than perceived by the eye. The filter, by passing more green light than yellow and blue, can lighten up grass and trees, and greatly improve their detail.

Remember when using filters in b&w photography that whatever is the *same* color as the filter will come out *lighter*. Alternately, a filter's *complementary* colors come out *darker*; blues are darker with a yellow filter, greens and blues are darker with a red filter, and reds and blues are darker with a green filter.

filters for color control

Under ideal conditions, color films should render an image close to what you see. But conditions are seldom ideal.

For instance, if a scene has a lot of reflected light, particularly near water, glass or concrete, the vibrant colors you shoot will often appear washed out in a print or slide. Or perhaps shadow areas will look bluish. Even worse, you might shoot a set of pictures that all look as though they were shot through a fishbowl.

Such a scene, teeming with reflected light, can be rescued with a polarizing filter. It passes only light rays of a certain alignment, thus giving darker skies and richer colors. It can be used for the same effect in b&w.

Bluish shadows can be reduced with a skylight filter. It looks like a plain piece of glass, but it warms up shadow areas and colors at a distance.

If you are shooting indoor film and move outdoors, an 85B filter will help restore color balance. If you shoot outdoor film indoors without flash, try using an 80A filter.

Under "cool white" fluorescent light, a 30M filter will bring you reasonably close to natural light.

RED FILTER No. 25A brings in tenuous clouds to complete the scene.

DRESS ON THE radiant bride below is a deep pink, but goes dark in b&w film. Red filter No. 25A lightens and softens the dress.

Refinishing furniture is easier than ever

By ROSARIO CAPOTOSTO

BEFORE REFINISHING, this book table is well-worn but proved to be a good quality piece of furniture.

WATER-RINSABLE remover is applied generously. Finish softens in 10 minutes to an hour, depending on thickness of coat.

SCRAPING BEGINS when wrinkles appear. Some spots need repeated application of remover.

WET TOWELING (or steel wool) and water is used to rub off remover and residue. Piece is then flushed clean with a hose.

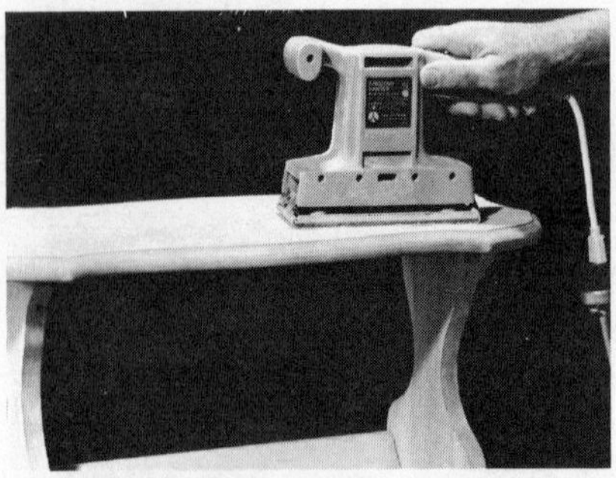

SANDING to bare wood—done when thoroughly dry—calls for smooth-cutting finishing sander and hand sanding.

BEFORE STAINING, wood is given a sealer wash coat so grain will accept stain evenly. Omitting this step can be risky.

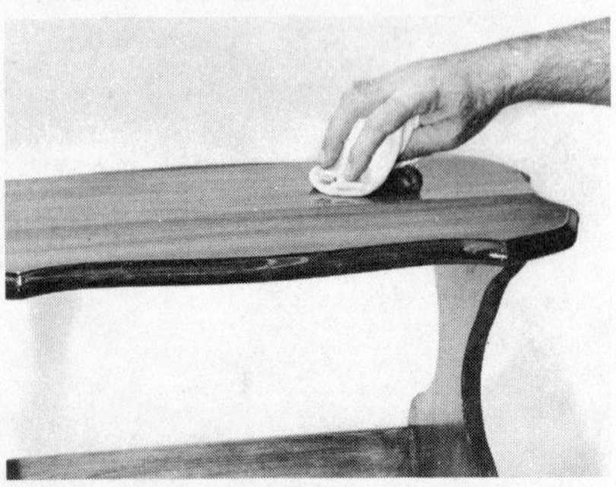

STAIN IS APPLIED with brush or cloth, then wiped down to even it out, let dry and followed by a coat of sealer.

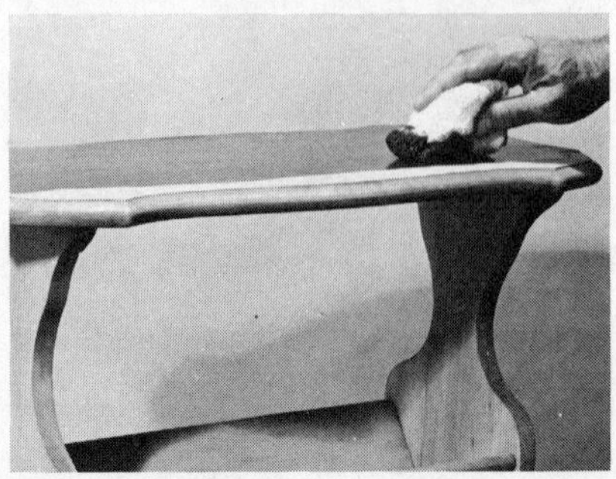

TWO COATS of wipe-on finish applied over sealer with cloth, like furniture polish, produce a beautiful semigloss finish.

AFTER THE REFINISHING steps are completed, the new finish, in simulated teakwood, is more durable than the original.

■ TIME WAS WHEN CLEAR finishing of wood was a tedious job reserved for the pro or the advanced amateur. But today's improved finishes have simplified methods and improved results to such a degree that practically anyone, with little or no previous experience, can turn out an admirable job the first time around.

A "hand-rubbed" finish used to be just that: high-gloss varnishes had to be rubbed down with pumice powder and oil to obtain a satiny sheen. Now you simply apply a top coat that has been scientifically designed to produce such an effect when dry! Improved brushing lacquers eliminate the need for spraying equipment and the pollution and dangerous fumes. Quick-drying natural varnishes and the remarkable polyurethanes, epoxies, vinyls and alkyds offer exceptional durability and easy-to-apply wood-enriching finishes.

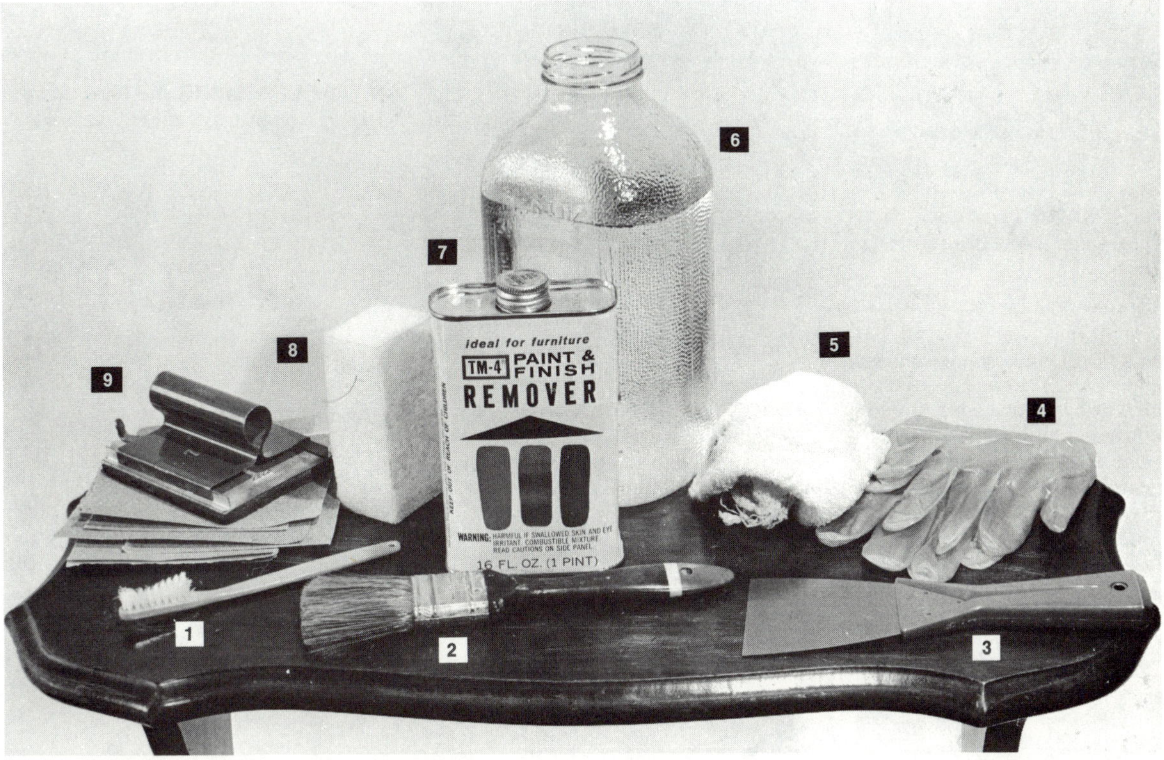

TOOLS AND MATERIALS required include: (1) toothbrush, (2) paintbrush, (3) scraper, (4) rubber gloves, (5) cloths, (6) water, (7) remover, (8) scrap of styrofoam (pad for sanding edges), (9) abrasive paper.

SEE ALSO

Abrasives . . . Furniture, care of . . . Joinery . . . Legs, furniture . . . Pad sanders . . . Sanding . . . Scrapers . . . Staining, wood . . . Veneering . . . Wood finishes

GRADES OF SANDPAPER	
Coarse	Used to remove old finish (paint, varnish, enamel, etc.), also deep gouges, scratches, stubborn stains and smudges. Coarse paper must always be followed by medium paper, then fine, since the scuff marks made by coarse paper are not only visible but sometimes magnified after a clear finish is applied.
Medium	Used to remove less severe scratches, stains, smudges, etc.; also scuff marks resulting from use of coarse sandpaper.
Fine	Used to obtain smoothness, and to remove slight traces of scratching or scuffing remaining after a previous sanding; also to remove raised grain resulting from sealing or bleaching.
Very Fine	Used to obtain maximum degree of surface smoothness—the key to the finest possible natural wood finish.

PRETESTING BOTH color of the stain and of the final coat material is good practice.

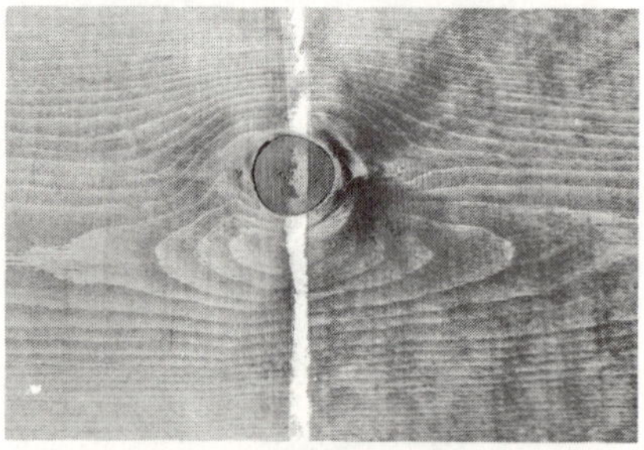

SEALER-WASH coat prevents blotchy stain job. Left was treated, right was not.

THOROUGH SCRAPING was done on chair (at right) when it was disassembled for regluing.

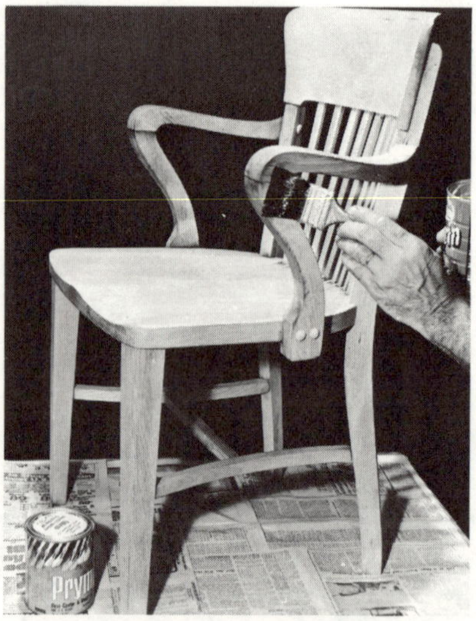

BEFORE CHAIR could be refinished,→ many dark coats had to be removed, but the true character of the wood now shows.

REGLUING MUST be done with care to avoid glue smears; they will not accept stain. Wipe off the smears immediately.

APPLICATION OF STAIN on the chair is best done with a cloth after all areas have been treated with wash coat of sealer.

AFTER REFINISHING, this chair proved to be handsomer than when it was new.

surface preparation

Generally your interest in finishing will concern new work, old work to be refinished, or old work which is too battered for successful refinishing, thus requiring a transformation. In the first two cases you'll be working on raw wood so surface preparation will require careful attention; a finish coat will accentuate rather than conceal surface defects such as insufficient, hurried sanding, scratches, dents and discoloration.

removing old finish

Paint and varnish removers have been greatly improved. The new water-rinsable types make the job easier and quicker than the old-fashioned kind. Now you simply lay on a generous coating with minimal brushing and let it stand about 10 minutes until the old finish peels and blisters or becomes gummy. Remove the old finish with a putty knife on all flat surfaces, steel wool in contoured areas and a toothbrush in carved sections.

Follow up with a water rinse, using a towel or sponge to remove the final traces of finish and remover. If feasible, a hosing is suggested. Stains that resist chemical removers must be bleached or scraped. The latter is laborious; do it only as a last resort. The chair shown on page 1194 needed such drastic action.

Veneer-lumber furniture must be handled with extreme care. Since most veneers are only 1/28 in. thick, it's obvious that scraping shouldn't be attempted. Use only a minimal amount of water for the final rinse, particularly if any of the veneer has splits or shows signs of having become separated from the core. The consequences could be disastrous.

sanding

Allow the stripped wood to dry thoroughly; then proceed to sand as with new work. Work with aluminum oxide, open-coat abrasive paper. Use a coarse 80-grit paper for heavy stock removal and work with progressively finer grits up to 220. A belt sander may be used for truing or leveling broad surfaces, followed with a power finishing sander charged with 220 paper and a light handsanding with 320 paper. Always sand with the grain where possible.

Always sand individual components of construction before assembly because it is practically impossible to do a thorough sanding job on inside corners. When refinishing, disassemble as many parts as possible, if the old glue permits, to allow better access for sanding.

Commercial finish stripping

The removal of old finish can sometimes be quite tedious and time-consuming. There is a shortcut available to you if you'd like to skip the chore. Simply take the piece to a stripper. They're listed in local directories under Furniture Stripping. Your piece will be dunked into a hugh tank of remover until every particle of finish is removed. A high-pressure water hosing and an application of a special "restorer" leaves the wood ready for finishing when dry. Prices are quite reasonable, depending upon the size of the piece.

PIECE TO BE stripped is dunked into a huge tank of heated chemical remover as a first step. It is then completely submerged and allowed to soak for a few minutes.

A LIGHT brushing, followed by a high-pressure water hosing removes the old finish and the chemicals. Pieces which can't take the hot solution (veneers, laminates) are treated in a special cold-process tank.

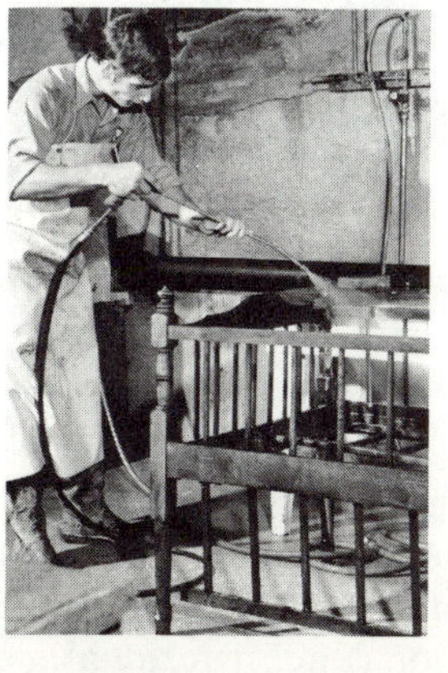

FINAL STEP in the process is a spraying with a special chemical which restores the wood and brings out the original color. These photos were taken at Yankee Antique Workshop, Inc., Huntington, NY.

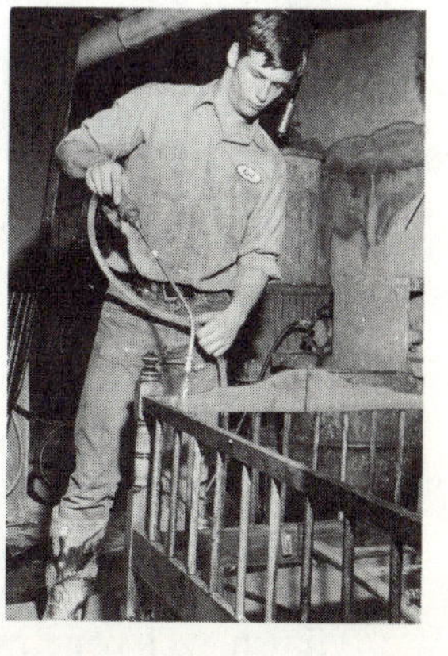

REWARD OF REFINISHING can be the restoration of a quality-built piece of furniture bought for just a few dollars at a sale. Those who know how to refinish furniture soon acquire a sharp eye for bargains. Surface scratches, stains and even coats of paint can, they know, be completely removed with patience and a little work.

When the major elements have been sanded they can be glued. Here you've got to exercise great care. No kind of transparent stain or clear finish will penetrate or conceal residual glue. Remove *all* traces of wet glue from the surface immediately; carelessness here will show up in the finished work. Scrape off the excess glue with a sharp chisel, taking care not to dig into the wood. Then wipe the spot clean with a dampened cloth. This will raise the grain slightly so

TOP COAT accentuates the figure and color of wood while adding a protective coating. Here it brings out the "fire" of a piece of mahogany.

FRESH SHELLAC dries faster. Make your own by simply dissolving shellac flakes in alcohol. The flakes can be weighed to the right amount on a postal scale.

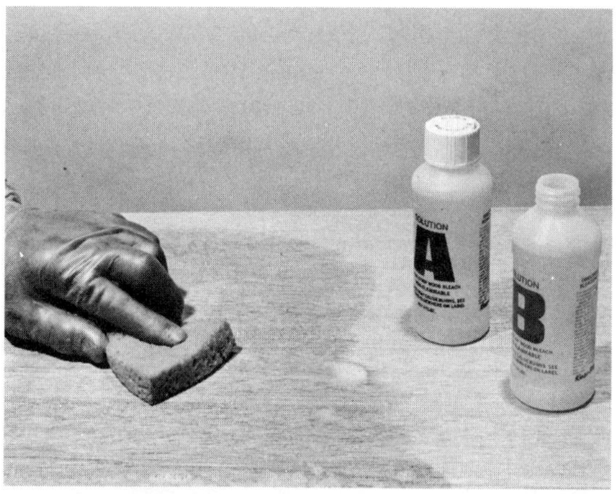

TWO-SOLUTION BLEACH is quick. After A has soaked for about 10 minutes, work B into the wood with a sponge. When it's dry, you then can sand it.

PRIMER-SEALERS prevent the top coat from darkening the wood. Note in the photo that the sealed half of the panel is lighter than the untreated portion.

WIDE RANGE of finishing products may confuse some beginners, but all materials are basically those described in this article. Shown are some of the top-quality products available today.

touch-up hand-sanding will be necessary. Never attempt to sand over wet glue as this will tend to push the glue farther into the pores. After sanding use a vacuum cleaner or tack cloth to remove all dust.

Slight dents in wood may be removed by placing a damp cloth over the area then heating it with an iron. The steam will swell the wood so it may be sanded level with the surrounding area.

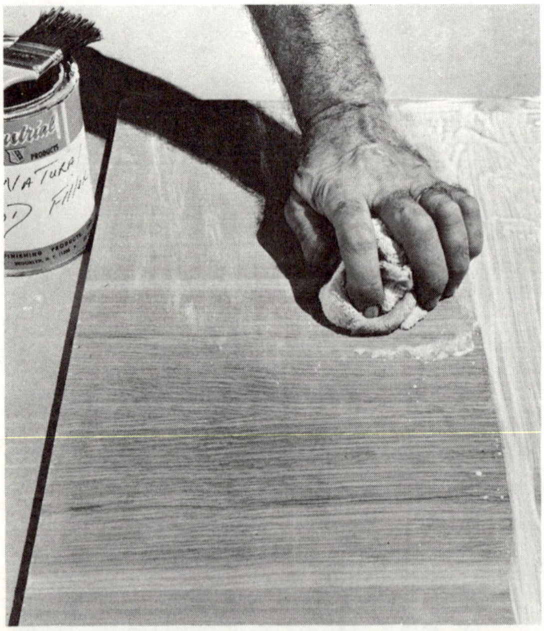

PASTE WOOD FILLER is used to get a smooth surface. When it begins to dry, just wipe it off across the grain with a rag. Finally, wipe lightly with the grain.

Paste filler check chart

Filler generally **used** on these woods	
ASH	OAK
CHESTNUT	ROSEWOOD
ELM	BUTTERNUT
HICKORY	LOCUST
MAHOGANY	WALNUT

Filler generally **not used** on these woods	
BASSWOOD	CYPRESS
CEDAR	BEECH
FIR	BIRCH
HEMLOCK	GUM
PINE	WILLOW
POPLAR	MAPLE
SPRUCE	SYCAMORE

Small chips and cracks will have to be treated by one of several methods at a later stage.

staining

Stain is used to enrich the color of wood, to reinforce the grain pattern, and frequently to imitate more expensive cabinet woods. The latter was done in refinishing the little bookshelf table illustrated. When the almost-black old finish was removed the wood revealed a very weak character. The problem was easily solved by applying a heavy coat of natural teak stain, then passing over it with a stiff dry brush to create a teak wood-grain pattern.

Amateurs often get poor results when they stain because end grain and soft spots soak up the stain unevenly and cause dark blotches. The simple trick of applying a wash coat of sealer to the wood *before* staining will prevent this common problem and assure an even coating. A wash coat is generally made by diluting a sealer in five or six parts of its solvent. Never apply the sealer full strength before staining—it will keep the stain from penetrating.

oil stains recommended

There are several types of stains but for home shop use the ready-mixed oil stains are highly recommended. They're available in numerous wood tones and colors. Water stains are difficult to control, they raise the grain and sometimes loosen glue. They're really for factory use.

Pretest the stain you plan to use on a scrap of wood of the same species as the job or on some concealed area of the piece to be sure of getting the desired color or shade. It's a good idea to go one step further and test the top coat because this too will have an effect on the finished job. Stain can be applied with brush or cloth, but the latter generally works better. Wipe off the excess before it gets too dry, using a clean lintless cloth. Drying time is usually overnight.

Now let's talk about the actual refinishing. Raw or stained wood is relatively porous and will absorb too readily any finish applied to it. Sealer "locks" the pores and acts as a foundation for the top coat so it stays on top where it belongs. It also keeps oil stain from bleeding through.

There are three basic types of sealers: lacquer-based sealer, shellac and a home-brewed varnish sealer made by diluting varnish with thinner. The lacquer type is by far the best to use because it's fast-drying, assures excellent adhesion for the top coat and prevents the finish coat from darkening the wood. Brush on a coat of

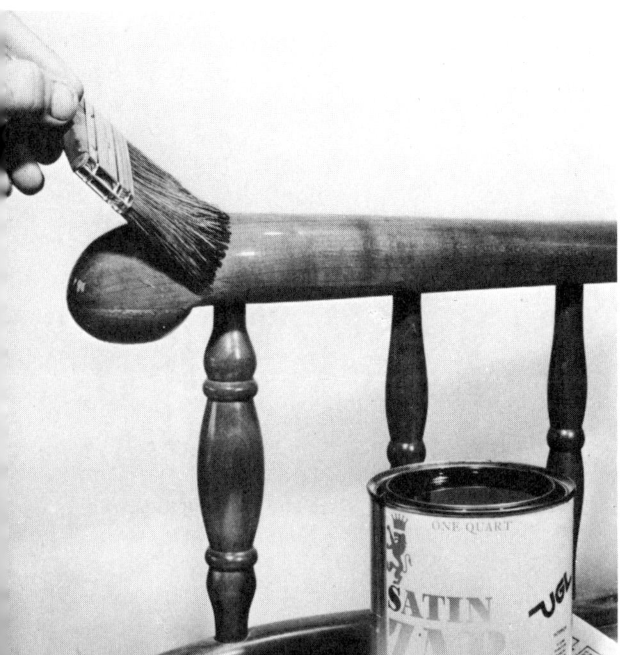

SATIN-FINISH top coat goes on nicely if you use a good-quality brush with flagged bristles. Apply the varnish liberally with a minimum number of brush strokes. You should finish each small area by lightly stroking it with just the tip of your brush.

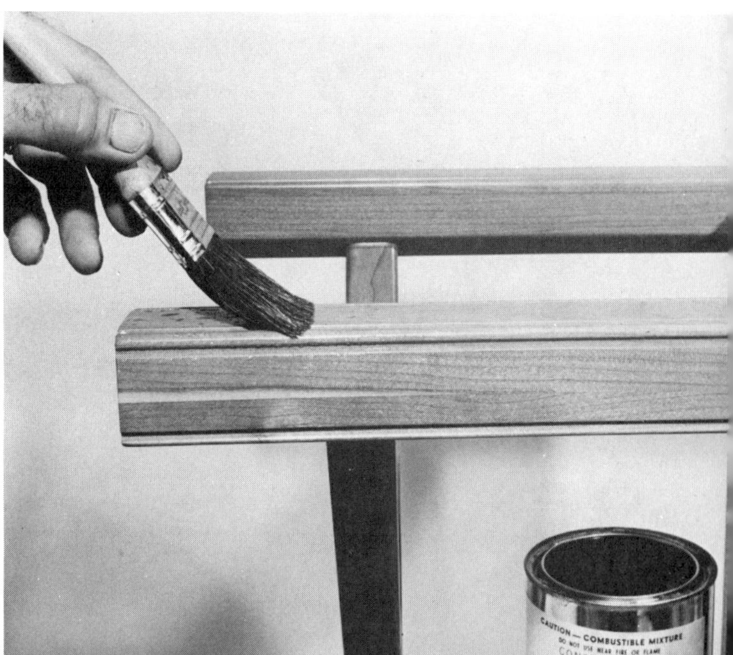

ALL-IN-ONE finishes combine the sealer and the finish coat. They require two or three single-solution applications. A two-coat job will usually produce a finish having a fine, hand-rubbed look to it.

How to repair dents and scratches

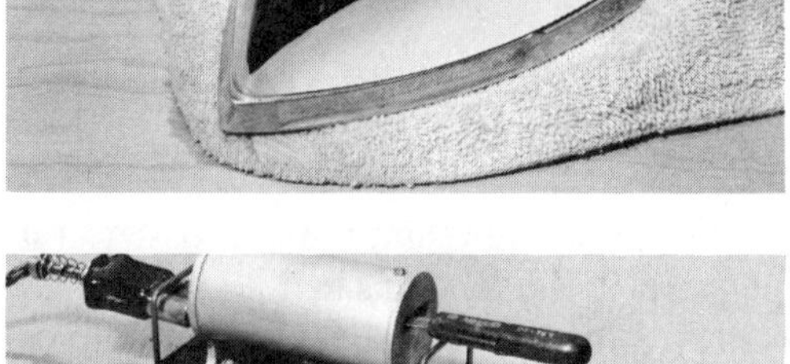

SHALLOW DENTS in wood can be removed by swelling the fibers. Place a damp cloth over the area and apply heat with an iron. Sand the area flush when it is dry.

PUTTY STICKS, available in many colors to match woods, are used to cover nailheads and small holes in a finished surface, but never used before application of the top coat. →

SHELLAC STICKS are used for repairing damaged surfaces (left photo). Heat flexible burn-in knife (or grapefruit knife) with smokeless alcohol or Sterno flame, touch it to material and press molten bead into hole or defect. Keep the knife moving to prevent burning the wood.

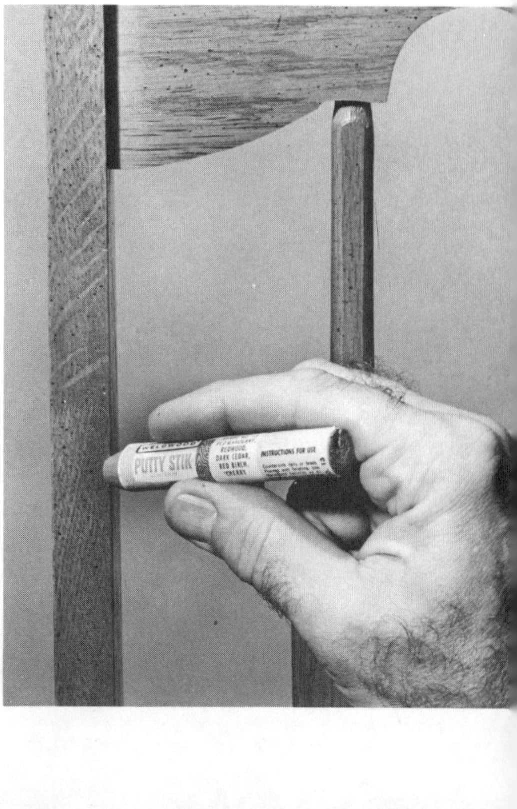

Before

How to simulate a wood-grain finish

FIRST FILL cracks and dents with wood putty or putty compound; lightly sand loose finish, don't remove firm finish.

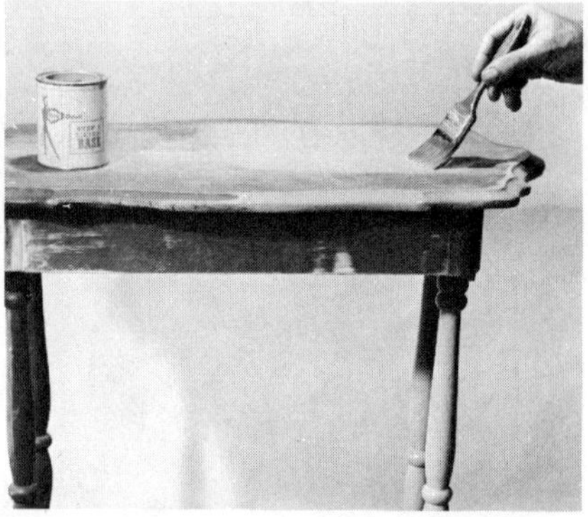

CLEAN OFF grime and sanding dust with turpentine. Then apply latex base (see text) and let dry for about an hour.

GLAZE GOES on next. Oil-based material dries slower than latex. Coat the area and do the next step before other parts.

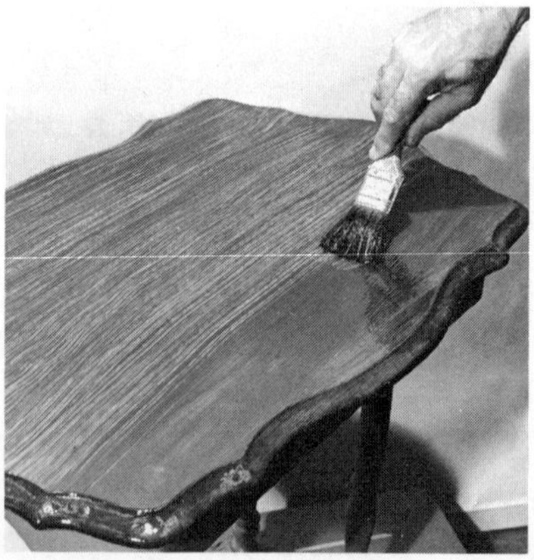

"COMB" A SIMULATED grain in the wet glaze with a stiff brush. Clear finish goes on last. (Edge shows ungrained glaze.)

After

sealer, lightly hand-sand with 220-grit paper and wipe off all sanding dust with a tack cloth. The surface is now ready for a filler and/or top coat.

filling open-grained wood

Some woods such as locust, mahogany, oak and walnut are open or coarse-grained and require filling in order to achieve a smooth flat surface. Paste wood filler, available in various wood colors, comes as a heavy paste which must be diluted with turpentine to brushing consistency. Brush the filler over a small area—about 2 sq. ft.—at a time. Work it well into the pores by brushing first with the grain, then across. Let it set until its "wet" look begins to dull. Don't let it get too dry. Wipe off the excess with burlap or other coarse cloth, first across the grain, then lightly with the grain using a soft, clean cloth. Let dry overnight. Sand surface lightly with very fine paper to remove excess surface filler.

bleaching, removing discoloration

The natural color of wood can be lightened by bleaching. Commonly used, commercially available wood bleaches contain two solutions which may be mixed or applied separately, depending on the formula. Bleach may also be used in localized areas to remove stains or other discolorations—always pretest it on sample wood. The chemicals are quite harmful to skin, so wear rubber gloves and goggles. Simply apply the solutions, let them dry; and then sand lightly to remove residual salts. Some methods require a water rinse.

applying the final finish

The top coat, or final finish, serves two purposes: It protects the surface and enhances the attractive color, figure and intricate grain patterns of the wood. Surface effects are optional—high gloss, satin smooth or flat. There are three basic types of natural wood finishes: surface—including shellac, varnish and lacquer—all-in-one and penetrating.

• *Shellac* is available in orange or white types. It is easy to use when fresh, but seldom is fresh because its shelf life is only about four to six months. Stale shellac is painfully slow-drying. You can make your own shellac, however, by buying shellac flakes and dissolving them in denatured alcohol as needed. A common dilution is "No. 2 cut" (2 lbs. of flakes per gallon of alcohol). Shellac dries fast in a dry atmosphere, but very slowly when humid conditions prevail.

White shellac does not deepen the wood color to any extent, but orange will impart a rich amber tone. Always apply several thin coats, sanding lightly after the first. Since shellac has poor resistance to water, alcohol and heat, it is desirable to rub the final coat with fine steel wool (000), followed with a substantial coat of rubbing wax for maximum protection.

• *Varnish* is available in the standard natural-resin type and in newer polyurethane and epoxy formulations. Standard varnishes are relatively slow-drying. The synthetics are easy to brush, fast-drying and have good resistance to wear, water, alcohol, acids and alkalis. A decided advantage of the polyurethanes is that humid weather has no adverse effect on drying as with standard varnishes. Actually, humidity promotes quicker hardening.

instructions for varnishing

Use a good bristle brush, dipping no more than one-third its length into the varnish. Flow it on liberally with a minimum number of brush strokes. Brush with parallel strokes, then quickly cross-stroke at right angles and finish by stroking lightly with the grain using only the top of the brush (almost dry). Never drag the bristles over the can rim to remove excess varnish because this will form tiny bubbles to mar the coating. Instead, gently tap the brush tip against the inside of the can above the liquid.

Regular varnish must be sanded with fine paper between coats, but the urethanes generally need not, provided each coat is applied within the time specified by the manufacturer. The time element is critical because chemical fusing between coats occurs only during the period indicated.

• *Lacquer*. Regular lacquers are extremely fast-drying and are meant for application only with spray equipment. Excellent hard-wearing brushing lacquers are now readily available for general use. These, too, are fast-drying so you must work more quickly than you would with varnish. Flow on liberal coats with the grain as evenly as possibly. Avoid over-brushing to prevent brush marks. Apply successive coats after light hand sanding. Be sure you have adequate ventilation.

• *All-in-one finishes* seal and surface-coat the wood in two or three single-solution applications. They require nothing under or over and dry to a medium luster simulating a hand-rubbed finish. Extra-fast-drying types should be brushed on like lacquer. Slow-drying types can be handled like varnish.

• *Penetrating finishes* are actually resin and oil sealer which penetrate deeply into the pores of wood where they harden to protect the surface from within. Not intended as a surface film, these finishes preserve and color the wood with a flat look typical of Danish Modern furniture. Application usually requires flooding the surface of the sanded wood and letting the solution penetrate about 30 minutes. Then apply a second coat and let it soak in about 15 minutes. Wipe the surface clean and dry with a soft, lintless cloth.

wood-graining and antiquing

Furniture too battered for bare-wood refinishing can be transformed into attractive pieces by wood graining or antiquing. Kits contain a base coat and glaze. You sand the pieces to remove loose, peeled finish and to smooth rough spots, then fill voids and cracks with wood putty or water putty. Apply the base coat and let it dry (latex type will dry within an hour). Brush on the glaze coat, then pass over it with a dry stiff brush to create a "grain" pattern. If you don't like the results, add more glaze and try again. With practice, you can get close to a new-wood clear finish.

How to choose and use fire extinguishers

By STEVEN J. HOWARD

One or two good extinguishers can keep a sudden fire under control until the fire department arrives. Here's how to select the right kinds and number of extinguishers, where to locate them, how to use them to best advantage

■ IF A GREASE FIRE breaks out in your kitchen, are you equipped to put it out? Do you know the three most common types of household fires and the quickest way to put each out? Since there are about 300,000 home fires annually, it makes good sense to equip your home—and family—with the extinguishers and the knowledge to combat common household fires.

Because fire can, and often does, travel extraordinarily fast, there is a procedure that fire departments strongly urge homeowners to follow:

SEE ALSO
Boating, safety . . . Electrical wiring . . . Emergencies . . . Safety, workshop . . . Wiring, electrical

First, evacuate the house.

Second, call the fire department.

Third, fight the fire if—*and that's a big if*—you have the right equipment to do so without endangering your life.

Besides an ordinary garden hose and water for use on many types of fires, this means you must have fire extinguishers carefully placed for maximum safety.

Fire extinguishers for the home are those that will put out class A, B and C fires. These classifications were devised by the National Fire Protection Assn. to distinguish the combustibles which feed a fire. Thus, unless you have a multipurpose fire extinguisher, you must know the class of a fire to fight it.

A, B and C Fires. Class A feeds on wood, cloth, paper and rubber; class B on flammable liquid and grease blazes, and class C fires are

DRY EXTINGUISHER (left) is for B-C (grease and electrical) fires. Water unit (right) is for A fires.

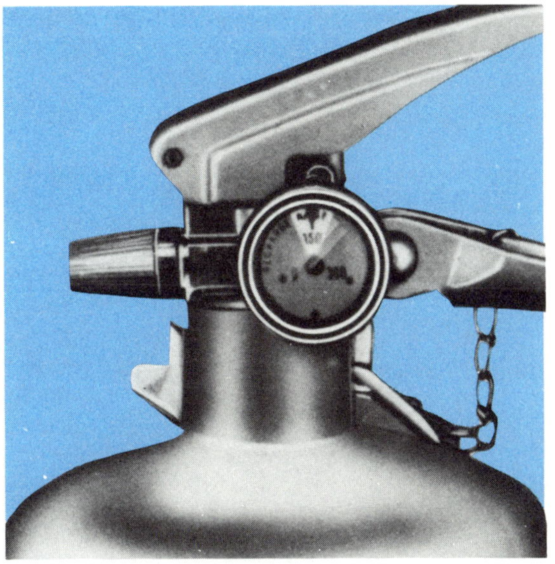

GAUGE OR INDICATOR on any extinguisher you buy is a must. It tells when repressuring is due.

MULTIPURPOSE EXTINGUISHER states on nameplate that it is usable for class A, B *and* C fires.

SOME TYPES have an indicator located at top of cylinder to show when pressure is inadequate.

electrical. If electricity is turned off, a class C fire is converted into a class A or B fire. (A fourth classification of fire (D), which feeds on combustible metals such as magnesium, sodium, titanium and zirconium, is unlikely to occur in the home.)

You have three options in protecting your home against the first three fire classes. One is to use a multipurpose extinguisher that fights all three. Your second choice is to use two different kinds of extinguishers. The third is to set up a water hose and supplement it with fire extinguishers to combat class B and C fires. Each option offers certain advantages the others don't and each has some special limitations.

For example, the multipurpose extinguisher, which uses monoammonium phosphate as the extinguishing agent, offers the very important advantage of speed. You can grab it and use it without stopping to think whether a fire you are fighting is of the A, B or C type. It extinguishes all three.

But you should recognize that monoammonium phosphate extinguishers that weigh 4½ pounds and more are the only ones listed by the Underwriters' Laboratories as "multipurpose." Those of smaller size have shown limited effectiveness against a class A fire and are listed as BC extinguishers.

You can use a smaller size monoammonium phosphate extinguisher against a class A fire, but you will also have to use water to completely extinguish a blaze of any proportion. Some misleading advertising of small-size monoammonium phosphate extinguishers would have you believe otherwise.

Of the three options, equipping a home with multipurpose extinguishers is the most expen-

CARBON DIOXIDE is used in B-C extinguishers, which require you to get in close to the fire.

sive. For example, a three-bedroom house with den, basement and garage, requires a minimum of four multipurpose extinguishers to provide for minimum protection: one for the bedrooms, living room, dining room and den; one in the kitchen; one in the garage, and one to protect the basement.

In choosing among the three options, there is an additional characteristic of the multipurpose extinguisher to consider. When monoammonium phosphate hits flame, it forms a tacky crust that smothers the fire. This crust has an insulating effect on electrical contacts that could damage electrical equipment if you have to fight a class C fire.

The second choice of home fire-extinguisher protection involves the use of two different types of extinguishers: *A* and *BC*. To use them, you must stop and think if the one you've picked up is the right one for the fire at hand.

For example, class A extinguishers recommended for home use employ water as the extinguishing agent. Never use a class A extinguisher on a class B or C fire. Water will spread a fire that is being fed by cooking fat, gasoline or other flammable liquid. It presents a danger of shock and electrocution if used on electrical fires.

Class A fire extinguishers are of two types: stored pressure, which keeps contents under pressure at all times, and pump tank. A pump tank extinguisher is a 2½ or 5-gal. container of water that you manually pump to bring water to bear on the flames through a hose. A stored-pressure class A extinguisher of 2½-gal. size weighs less than a pump-tank type, which makes it easier to handle. However, it costs more than the pump-tank extinguisher.

Additionally, the extinguishing agent for a pump tank is right in your kitchen or bathroom. If you discharge a pump-type extinguisher, you simply refill it at the sink. (A stored-pressure extinguisher has to be refilled and repressurized by a fire equipment service shop.)

BC extinguishers use carbon dioxide, sodium bicarbonate, potassium chloride, or potassium bicarbonate as the extinguishing agent. Carbon dioxide doesn't leave a residue like the chemical powders. However, its range is more limited; you have to get in closer to fight a fire.

A carbon dioxide extinguisher costs practically twice as much as a dry chemical BC extinguisher of comparable size. And it has still another drawback: It has to be weighed and possibly repressurized every six months by a fire equipment service shop. Thus, homeowners are better off if equipped with dry chemical extinguishers.

Incidentally, in an emergency you can use a BC-type extinguisher against a class A fire. The chemical agent will knock down the flame, giving you time to get water to the blaze.

what to buy

Buying individual class A and class BC extinguishers for the home is less expensive than buying multipurpose extinguishers. Again, assuming that same same three-bedroom home mentioned earlier, you will spend $65 to $85 for minimum protection, depending on whether you get a stored-pressure or pump-type, class A extinguisher, as follows:

- One class A extinguisher to cover the bedrooms, living room, dining room and den. Cost: $20 to $40.
- Three BC extinguishers to protect the kitchen, garage and basement against flammable liquid fires and all areas of the home against electrical fires. Cost: $15 each—$45 total.

The third and least expensive option open to you is to equip the house with a garden hose for class A fires and with BC fire extinguishers. Make sure the hose is long enough to reach to the farthest part of the house. You can store it rolled up near the water source, such as in a kitchen cabinet beneath the sink. But you should bear in mind that a fire may keep you from reaching the hose.

The hose should have a nozzle so that a high-pressure spray can be played on the fire, and the connection should be of the quick-connect type. They're available in hardware stores for about $2.

The coupling has two parts: a female adapter connected to the hose, and a male adapter that connects to the water faucet. Unfortunately, this awkward piece of hardware must stay connected to the faucet to assure quick hook-up in case of fire.

In selecting multipurpose or BC fire extinguishers, there are several important points to note, such as size. BC extinguishers contain a charge of anywhere from 1 to 30 pounds. Naturally, the greater the charge that an extinguisher has the greater amount of extinguishing agent that can be brought to bear on a fire. But, of course, large-charge extinguishers also weigh more.

The Fire Equipment Manufacturers Assn. says, "Pick the largest extinguisher that can be handled by everyone in the family who may have to fight a fire."

Incidentally, the numeral classification that precedes the letter classification on a nameplate, such as 2BC, indicates the size of the Underwriters' Laboratories (UL) test fire which the extinguisher can handle. The numeral is academic since no authoritative agency has established standards for the home which use UL-test-fire sizes as a basis.

CYLINDER in this type of extinguisher for B-C fires is replaced rather than recharged.

Make sure that class A stored-pressure, multipurpose and BC extinguishers have direct reading gauges or indicators that tell if the extinguisher is pressurized and ready for use. One type of indicator is a button-type device that you press in to test the extinguisher. If it pops out, pressure is okay. If it stays in, the extinguisher should be repressurized.

You may encounter cartridge-type extinguishers. These have gas stored in a separate container that must be ruptured before the extinguisher can be used. They are not recommended for home use by the Fire Equipment Manufacturers Assn. because they don't have pressure gauges or indicators and must, therefore, be weighed periodically. Select extinguishers that specify they have been listed by the Underwriters' Laboratories (which has set standards of construction and performance).

what not to buy

As for non-UL-listed equipment, the National Fire Protection Assn. says: " 'Beer-can'-size extinguishers are a poor choice. These are tin cans, aerosol containers, plastic shakers, or squeeze bottles that hold less than a pint of liquid or 12 to 16 oz. of a dry powder. Besides their small capacity, these devices are of uncertain reliability and their range is dangerously limited."

An extinguisher is worthless if you can't get to it, so keep these points in mind:

Mount extinguishers so they're near an escape route. This gives you flexibility. You can fight the fire or get out if heat and smoke become intense.

Don't locate an extinguisher in a stairwell. Rising heat and smoke may make it inaccessible.

In garages, workshops and kitchens, avoid putting the extinguisher on a wall nearest a likely fire source. For example, don't mount one over the stove.

Become familiar with the use of your extinguisher by reading instructions on the nameplate. And check that gauge or indicator often to make sure the equipment has sufficient pressure.

Although do-it-yourself repressurizing kits are available, do not attempt to repressurize a stored-pressure extinguisher yourself. It's too dangerous. Containers have exploded and caused injury.

Some extinguishers use replaceable cylinders which can be safely handled. If the extinguisher loses pressure, the spent cylinder is unscrewed from the valve assembly and a new cylinder is attached in its place.

Warm up to a patio firepit

By CLEMENT D. HELLYER

SEE ALSO

Barbecues . . . Benches, deck . . . Cookout bars . . .
Garden shelters . . . Gazebos . . . Grills . . .
Insect traps . . . Patios . . . Planters . . .
Screened summer rooms

■ WHETHER it's used to grill a sizzling steak, toast marshmallows or provide a cozy campfire around which to congregate on a chilly evening at poolside, a patio firepit can be a lot of fun whatever the occasion.

I built the one you see here for roughly $15 which is what I paid for 111 bricks, a half sack of cement and four buckets of sand. A couple of common lath will be needed too, plus a length of clothesline. As you see, I also bought a valve and burner so I can ignite the logs with butane gas.

You can make the pit as high as you want although three tiers provide a convenient seat height and will give enough depth to build a good wood fire or bed of coals. A 30-in. inside diameter will accommodate a regular fireplace grate or basket.

Each tier requires 37 standard paver bricks (2½ x 3¾ x 8⅛ in.), and after a circle is drawn

FIRST DRIVE A NAIL and swing a 30-inch circle with chalk and string. Bricks are placed around the circle.

BRICKS ARE SPACED at the outer edge by inserting wood spacers, then tying the circle of bricks with cord.

A BRICK AGAINST the lath dam prevents the mortar from pushing out the dam when you fill the joint.

JOINTS LEFT OPEN in the bottom tier provide drain holes. Note the gas valve in the second tier.

with chalk the bricks are placed on edge (without mortar) around the outside of the circle. The bricks touch at the inside but fan out at the outside, evenly spaced with mortar dams of 1⅜-in. lath between the bricks. The dams are inserted completely around the tier and when they are all in place, the tier is wrapped with cord and drawn up tight to hold the wood spacers in place flush with the ends of the bricks.

The pie-shaped pockets formed by the dams are now filled with mortar. A good mix is sand, 3 parts, and cement, 1 part. Bag mixes which need only water, such as Sakrete, are also available. The mortar should be wet enough to settle and tamp firmly in the spaces. Be sure to see that you don't get it either too dry or too soupy. It's important, too, that the bricks be soaked in water first so they will not absorb moisture from the mortar. Also, avoid laying the pit in the hot sun. Try to shade the area and, if you have to leave the project, protect the mortar from rapid drying by covering the work with damp burlap. Leave a couple of joints open in the bottom tier so there's a drain. Succeeding tiers will help bond these unmortared joints.

Let the mortar set a few hours before untying the cord and removing the dams. Then wash any mortar stains from the tops of the bricks and start your second tier. Place these bricks over the mortar joints below. You'll notice that the ⅜-in. thickness of the dams produces a pleasing "pointed" or recessed joint which gives an interesting shadow effect. A brick placed against the dam when filling the joint will keep the dam from being pushed out by the cement.

If you are planning on using butane gas to light your logs, it's a simple matter to install it. Just mortar the valve into the second tier. Then construct the rest of the firepit around it and connect to an underground gas line.

How to have a smokeless fireplace

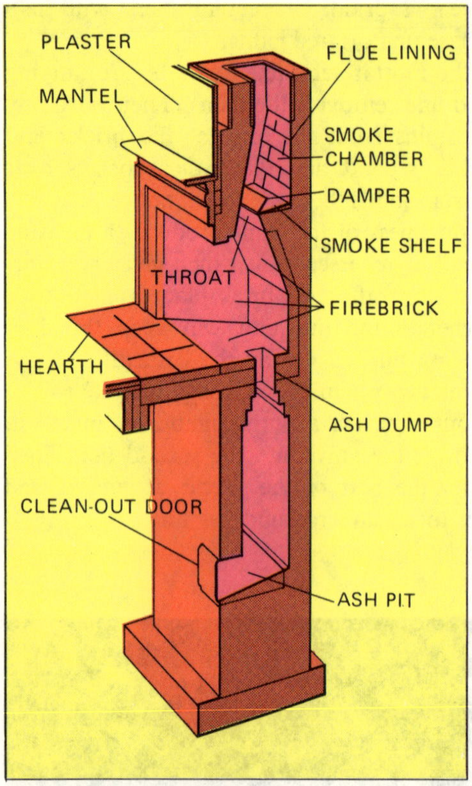

Fireplace construction

To function properly, a fireplace must be proportionally designed within certain limits: Size of throat, flue-effective area and firebox height, width and depth are all relative to each other for good draft. Often a design defect can be corrected by a simple alteration—for example, addition of a hood or lintel, as shown in the drawings on these pages.

THE ENJOYMENT of spending a cold evening in front a well-laid fire is often marred by a familiar problem: The fireplace spills smoke into the room rather than curling it up the chimney. Routine steps you can take to minimize this problem include periodic inspection of the flue to be sure there is no excessive soot and scale buildup and being selective as to what you burn. Do not burn too much pine or fir because they cause a disproportionate amount of soot buildup in the chimney. Rather, stick to hardwoods. Another cause of smoking is chimney blockage. Usually, it's a fallen nest or brick (in a new home) lodged in the throat. Other smoke-producing causes—and their cures—are described and illustrated here.

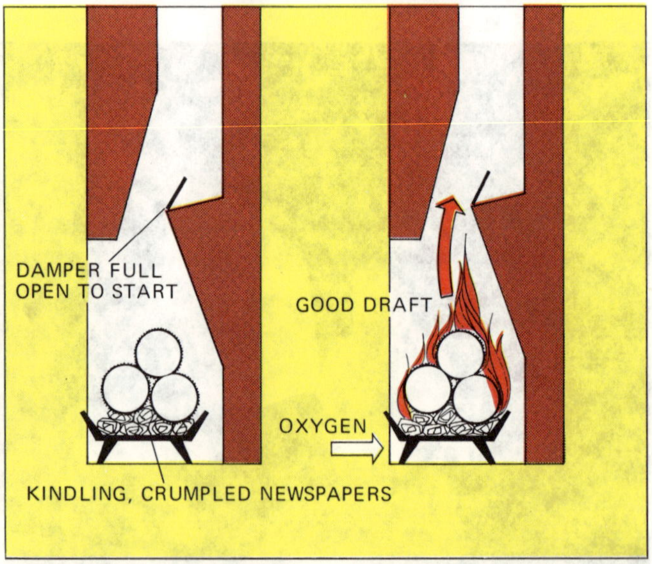

How to get (and keep) a good fire going

Place crumpled newspapers on the grate, add dry kindling, then stack logs so that flames can curl upward around them. (Three logs burn better than two.) Before lighting the fire, get a draft moving up the chimney. Open the damper, insert three sheets of newspaper in the chimney and burn them completely. Now, light your fire. For good burning, you may want to open a window slightly to keep oxygen flowing into the room.

If the flue is too small

The flue should be about 1/12th the area of the firebox opening (height x width). To replace it involves tearing down the chimney. Instead, try adding a metal hood or new lintel. To determine the correct opening, with fire burning and smoke rolling out at the top, hold a piece of metal across the top of the opening. Gradually lower the metal until there's a good draft and no smoke. That opening is the correct one.

SEE ALSO
Firewood . . . Heaters, space . . .
Heating systems, home . . . Stoves, wood-burning

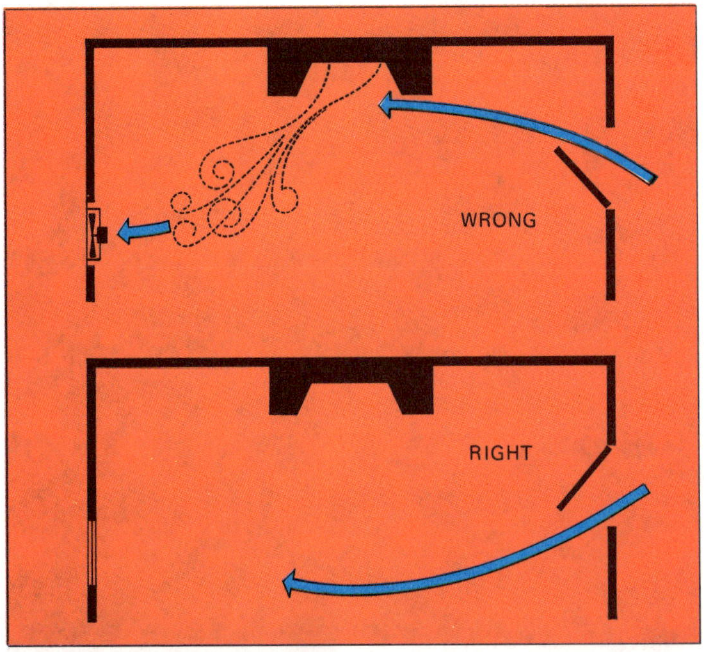

Check out the room's airflow

A door in the room may be so located that, when it's open, it causes a draft *across* the fire. Either rehinge the door on the opposite jamb or use a fire screen. Similarly, an exhaust fan in the fireplace room can cause smoking. Leave it off when using the fireplace.

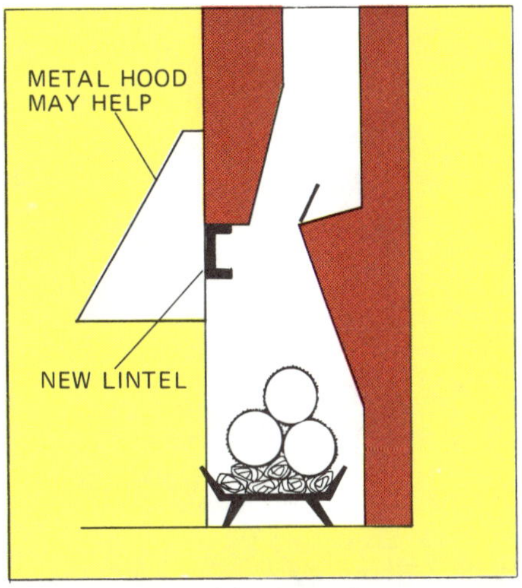

Damper located improperly

If the front edge of the damper is used as a lintel, the damper is too low. The lintel—a separate piece of angle iron—should be 6 to 8 in. lower than the damper. There's a good chance that a metal hood or a new, lower lintel may correct this fault. A much more drastic solution is to rip out the brickwork and raise the damper to a proper height, then rebuild the back wall to line up with the new damper position.

Chimney not high enough

On a house with a peaked roof, the chimney should be at least 2 ft. above the ridge; for flat or slightly pitched roofs the figure is 3 ft. If it's not that high, the chimney should be raised. Make certain that the extension is no smaller inside than the diameter of the existing flue. Tall trees, surrounding hills and nearby chimneys cause downdrafts too. A shield hood and cap—with the shield toward the wind—usually will eliminate downdrafts from these sources.

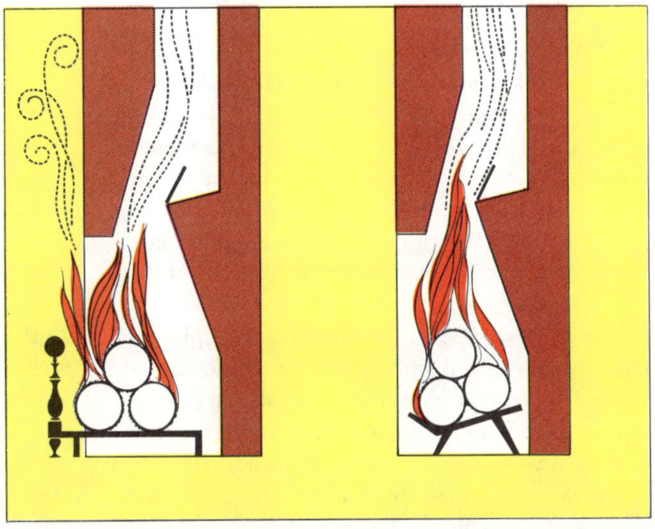

Firebox is not deep enough

The easiest correction for a too-shallow firebox is to use a narrower grate to keep the fire well back in the firebox. Precaution: If you see smoke coming out of the chimney anywhere but at the top, don't use the fireplace until the leak is checked out and, if necessary, repaired by an expert.

HANDSOME prefab fireplace serves as room divider. This design is by Ira Grandberg, AIA, and Robert Brooks.

Give a prefab fireplace a custom look

TODAY'S FIREPLACE doesn't have to sit with its back against the wall. Prefabricated units can be used in new and creative ways. The design problem in this house was to make the most of the available living space. Architect Ira Grandberg chose to maintain an open, spacious feeling in both the living room and snack area/dining room by separating the areas with a low-profile, free-standing fireplace.

The easiest type of prefabricated fireplace to customize is a built-in model. This type is engineered for zero clearance—so that combustible materials can touch its sides, back and bottom without fear of fire. For our installation we chose a Preway unit called the Energy Mizer that uses outside air for combustion and reheats and recirculates room air for added energy savings.

The first step in any fireplace installation is deciding where you want it. Don't put it where it will be in your way or disrupt convenient traffic patterns. Also, choose a spot that will give the most heat benefit. Ideally, as in our installation, a fireplace should be located smack in the middle of the most-used space on the first floor, or in the basement of your house. Since warm air rises, putting it near a stairwell provides you with ready-made ducting to warm the upper floors. Another consideration is proximity to combustibles. Even with zero-clearance units, remember that the fireplace should be located so its opening is at least 30 in. from combustible furniture or walls. Finally, choose a spot where the chimney can be installed without cutting into your rafters or ceiling joists.

After you choose a location, position the fireplace and then use a plumb bob to mark the center point for the chimney opening on the ceiling. Push a wire marker through a hole drilled at the center point and check the space above the cutout to avoid cutting wires or plumbing above the ceiling. Then cut a hole in the ceiling to suit the chimney with a keyhole or sabre saw.

Fit the first section of triple-walled pipe onto the top of the fireplace. Then add sections as you continue toward the ceiling, rotating each section until seams are aligned. To support chimney at the ceiling penetration, use ceiling support box

SEE ALSO

Energy, saving . . . Family rooms . . . Firewood . . . Heaters, space . . . Heating systems, home . . . Home improvement . . . Insulation . . . Remodeling . . . Winterizing, homes

for free-standing fireplaces. Next, cut a hole in the roof and proceed to install the rest of the chimney, its flashing, storm collar and rain cap. The finished chimney must be at least 3 ft. above the high point of the roof cutout and at least 2 ft. above the highest point of the roof that's within 10 ft. of the chimney.

The air intake ducts to a unit like the Energy Mizer must terminate outside the house. *Do not* draw air from the attic, other rooms or from the garage. Once the outlet positions have been located, cut the required holes for the combustion air ducts and connect the ducting to elbows fit into the stove.

Don't forget a hearth extension. It's an important safety feature that guards against errant sparks and embers. The hearth extension should extend at least 16 in. in front of and at least 8 in. beyond both sides of the fireplace opening. It must be composed of a noncombustible material such as brick, tile, slate or concrete.

The surround is basically a straightforward job of framing with 2 x 4s and skinning the framework with plasterboard. Start by laying out the walls for the surround in the spot you have chosen for the fireplace.

Next, you position your unit. Then precut all studs and plates to length as determined by your stove's base and height dimensions. Be sure to follow your fireplace manufacturer's installation manual carefully for safety and efficiency.

Nail down the end soleplate first and then preassemble the front and back walls—and erect each as a single unit.

Next, install the drywall and set the ringed nailheads slightly below the surface (i.e., dimple, but don't break the plasterboard paper). Tape and compound all joints and nail depressions.

You will require only one coat of compound if you plan to finish the surface with Ruff-It as we did. Once the plasterboarding is completed, nail on the plyood top—with the chimney hole cut out beforehand. Bond the high-pressure laminate to the plywood and trim around the mantle and the fireplace opening with 1 x 4 pine.

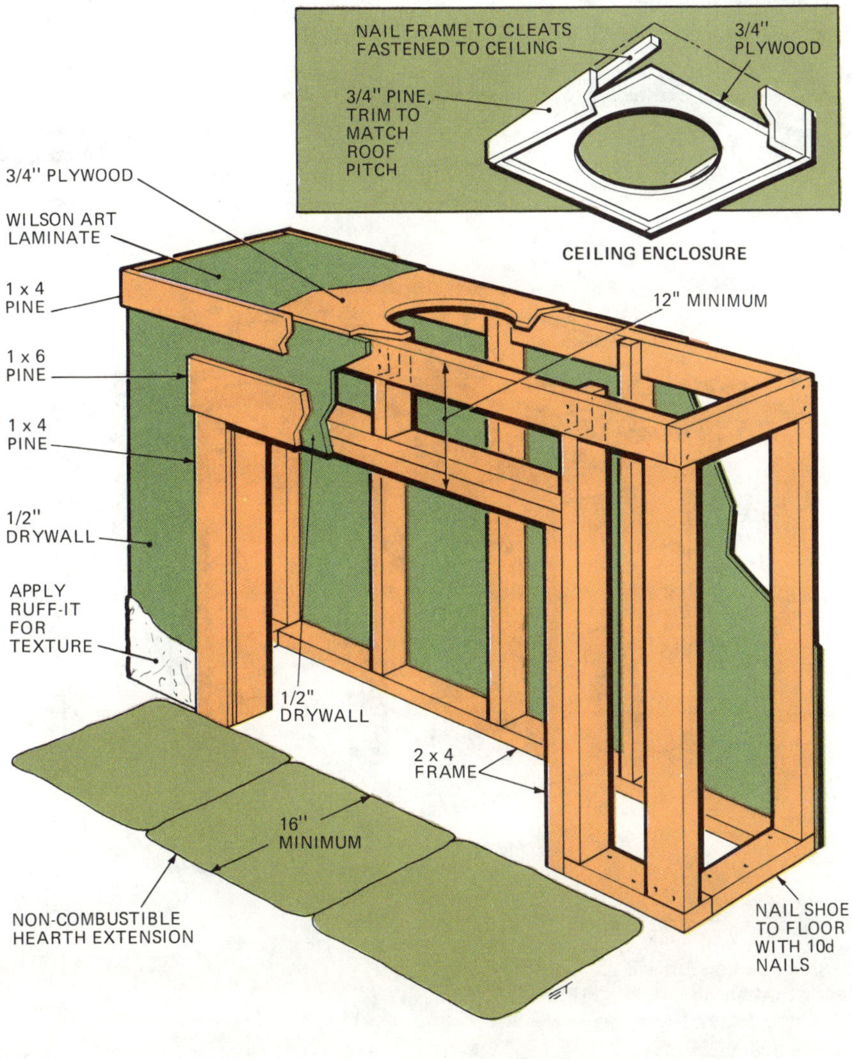

Build in a woodbox

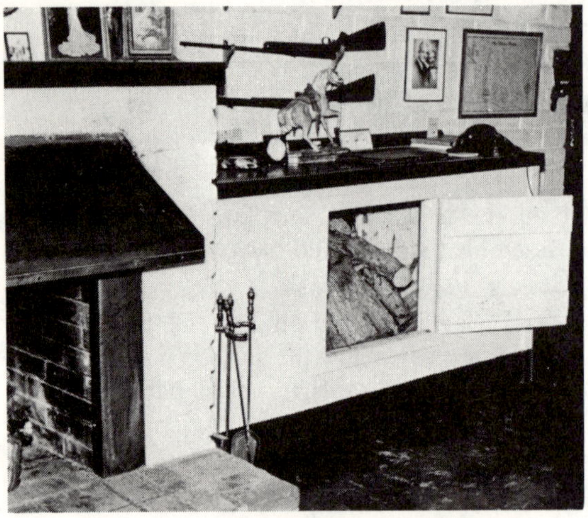

■ WITH THIS dual-access box next to your fireplace, there will be no need to run out in the cold for a log or two. Just fill it every third or fourth day and firewood will always be indoors and handy.

First step in construction is to cut an opening in the wall of the house. Then frame it in and add a suitable hinged door. Be sure to make the opening large enough to allow passage of logs cut to fit your fireplace.

The rest of the bin should be framed with 2x2s and finished to suit the interior of the house. Do not omit the 2x8—it prevents any tossed logs from knocking off the siding.

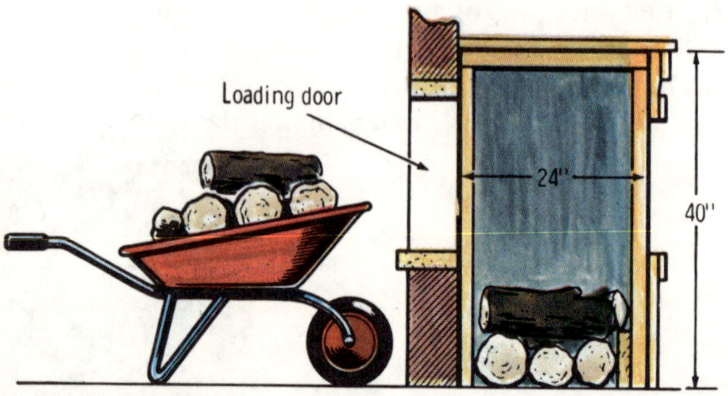

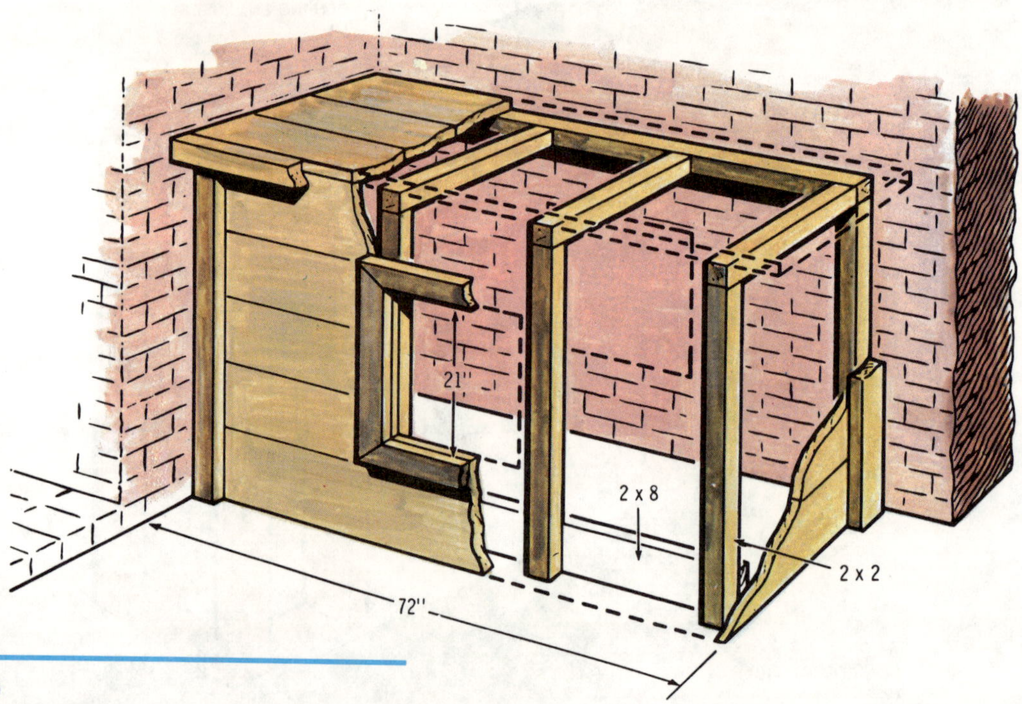

SEE ALSO

Chain saws . . . Firewood . . . Log cutting . . . Sawbucks . . . Stoves, wood-burning

How to cut firewood and use a fireplace

By HARRY WICKS

■ THE WELL PLANNED USE of your fireplace this winter can be a practical complement to your home's heating system. A small fire can provide enough warmth to take the chill out of an early morning or damp evening. When it does, your furnace will work less, saving expensive fuel.

Though there are occasions when you may use charcoal, coal or commercial pressed "logs," it's a pretty safe bet that you, like most, actually prefer to use real wood. Thus, with the cost of firewood being what it is today, it's just about a must to know how to select, cut and stack logs as well as how to use them properly in the fireplace.

Softwoods like pine, fir and spruce are easy to ignite and burn very fast with a hot flame. The very speed with which softwoods burn makes them less desirable, though. Such a fire needs constant attention and replenishing. Also, burning softwood over a period of years can build up a dangerous coating of tars in the chimney.

You should avoid using scrap lumber and refuse. These materials, especially when excessively dry, produce sparks which escape up the flue and are a fire hazard.

The best fire—one that burns long and gives plenty of heat—is produced by combining softwoods with hardwoods such as maple, oak, birch and ash. The hardwood species burn less vigorously and with a shorter flame; thus, they burn more slowly. For aroma, add woods from fruit and nut trees: Apple, cherry, hickory and

SEE ALSO

Chain saws . . . Crosscut saws . . . Fireplaces . . . Log cutting . . . Sawbucks . . . Saws, buck . . . Stoves, wood-burning

FUEL SAW over ground that offers no fire hazards; keep fuel in marked can.

TO SLICE small-diameter log, open throttle before touching log. Cut with bumper snugged against log. Release throttle as soon as cut is completed.

AS YOU CUT a log, keep in mind that it weakens and bends at the cutting point. To avoid pinching the saw's bar and chain, support the log as shown here.

pecan, for instance, all give pleasant scents. Generally, wood smoke's scent resembles the fragrance of the tree's fruit.

If you buy firewood, be aware that it is sold by the cord, a stack that measures 4x4x8 ft. The price depends on your locale and the species you order. For many homeowners, burning a cord of wood they have cut themselves will just about amortize the cost of a quality chain saw. Given reasonable care, that same saw will be cutting firewood for many years. But if you must buy logs, try to order from a dealer who can supply a mixture of wood species.

Try to select and work with logs of a length that you can handle easily. Then simply slice the logs up into fireplace lengths; for most fireplaces this is 24-in. The diameter of logs you buy should be governed by your chain saw's capacity. Using a saw with a 14-in. guidebar, for example, you can comfortably cut logs that are up to 20 in. in diameter.

When selecting wood, try to pick out straight-grained, knot-free logs, because they're easier to split than lengths with crooked grain. Keep in mind that wet or green wood is more easily split than seasoned wood. In general, softwoods can be split with less effort than hardwoods. Split logs after you have cut them to length.

Andirons should be spaced about 12 in. apart and equidistant from the hearth's centerline. Lay a generous amount of crumpled newspaper on the hearth between the andirons. Next, arrange a crisscross pile of kindling—pine and cedar work fine—on the newspaper.

Position the longest and thickest log across the andirons toward the rear of the fireplace. *Do not* let the logs butt tightly against the back wall. Leave about ½ in. of air space between them. Place a second piece, preferably a split log, in front and a third split log on top to form a triangular pile.

If you use a fire basket instead of andirons, the fire-laying procedure is the same—just place crumpled newspaper below the basket.

Light the fire with the fireplace damper open all the way. When the fire has started, close the damper until the fireplace starts to smoke, then open it just enough to stop the smoking.

For your fire to burn brightly, it must have a supply of fresh air. If your house is tightly weatherstripped and storm-windowed, it may even be necessary to open a window several inches. Ideally, that window will be located on the wall opposite the fireplace rather than to one side where it may create a cross-draft.

Also keep in mind that any exhaust fans going full blast in the kitchen and bathroom can create a smoking fireplace by pulling air down the chimney.

If your fire hasn't burned out and you're ready to retire or must leave, use the fireplace tongs to stand all unburned logs on end in the back corners of the fireplace. Standing this way, the logs will burn out quickly.

Do not close the damper if there is any smoking wood in the fireplace. The fireplace screen should be fully closed before you retire to keep sparks off rugs and floors.

Don't clean out your fireplace after each fire: Ashes about 1-in. thick should be left and spread evenly over the entire hearth. These will insulate the cold hearth and make the next fire easier to start.

Don't build too big a fire. Three or four logs will usually provide all the heat and flames you will want. As top and front logs burn up, turn them with tongs and, if necessary, place another split log on top.

TO SAW larger-diameter logs—but still less than the length of the saw's bar—use this technique: Start with the saw's bumper (circle) pressed against a log with the blade held at a slight angle. Open the throttle to full speed and slowly lower the traveling chain into the log by pivoting the saw with its bumper kept against the log. Keep the throttle fully open throughout the cut; release the throttle as log starts its drop.

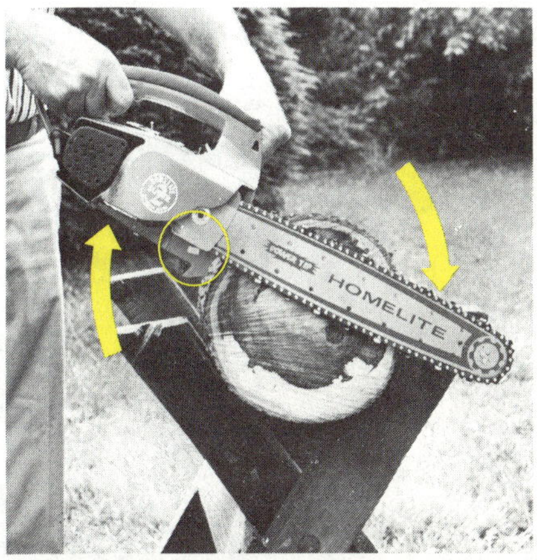

YOU CAN split logs—preferably when they are green—using either a splitting ax, as at left, or a steel splitting wedge and a sledgehammer, as above. For larger logs, the latter method is recommended.

GOOD CIRCULATION through and around pile makes this a good way to stack logs for seasoning. When the logs are split into similarly dimensioned pieces, you can pile from 12 to 16 pieces in such stacks.

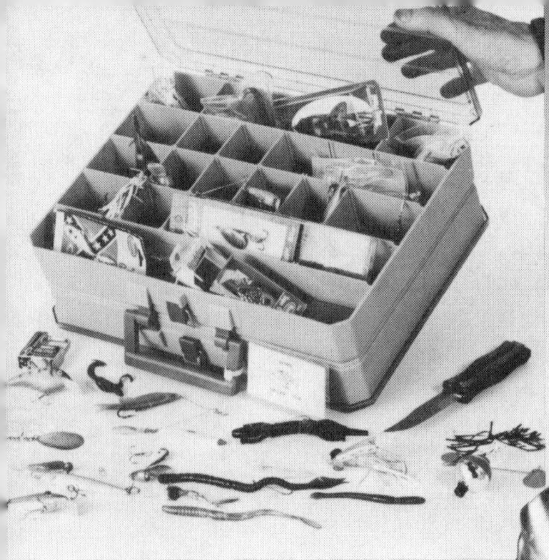

POPULAR tackle boxes like Magnum 1146 (above) by Plano, have adjustable compartments, see-through lids. Recommended rods (top to bottom) are:

- Zebco Pro Combo with Omega One reel, Stren line, PS10 Pro Staff 6-foot rod;
- Garcia Ambassadeur 5000 bait-casting reel, 8315-A Ambassadeur 5-foot rod;
- Daiwa GF-13 graphite 7-foot rod with Silver 1300C skirted-spool spinning reel.

Tackle that lands the lunkers

By MARK SOSIN

■ GETTING YOUR YOUNGSTER, wife or friend started in fishing is easy if you follow two basic rules: Make sure they catch fish the first time out, and urge them to use tackle that fits the situation. Each rod and reel combination is suited for a particular phase of the sport, and there is no universal outfit that is ideal for every type of fishing.

First, a beginner should consider his needs: the type of fishing he plans to do, weight of lures and bait that will be cast, size of the fish that might be caught, and conditions under which they will be taken. An outfit must be balanced. That is, the breaking strength of the line determines the size of the reel, and the reel must match the rod.

Though many people choose the rod first, it's better to decide on the breaking strength of the line you'll need. Ten-pound test is a good starting point for most freshwater fishing. If you are going to battle largemouth bass or big northern pike, you may want 12 or even 15-pound test. Should you decide to cast very light lures or fish very clear water, you might use eight or even six-pound test.

choosing a rod

Once you select the line, you pretty well determine the lures and baits that can be cast with it and can focus on the rod. Most rods today are fiberglass; yours should be tubular with enough backbone or reserve power to handle the line of your choice without having the rod collapse.

Spinning tackle is most popular and your choice is between closed-face and open-face reels. Closed-face hides the spool of line behind a bell-shaped projection. It is usually operated with a pushbutton on the back and fits on a rod with a recessed handle and guides facing upward. It's probably the easiest reel to use.

Open-face spinning is better for longer, controlled casts, and an angler can "feather" the line as it comes off the reel. Since the reel has more line capacity, it is better for bigger fish. Learning to cast is easy, but there are more operations than for pushbutton closed-face spinning. Open-face reels hang below the rod and are cranked with the left hand for right-handed casters.

The trend in open-faced spinning reels is toward fully skirted spools and high-speed retrieve of 4:1 or more. Higher ratios are also becoming standard on closed-face reels, and some are now made with longer "power" handles for easier cranking. Rod lengths vary with type of tackle, but 6 to 7 feet will handle most freshwater action for open-face spinning; closed-face rods are 5 or 5½ feet.

In the past few years, new graphite rods have begun to offer many advantages over fiberglass, but are still extremely expensive for the beginner. Graphite, more sensitive than glass, gives a much better feel of a lure working or a strike.

Spinning tackle is most popular, but bait casting is staging a strong comeback. It takes longer to learn to cast with revolving-spool reels, but it can be more fun, though more expensive.

Better rods usually have at least five line guides plus the tiptop. Check the reel seat, grip, guide wrappings and rod finish for quality. Rods and reels should be impervious to corrosive elements, including saltwater, even if you usually fish in fresh.

Saltwater fish are generally larger and require heavier gear. Open-face spinning tackle is good as a start for casting; closed-face frequently does not have enough line capacity or a quality drag. Line of 12-pound test is a reasonable beginning for saltwater.

A conventional boat rod and revolving-spool reel is standard for the bottom fisherman; sophisticated rods are for offshore trolling.

Monofilament line may be better for most assignments, and certainly in breaking strengths under 50 pounds. There are many monofilaments, but a premium line is a better investment. You can save money by buying bulk or one-shot filler spools. Lines should be changed at least once a year and abraded sections discarded.

SEE ALSO
Boat camping . . . Camping . . . Casting, fly . . . Fly fishing . . . Ice fishing . . . Lures, fishing

BY FLEXING ROD carefully, Ned Segar notes rub of line on blank as he checks position of the line guides that are temporarily taped to the rod.

Make your own take-along rod

By BOB STEARNS

PERSONALIZED ROD requires a few simple supplies and about five hours of work. Blanks, guides, grip, epoxy, wrapping thread, stand and wax are essentials.

SEE ALSO

Boat camping . . . Camping . . . Casting, fly . . . Fly fishing . . . Ice fishing . . . Lures, fishing

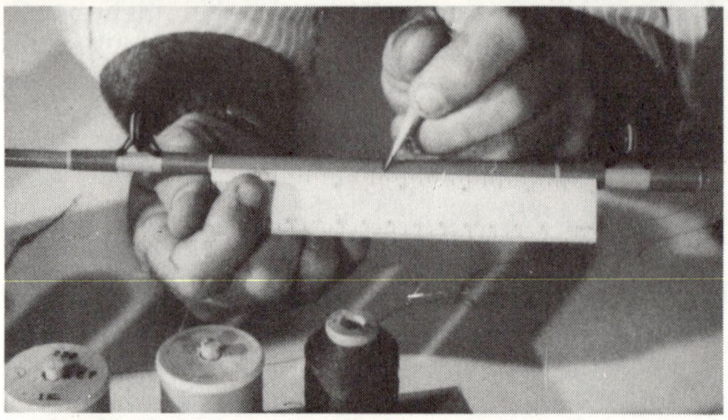

CUTS FOR FERRULES in new or old rod come after measurement and can be made close to line guides or between them to divide rod into lengths for packing.

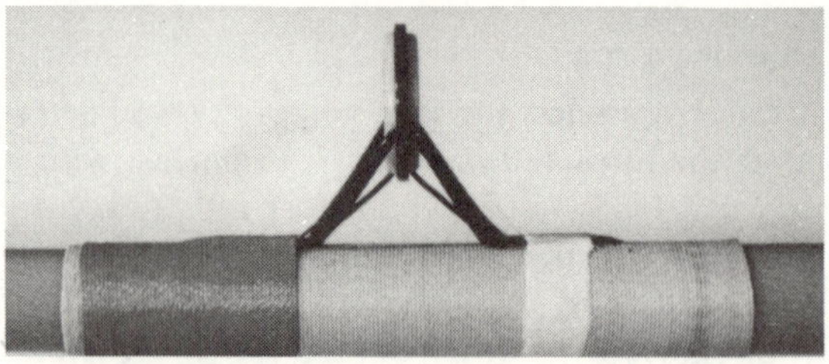

AN UNDERWRAP BASE for the feet of the line guide provides an added contrasting color. Guide is held in place with tape as each foot receives wrap.

DIVIDED AND FERRULED into lengths to suit travel needs of its owner, custom rod has attractive diamond wrap next to the grip.

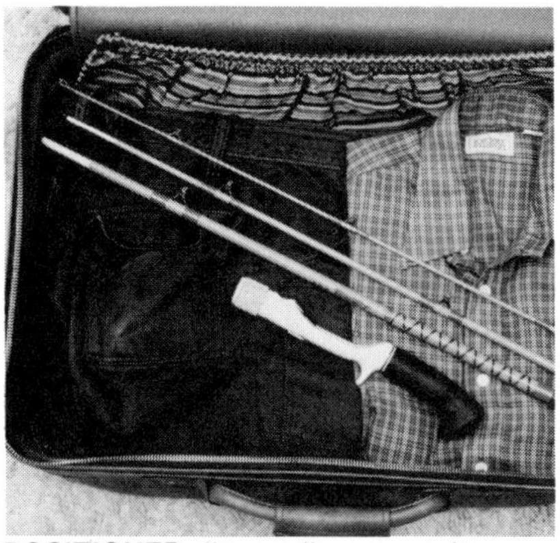

POSITIONED diagonally, your suitcase rod will be protected without rod case, and fits under an airplane seat.

AFTER GUIDES are taped on rod blank, equal lengths are marked on each side of guide feet for underwrap.

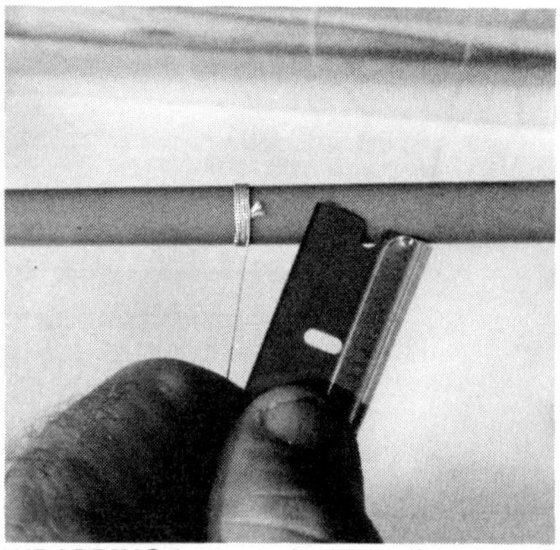

WRAPPING is started with end tucked under to anchor it. Frayed tip is trimmed, wrap wound to other mark.

TO FINISH a wrap, thread loop can be positioned near end, covered with wraps to mark. End is threaded in loop.

PULL LOOSE end of loop with wrap end threaded through; end then anchors out of sight and is trimmed off.

PLUG, cut from solid white fiberglass blank, has been sanded; larger taper will be epoxied into hollow blank.

IF YOU'RE LIKE most fishermen and must travel to get to the water, you'll find this compact, customized suitcase rod particularly handy. You needn't bother with the usual long fishing-rod storage and shipping tube or case—just pick a length that will be most suitable for stowing in your bag.

Almost any rod, even your present ones, can be converted into a compact model by means of fiberglass ferrules, but the best rod of all is the one that is designed from scratch for this purpose. The technique is quite simple and can be used for spinning, baitcasting and fly rods. Don't try it, though, with graphite rods or rod blanks. The ferrule systems that fit together sections of graphite rods are complicated and the work must be done at the factory. Otherwise there is greater danger that you may split an expensive blank.

Internal fiberglass plug ferrules are extremely tough and will not weaken the rod if installed correctly. The rod will actually become stronger at the joints and, because the ferrules themselves are fiberglass, too, unwanted stiffening at ferrules is markedly reduced. This allows the rod to retain most of its natural action.

We went to Ned Segar of Rodmakers Supply in Miami, FL, for a how-to-do-it demonstration. He is considered one of the top custom-rod creators in the country. For a suitcase model, he selected a Lamiglas SC-69-1F blank to be mated to a Fiji Speed Casting Handle (Model OCB). The 5½-foot blank has light action for casting light lures. With the handle, the finished rod totals 6½ feet, yet when disassembled. the longest piece is just 26 inches. This lets the rod be easily fitted diagonally into a 24-inch suitcase that will slide under an airline seat.

Construction of the rod shown took about five hours. If you want to do further customizing with more diamond wraps in various colors, you can lavish extra hours on your project. The cost of components was approximately $30. The same rod from a custom builder would cost $65 to $85 or more.

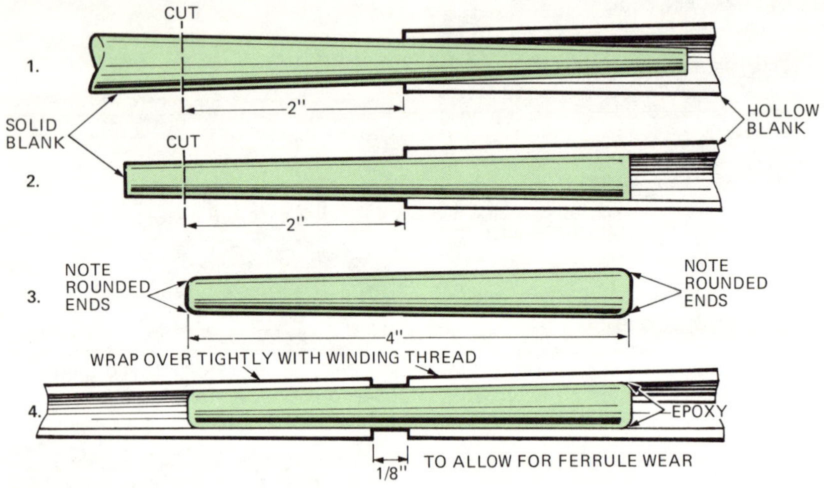

AFTER ROD has been cut at ferrule position, solid blank is fitted into larger section and cut 2 inches on each side of its center. Tight fit and gap allow for wear.

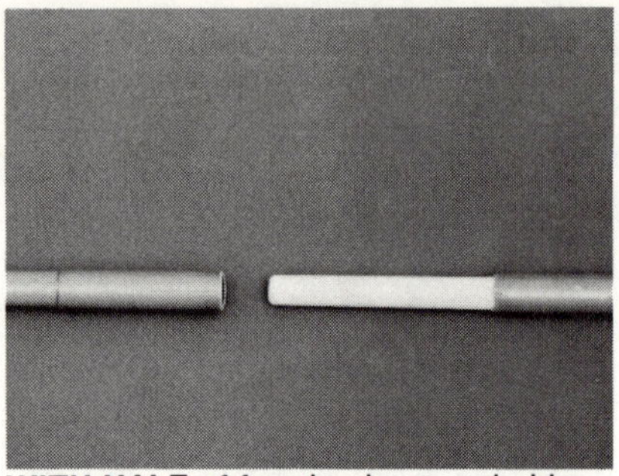

WITH HALF of ferrule plug epoxied in larger rod section, smaller taper end is rounded, sanded for tight ferrule fit.

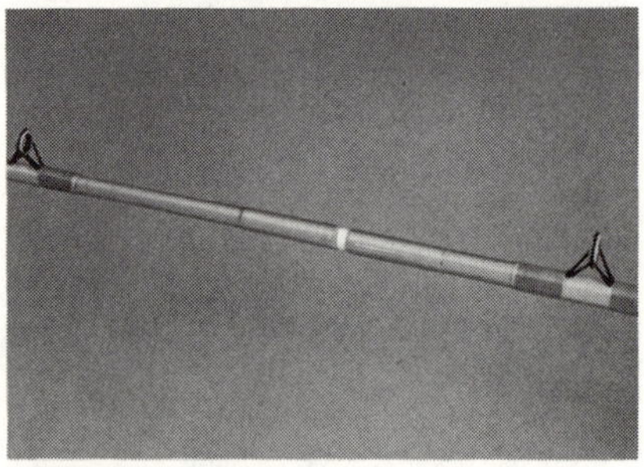

ABOUT 2 inches on each side of cut have been wrapped with same color thread; reinforcing of ferrule hardly shows.

First and most important step is to determine how many sections the rod must be divided into for manageable packing. For the rod shown here, three sections requiring two ferrule joints were sufficient, since the handle would also come off and attach to the rod with a Fuji adapter ferrule sold just for that purpose. This particular blank had a relatively slow taper near its light tip, so it was better to avoid ferruling it too close to the tip. Blanks of faster tapers can be ferruled at points along the blank that divide the sections almost equally. Longer blanks, such as fly rods, may need to be ferruled at four or five points, while shorter rods might get by with a single ferrule in the middle. Careful preplanning is as important as the final finishing.

Ned Segar begins by flexing the blank in order to determine proper position for the guides. Next, the guides are temporarily held in place with masking tape and a line strung through the guides. The rod is then bent to be sure the placement of these line guides is correct. If guides are too far apart, the line will not stay on top of the rod when under load. Casting distance will be reduced, since the line will slap the rod as it is flexed during the casting stroke. Segar selected seven Fuji speed guides and a speed tip for our suitcase rod blank.

securing the guides

Wrapping holds the guides in place and provides the opportunity for colorful customizing. You'll need nylon wrapping thread, a wooden rod wrapping stand (which you can easily build or order from Rodmakers and others), epoxy glue and Q-tips for applying it, a solid glass rod blank of about the same rate of taper as the rod, and a block of household wax to help the ferrule plugs fit.

With the guides carefully positioned along the rod, they can be secured right on the rod or on an underwrap, as we selected. Marks were made ⅜ inch beyond both ends of the foot of each guide and the wrapping started with a few turns back over itself to anchor the loose end. The wrap is continued almost to the second mark, where a thread loop is placed and wrapped over. At the mark, the wrap end is threaded through the loop and then pulled back under the wrap to secure it. The guides are then placed on the underwrap and the feet secured in the same way.

Now, with all guides in place, cut the rod carefully with a hacksaw at the spots marked for ferrules. Slide the smaller end of the solid blank into the larger diameter of the cut rod. Mark where it fits and then cut off the plug 2 inches on each side of this mark. Sand, then epoxy the larger end of the plug into the larger section. Wrap, using the same color as the rod, for 2 inches on each side of each ferrule to prevent splitting. *The Rod Builder's Guide and Catalog,* from Rodmakers Supply, 10346 Southwest 187th St., Miami, FL 33157, lists all supplies.

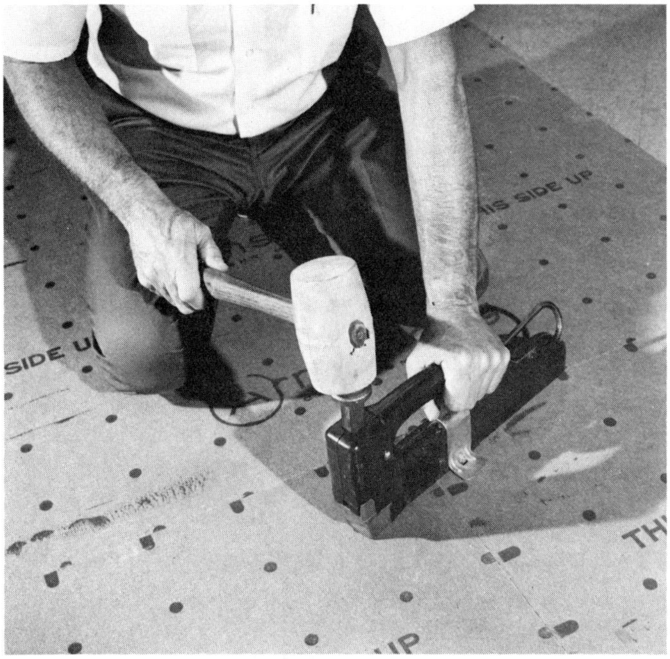

Photo courtesy Armstrong Cork Company

How to install underlayment

By ARTHUR MIKESELL

Any resilient floor covering requires a smooth, firm foundation. This quick course in underlayment covers the three materials you can use under tile or sheet flooring

THE BEST TIME to learn about underlayment is *before* you add that extra room, *before* you remodel the kitchen or *before* you convert the garage into a family room. Otherwise, you may discover too late just how important this special foundation is to a new tile or sheet floor, and that's the most expensive way to learn.

Today's resilient floor coverings are all relatively thin. Under the pressure of normal wear, they soon lose that fresh-from-the-carton flat surface and settle to conform to the contours of the surface on which they have been laid. If you have a good underlayment installation, you have nothing to worry about since the surface is perfectly flat.

On the other hand, if the surface is an improper underlayment installation or if you've omitted underlayment entirely, your new floor will soon begin to show high and low areas. High spots automatically receive more than normal wear and they don't take long to show it. Cracks may develop. The floor loses its like-new appearance long before it should and ultimately will have to be replaced much sooner than would otherwise have been necessary.

Underlayment not only provides the necessary smooth and firm foundation for your resilient floor, but also adds a certain degree of stiffness. While not a structural member, the sheet nature of the material has the effect of spreading the load over a larger area, a fact of particular importance if you're putting down resilient floor covering over an old wood floor.

There are other advantages to underlayment not directly related to the floor covering it supports. Insulation, for instance. That extra layer of material can make a big difference, especially if the floor happens to be located over a crawl space.

Underlayment also cuts down on noise transmission. That noisy game of table tennis in your basement rec room will seem much quieter to anyone in the room above if the sound has to penetrate through another layer of material. Likewise, an upstairs nursery having a resilient floor covering laid on underlayment will be better insulated from downstairs noise than if the underlayment were omitted.

Underlayment can be any of three different materials: plywood, hardboard or particleboard. All are specially manufactured for use as underlayment.

Plywood underlayment, for instance, has a "C" plugger face ply which has been fully sanded for maximum smoothness. Under this is a "B" or "C" veneer designed to reinforce the face ply and resist puncturing. For reasons of economy, the remaining veneers and back are "D."

SEE ALSO

Hardboard . . . Home improvement . . . Nails . . . Plywood . . . Remodeling . . . Tile, floor

TYPE OF APPLICATION

OVER WOOD SUBFLOOR. When an underlayment is being installed directly above a damp basement or an unheated crawl space, apply a suitable vapor barrier between the subfloor and the underlayment material.

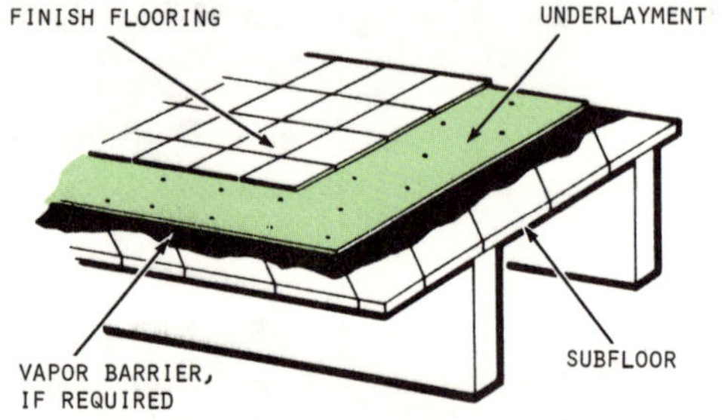

OVER OLD WOOD FLOOR. Remove the base shoe and check the existing floor for flatness and freedom from any protruding nails. The underlayment is stiff enough to bridge small irregularities, such as those that exist in a washboard floor, but any large gaps or low portions should be filled and all high spots should be cut down to furnish a solid base.

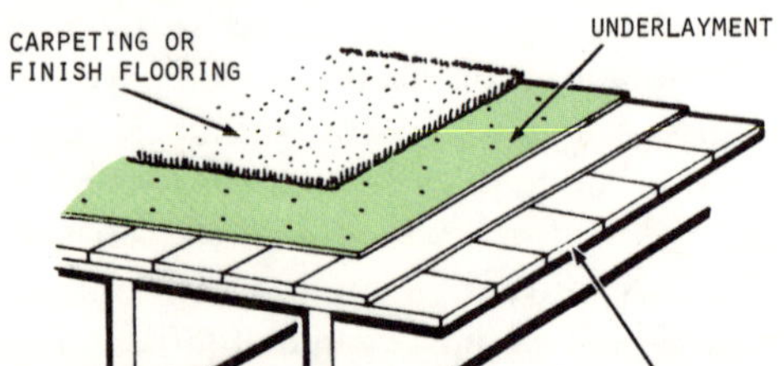

OVER OLD TILE FLOOR OR FILLER LAYER. When it's necessary to build up a new floor to the level of an adjacent floor, asphalt-impregnated insulation board of the required thickness may be used as a filler between the subfloor and the underlayment. Of course, this is assuming that you anticipate no more than normal traffic and average loads. If you expect heavy concentrated loads, you'll need a dense filler, such as additional layers of underlayment. Fasten the filler material to the subfloor, then use at least 1½-in. underlay nails when installing the underlayment. You may install an underlayment directly over an existing tile or linoleum floor, provided that you first remove any loose pieces. However, be sure that it's dry and free of protruding nails.

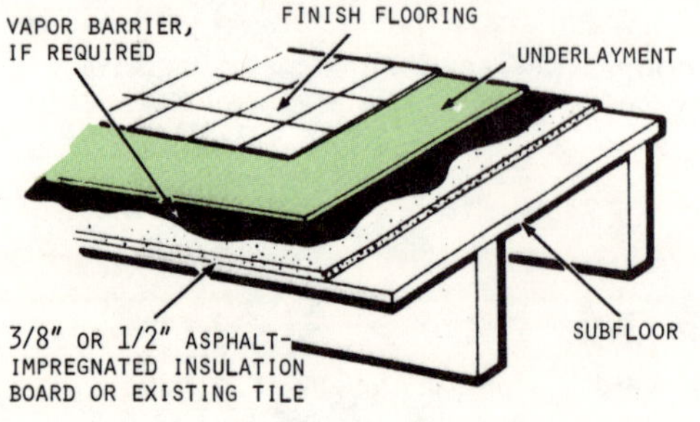

You can also buy plywood underlayment of the same construction bonded with exterior-type glue for use where unusual moisture might otherwise create a problem.

If you decide to use plywood, be sure to buy underlayment grade. Don't be tempted to go to the more economical "C-D Plugged." This is similar to underlayment, but that veneer beneath the face ply is "D" instead of "B" or "C." This means that knotholes measuring up to 2½ in. are permitted, so it's not as well suited to resist dents and concentrated loads.

combination product

Incidentally, in new construction you can use a special 1⅛-in. plywood which combines subfloor and underlayment. This "2-4-1" grade not only saves time during installation but performs just as efficiently as separate subfloor and underlayment layers of plywood.

Hardboard underlayment is made by "felting" selected wood fibers, then consolidating them under heat and pressure. The resulting material is dense, grainless and moisture-resistant.

Masonite's hardboard underlayment features the normal smooth hardboard surface on one side, while the other is planed smooth to provide uniform thickness. Printed on each panel are installation instructions, nailing locations and edge alignment marks.

Georgia-Pacific's hardboard underlayment has a coarse-sanded surface to increase adhesive bonding properties.

INSTALLATION TIPS

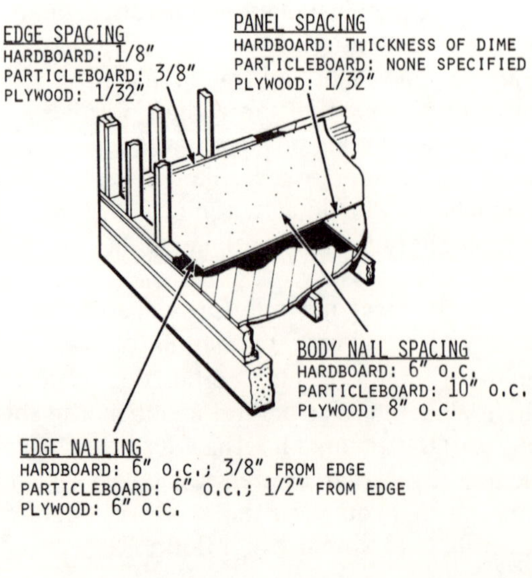

As noted in the table, some floor-covering manufacturers specifically recommend bonding their products to either the smooth or rougher side of hardboard underlayment, so be sure to check this before you begin the installation.

Particleboard underlayment is made up of matted wood fibers which have been compressed to uniform density and bonded with special adhesives under heat. It's hard, durable, resilient and will resist sharp blows.

When installing underlayment, be sure to stagger the joints in bricklayer fashion. Also, be careful not to locate these joints so that they will coincide with joints in the subfloor. Ideally, the long axis of the underlayment should be at right angles to that of the subfloor.

Detailed instructions for installing each of the three types of underlayment may be obtained from your lumberyard or directly from the manufacturer.

FACTS ABOUT UNDERLAYMENT

DESCRIPTION

HARDBOARD	PARTICLEBOARD	PLYWOOD
3x4′ and 4x4′ sheets ¼″ thick	4x8′ panels in thicknesses of ¼, ⅜, ½, ⅝ and ¾″	4x8′ panels in thicknesses of ¼, ⅜, ½, ⅝ and ¾″. Face ply, plugged C; back ply, D

PRELIMINARY WORK

HARDBOARD. Existing subfloor should be clean, dry, securely fastened and free of protruding nails. Where floor is irregular over large areas, low portions should be filled or high spots sanded to provide solid base. (Joint fillers are not recommended.) If atmosphere is abnormally damp due to wet concrete, wet plaster or other temporary conditions, wait until room has dried out before beginning installation. When humidity conditions are close to normal, unwrap panels and stand them on edge separately around the room for at least 24 hours to stabilize to existing conditions.

PARTICLEBOARD. Same precautions as for hardboard concerning atmospheric moisture, condition of subfloor and stabilizing period. For installation over unexcavated crawl space, make sure foundation is well-vented and install a vapor barrier directly over the ground. Never apply directly to concrete or below grade. Hot-air ducts and area over furnace must be well-insulated to prevent localized drying of floor components. Vapor barrier must be installed over subfloor if it's square-edged dimensional lumber. (This is recommended as "good practice" even when subfloor lumber is tongue-and-groove.)

PLYWOOD. Where floor may be subject to unusual moisture conditions, use exterior-grade panels. Choose ¼″ for installation over plywood subfloors or lumber subfloors in which the boards are 3⅝″ wide or narrower. With lumber subfloors made up of wider boards or those that are particularly uneven, go to ⅜″ thickness.

FASTENING

HARDBOARD. Use 1¼″ ring-grooved underlay nails or 4d cement-coated sinker nails. Begin nailing at the center of each panel and work out toward the edges. Nails should be spaced 6″ o.c. throughout, but no closer than ⅜″ to edge. Drive nailheads flush with surface. You can also use staples to fasten underlayment, but you'll need a "spotnailing" machine. Recommended are etched or galvanized divergent chisel-point or plastic-coated staples ⅞″ long, such as those made by Spotnails, Inc. These should be spaced 6″ o.c. throughout the body of the panel, but only 3″ apart along the edges and no closer than ⅜″ to edge.

PARTICLEBOARD. Nails or staples should be long enough to penetrate subfloor at least ¾″. Begin at center and work outward. Use 6d ring-grooved nails for ⅜″-⅝″ thickness, spacing them 10″ o.c. throughout body, 6″ o.c. along edges and no closer than ½″ to the edge. If stapling, use 1⅛″ galvanized divergent chisel-point staples for thicknesses to ⅜″, 1⅜″ length for ½″ thickness and 1½″ for ⅝″. Staples should be spaced 6″ o.c. throughout body, 3″ o.c. around the edges and no closer than ½″ to the edge. Staples should be countersunk.

PLYWOOD. If nailing, use 3d ring-shank nails for thicknesses to ½″ and 4d nails for ⅝ or ¾″. Space them 8″ o.c. throughout the body and 6″ o.c. along the edges. Staples should be 16-ga. (18-ga. for ¼″) and long enough to penetrate at least ⅝″ or completely through subfloor. Staple spacing is 6″ o.c. in body and 3″ o.c. along edges. Unless subfloor and joists are thoroughly seasoned material, countersink nailheads 1/16″ just prior to laying the finished floor to avoid nail popping. Staples should be countersunk 1/32″.

APPLICATION

HARDBOARD. Start in one corner, fastening each panel securely before laying adjoining panel. (Note: Some floor-covering manufacturers specifically recommend bonding their products to the smooth surface or the rough surface. Check this before installing first panel.) Stagger panel joints in one direction. If subfloor is lumber, plan layout so that continuous joints in underlayment are perpendicular to the direction of boards in the subfloor. Avoid placing underlayment joint directly over joint in subfloor. Allow ⅛″ space between wall and underlayment. Fit panels loosely, leaving space about the thickness of a dime between adjoining edges. Before putting down finish floor, check all joints for rough edges caused by cutting and use sandpaper or a block plane to smooth any rough areas.

PLYWOOD. Stagger all joints with respect to subfloor joints. For maximum stiffness, place face grain of underlayment across supports and end joints over framing. Allow 1/32″ space between panels. Fill any damaged or open areas (joints or splits wider than 1/16″, for instance), but don't bother filling nail holes. Sand down any surface roughness around nails or along joints before installing finish floor.

How to lay hardwood flooring

By ROSARIO CAPOTOSTO

IT SEEMS as though hardwood was put on earth to be used for flooring. It finishes well, will last for generations given proper care, can be cut into interesting patterns and is beautiful—a perfect material. Many flooring products are now being geared to the handyman.

Durable factory finishes on parquet and plank flooring have eliminated the tough, painstaking task of sanding and finishing, which generally proved to be the amateur's downfall. A variety of excellent adhesives and fasteners are now available to permit easy installation over wood, concrete or resilient flooring. Power nailers let you finish nail installations in considerably less time. And for the ultimate in installation ease, there are self-stick parquets.

SEE ALSO
Additions, house . . . Nails . . . Quarry tile . . . Remodeling . . . Tile, floor . . . Wood finishes

Hardwood flooring is available in a variety of classes, including red and white oak, beech, birch, maple, pecan, Asian rosewood, teak and walnut; prefinished as well as unfinished. Finishes are practically as varied as are the parquet and plank patterns that are supplied by the different manufacturers.

Aside from common shop tools such as hammer, rubber mallet, putty knife, pry bar, tape measure, chalkline, crosscut saw, drill, sabre saw, belt sander and broom, you may need the following:

1. A *power nailer* is used for blind-nailing of tongue-and-groove flooring. It can be readily rented for about $8 per day from tool rental or flooring supply dealers. Tongue-and-groove strip or plank flooring can be secured manually with a hammer and cut or screw nails, but a power nailer is easier to use, does a much better job and sets nail heads automatically. This tool drives a special barbed fastener, fed into a chamber like

staples, right through the tongue of the flooring at the proper angle.

2. *Sanders and concrete surface grinders* used to prepare surfaces for installation can also be rented.

3. A *150-pound roller* is required when installing plank or strip flooring with adhesive to insure good contact. The roller can be replaced by the footsteps of a person weighing 150 pounds or more, provided every square inch of surface is covered.

4. A *notched trowel* is used for an adhesive installation. Don't use just any trowel with notches, but the one recommended by the manufacturer. This insures distribution of the correct amount of mastic for optimum adhesion.

Aside from style considerations, flooring should be specified according to where it will be put. Most manufacturers do not recommend installing solid types of planking and parquet below grade level (in basement recreation rooms).

SLATE PARQUET (right) in antique color from Sykes works well in a Victorian setting.

PLANKING COMES in solid type (opposite page) or laminated glue- or nail-down version (below).

JEFFERSONIAN PARQUET (below, right) will complement modern, as well as colonial furnishings.

PREPARING RESILIENT FLOORS FOR GLUING DOWN PARQUET

TO REMOVE base shoe from baseboard, insert scraper with stick fulcrum behind blade and pry off the molding.

MOP WITH wax-remover to clean wax from resilient flooring. Scrub brush may be required on spots thick with wax.

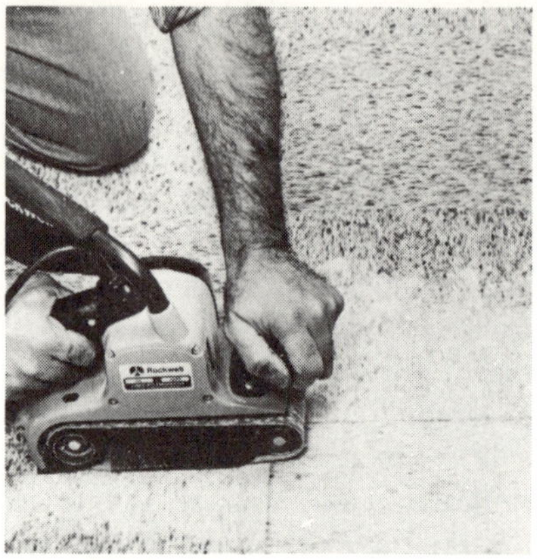

USE BELT sander to remove traces of wax and to roughen floorcovering's surface to provide tooth for mastic.

INSTALLING HARDWOOD FLOORING OVER A CONCRETE SLAB

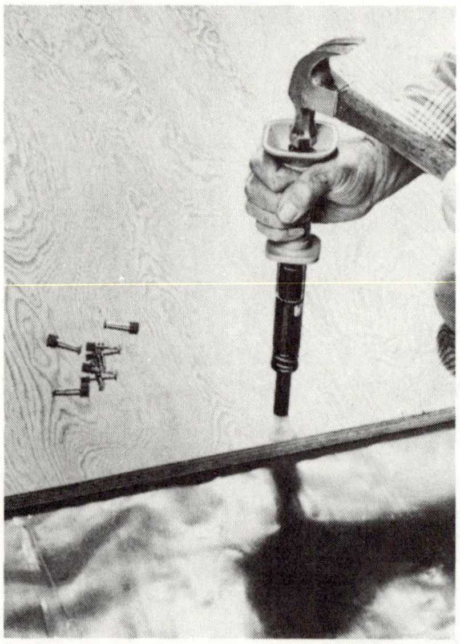

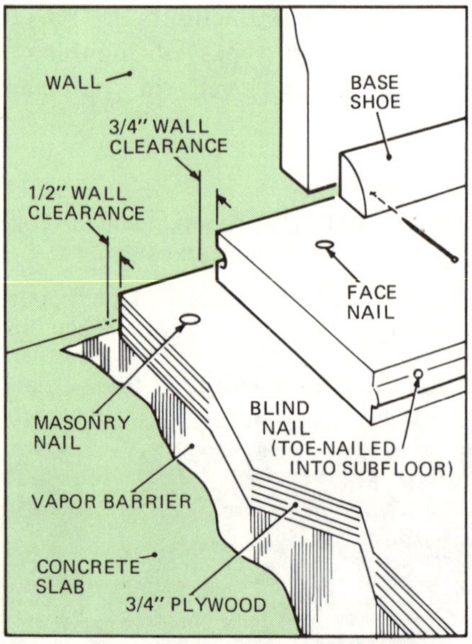

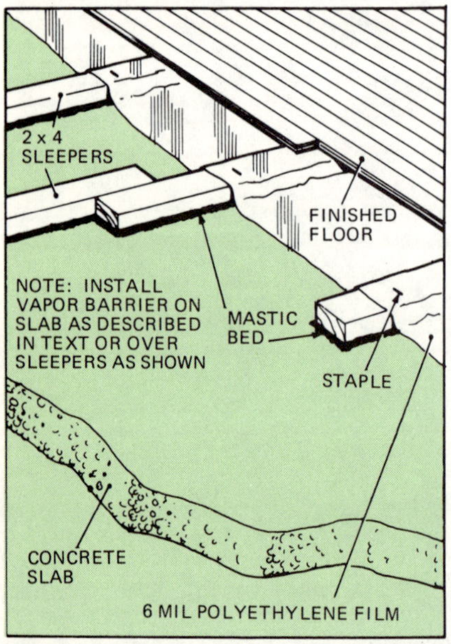

WHEN INSTALLING a floor directly over concrete, first level off the high spots with a heavy-duty disc sander (left). Plank and strip flooring usually require a nailing surface. Power-actuated nailer makes the fastening of plywood easier (middle). Plywood-on-slab method of installing strip or plank flooring is shown on right. A vapor barrier (see text) is required. Alternate method, utilizing sleepers to raise floor above slabs (below), is preferred.

BEFORE LAYING block parquet in square pattern (opposite page), be sure angles at intersection are 90° by using 3-4-5 test. To apply in diagonal pattern, lay out as shown at far right. Once again, test angle for squareness.

HOW TO INSTALL PLANK OR STRIP FLOORING

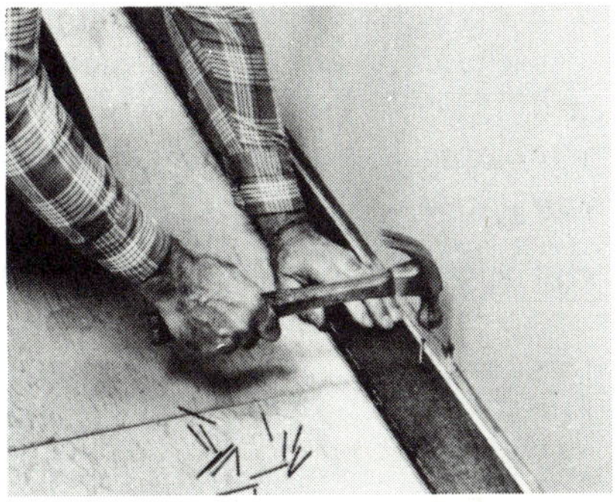

ALIGN first plank with line struck parallel to wall. Allow clearance and nail through predrilled holes.

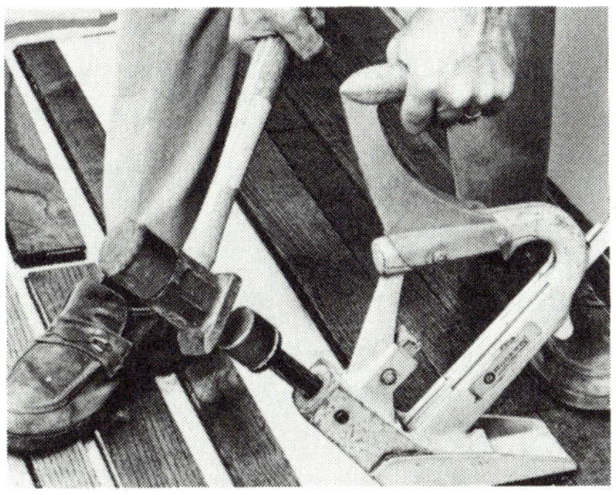

MAJORITY of nailing can be speeded with power nailer. It drives and sets each nail, saving you time.

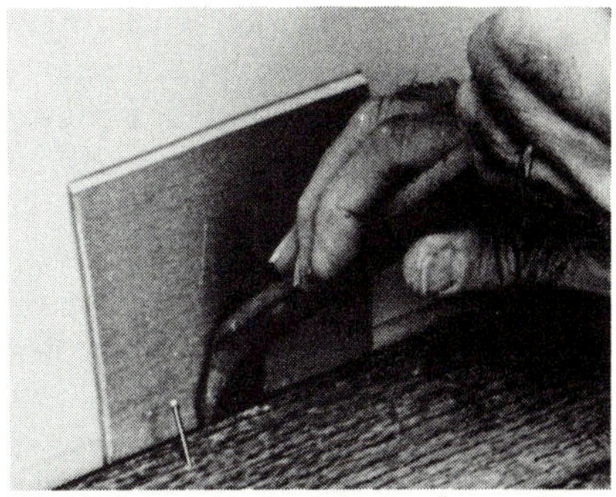

NUDGE the last planks into place with a pry bar. Use scrap of plywood behind tool to keep it from marring wall.

HOW TO INSTALL HERRINGBONE PARQUET

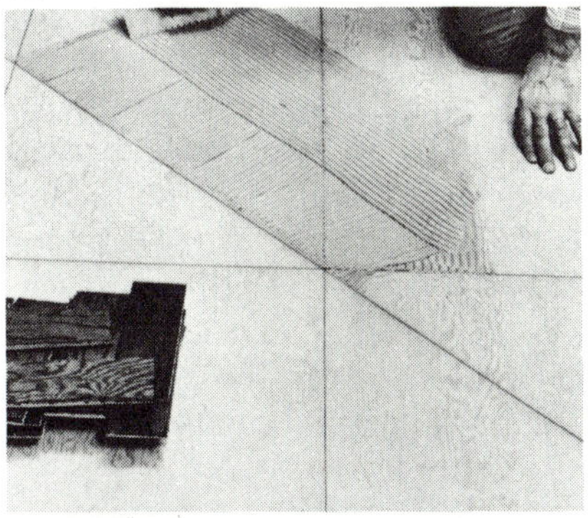

SPREAD ADHESIVE to one side of base line. See diagram at right. First locate centerpoint C; mark points A and B, and connect. Then strike base line between midpoint D of segment AB and C.

ALIGN FIRST block carefully. Press subsequent blocks straight down—do not slide. Use plywood panel as stepping stone across newly installed areas. Use sabre saw to trim blocks at wall.

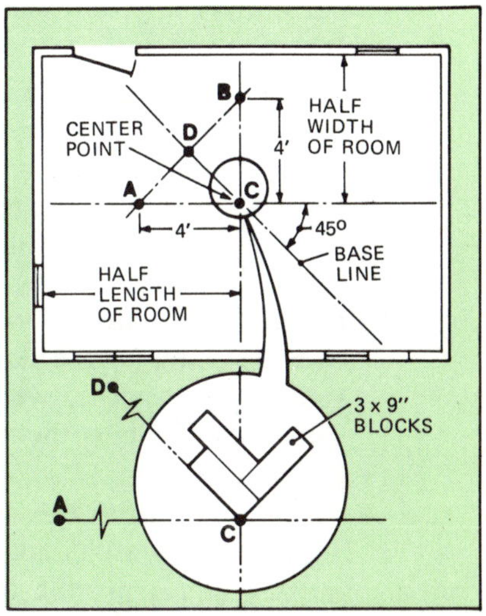

HOW TO INSTALL PARQUET BLOCKS

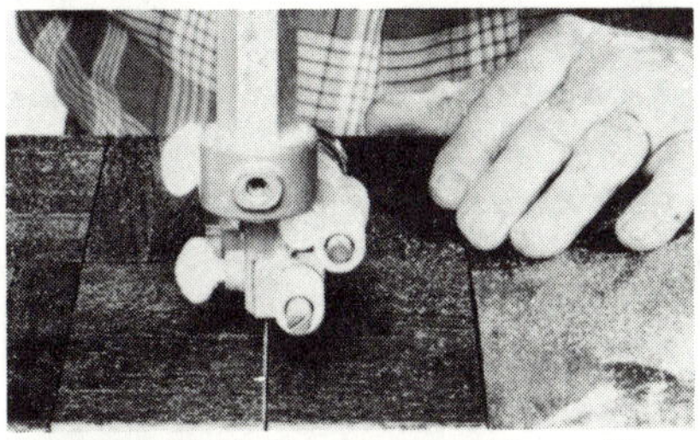

BANDSAW is the ideal tool for cutting odd shapes in parquet to fit around jambs, counters and obstructions.

SELF-ADHERING, prefinished parquet from Hartco is alternative to working with adhesive. Backs are foam-cushioned.

hardwood flooring, continued

REDUCING THE LEVEL OF NEW FLOOR TO EXISTING FLOOR

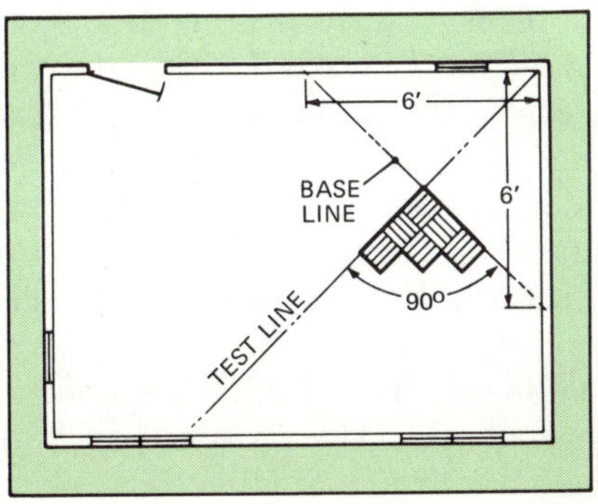

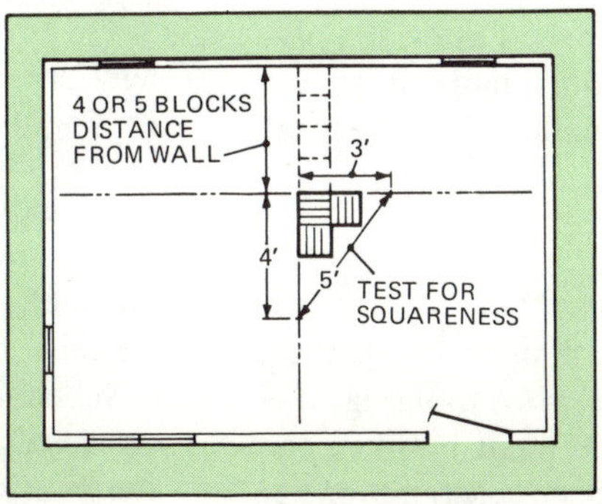

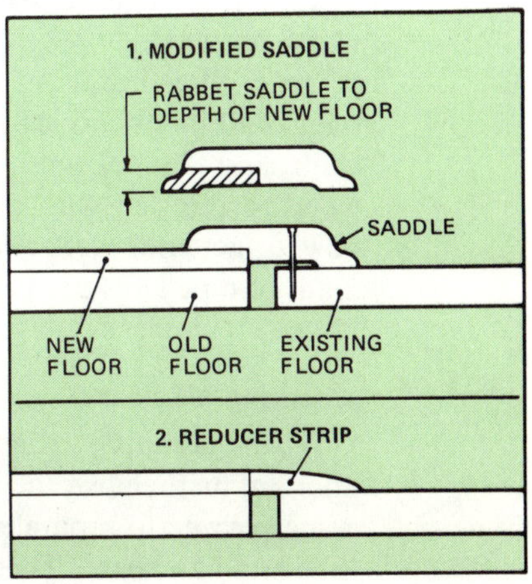

If you intend to lay the floor over a concrete slab, either on or below grade, you must choose a glue-down type of planking or parquet. If you are willing to install a plywood nailing surface or sleepers over the concrete, nail-down types of strip and plank flooring can be accommodated.

Parquet installations over linoleum tile are possible, but with some risk. There is always the possibility that the old tile adhesive will fail when subjected to the stress of the new floor. Parquet installations are not recommended over existing cork or rubber tile floors. Installation over sheet-type resilient flooring is possible.

Hardwood floors can be installed successfully over a concrete slab, provided it is thoroughly cured (dry), level and smooth, and free of grease, oil stains and dust.

If the floor is uneven, sand or grind it level. Fill depressions with a concrete patching compound.

For flooring which does not require a nailing base, lay a vapor barrier next. One method, using 6-mil polyethylene, requires that you prime the slab with asphalt primer and spread cold-type, cutback asphalt mastic with a straightedge trowel over the entire surface. After 30 minutes you unroll the polyethylene, overlapping the edges 4 in. Then, walk it into the mastic, eliminating all large air bubbles.

A vapor barrier can also be made with two layers of 15-lb. asphalt paper (not felt). Prime the surface and apply the asphalt with a notched trowel at a rate of one gallon per 50 sq. ft. Let it set two hours, then roll out paper, overlapping edges 4 in. Apply a second coat of mastic at the same rate. Lay another layer of asphalt paper in the same direction as the first.

Glue-down tongue-and-groove types of flooring can be installed directly on the vapor barrier in mastic. Nail-down types of flooring require either a ¾-in. exterior plywood or a pressure-treated 2 x 4 nailing base (in addition to the vapor barriers).

Note: When installing a plywood nailing base, stagger all joints and leave a clearance of ½ in. at walls, and ¼ in. between panels. Fasten the plywood to the slab with masonry nails or with a powder-actuated concrete nailer. Use a minimum of nine nails per panel.

preparing old floors

When installing a new floor over existing flooring, first remove the base shoe molding. Use a sharp knife to separate the paint between the shoe and baseboard. Then insert a scraper or flat pry bar between the two to pry out the shoe molding. Place a small stick behind the scraper blade to serve as a fulcrum and prevent damage to the baseboard. If no shoe molding exists, use quarter-round molding to conceal the finished floor's expansion joint.

Doors present special problems. First, use a piece of flooring to check whether or not the door will have to be trimmed at the bottom to allow clearance from the new floor. Then use the same piece of flooring as a saw guide for cutting back the door stop, jamb and casing. This also will provide enough space at the jamb to allow clearance for floor expansion.

If the existing floor is of the resilient-sheet variety, all wax must be removed before laying new floor. The best way to prepare old linoleum tiles is to lay ¼ in. plywood over the existing floor. Use an ample number of ringed nails to fasten plywood securely to the old floor. Or, if this raises the floor level too high, remove the old floor covering to the subfloor before proceeding.

Old wood floors should be renailed before reflooring if any of the boards are loose or squeaky. If the floor is in poor, unsound condition, a ¾-in. plywood subfloor should be installed.

general installation procedures

Regardless of the type of flooring, all installations begin with the snapping of two (or more) chalk lines to guide the placement and alignment of the first course. Recommended procedures vary, according to the style and type of flooring and to different manufacturers. Essentially, however, a starting base line is snapped with a chalk line.

A second intersecting line is snapped at an exact 90° angle to it. This second line serves as a test line to help keep the pattern straight as the installation proceeds. The 3-4-5 method is used to test for squareness of the lines: Measure 3 ft. along one line from the intersection, and 4 ft. along the other. The distance between these points will be 5 ft. if the lines are true.

Install new plank or strip flooring at a right angle to the old floor boards and stagger the end joints. Snug each plank, using a rubber mallet before adding the next. Use spacers to leave ⅓₂-in. expansion gaps between planks if required by the manufacturer. Glue, screw or nail ends to the subfloor, according to the manufacturer's directions.

When installing parquet, don't walk directly on freshly covered areas. Use plywood panels as stepping stones.

Lay a floor that outlasts your house

By MIKE McCLINTOCK

■ HERE COME the wet boots and mittens, dripping snow shovels and occasional stray snowballs. When you lay a sturdy tile floor that water can't damage, you can forget about the drips and spills.

Mud-set tile is the Cadillac of floor installations. It will work over any concrete slab whether it's a basement, garage entryway, or utility room floor—even one that's old, cracked and out of level. It also makes a great fireplace hearth.

"Mud" is a mixture of sand and Portland cement. The ratio is 40 shovels of sand to one bag of Portland, mixed with water to a thick but workable texture. When it hardens, the tile is supported firmly and uniformly.

A mud set, usually between ¾ and 2-in. thick, will overcome all the shortcomings of a concrete slab.

Low spots take a little more mud, high spots a little less, but the surface comes out level. Check your floor with a flat 2 x 4 (long enough to span most of the room) and a level. By moving the 2 x 4 to different locations, you can determine the highest spot. If your floor has major cracks and substantial level changes (like two or three inches from one side to another) you should lay reinforcing wire under the new mud to strengthen it.

setting up the job

Good preparation will make the job go smoother and faster. Here's a checklist for starting up your tile job:

■ Have all your materials on hand.
■ Clean the floor completely.
■ Make your mud mixture with 40 shovels of concrete sand to one bag of Portland cement.
■ Make a "dry" mix by adding 3½ gallons of water for each bag of cement. Pros never rely on a strict formula. If the concrete sand (some aggregate comes mixed in for strength) is very moist,

SEE ALSO
Additions, house . . . Finishes, wood . . . Garage remodeling . . . Nails . . . Quarry tile . . . Remodeling . . . Tile, floor

1. PREPARE CONCRETE SLAB: Clean floor completely, then brush on a creamy-textured mixture of pure Portland cement. This bonds new "mud" to old concrete floor. 2. Set up the mud: The 1 to 2-in.-thick mixture (40 shovels to one bag Portland) can be smoothed and leveled with a straight board.

3. SMOOTHING TECHNIQUE: First tamp the edge of the board firmly across the surface. Then change to gentle figure-eight patterns. 4. Leveling the concrete: Check for level across the top of your board. Use a hand trowel to shift the mud until the smoothed surface is completely level.

5. TOUCHING UP: A long board may leave small voids in the concrete. After filling, use circular strokes with a trowel or short 2 x 4 for smoothing.

6. LAYING TILE: Work on a small area (2 x 6 ft.) at a time. Start full tiles along wall edge to minimize cutting. Use board for straightedge, space by eye.

7. USING FULL TILES: The more tile you lay, the easier it will be to judge the spacing and alignment. Save edgecutting until later.

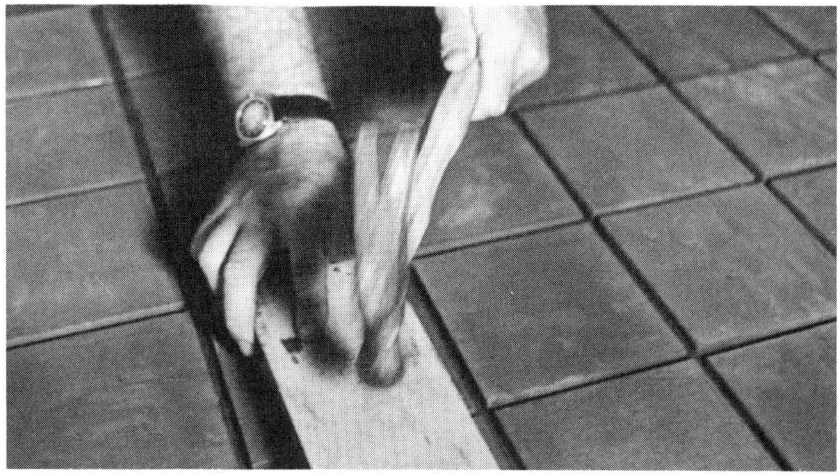

8. ALIGNMENT: Pros use 8-ft. magnesium rules. You get same results with a straight 1 x 4 pine board. Tiles will move easily. 9. Seat tiles: 2 ft. 2 x 4 block is laid across several of the tile joints and tapped firmly with a hammer to seat the group of tiles uniformly. Then move on to next row.

they might add less water. If it's very dry, up to 4 gallons maximum. The test is to take a handful of the mix and squeeze it. When you open your hand, the mix should keep the shape of your fist. You'll need about one shovel of mix for each square foot of space.

one step at a time

To assure a good bond between the old concrete floor and the new mud mixture, brush on a thin layer of pure Portland mixed with water. Then start troweling out enough mud to cover about a 2 x 6-ft. area. Use a straight length of 1 x 4 to level and smooth out the mix.

It's good policy to start laying out full tiles from the most visible corner of the room. You can use a short block (about ⅜-in. wide) to standardize the spacing between tiles or judge the spacing by eye. After you've completed a few sections, use a straight board to line up the joints.

To make sure that the tiles stay flat and level, lay a 2 x 4 block across the joints, tapping it firmly with a hammer.

edging and grouting

Crystalline-finished tiles can be cut with a scorer which weakens the surface so that the tile can be snapped cleanly along the scored line. Cutting quarry tile is another matter. The best option is to use a water saw. This machine cuts the tile with a water-lubricated friction blade. There are more ways to cut your edge pieces: If you mark the tiles, many suppliers will make the cuts for you at their shop. If you can't rent a water saw, a slate cutter is a good second choice. Although it's harder, you can cut the tile with a masonry nipper.

For quarry tile, make your grout mixture from equal parts of cement and masonry sand (a finer grade than concrete sand) and force it into the joints with a trowel or squeegee. Rub away the grout residue with heavy burlap rags.

After one week, the final mortar residue can be removed with a 20-percent solution of muriatic acid. A final sealer of lemon oil can be mopped on one day after the acid cleaning to bring your floor to a lustrous, water-repellent finish.

10. EDGING: At left, full tiles are setting up. A water saw (rent from tile suppliers) easily cuts edging pieces with a water-lubricated friction blade. A slate cutter or masonry nipper can also be used for cutting.

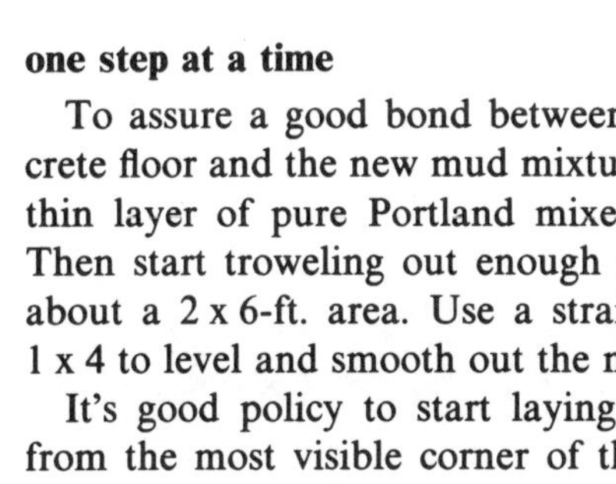

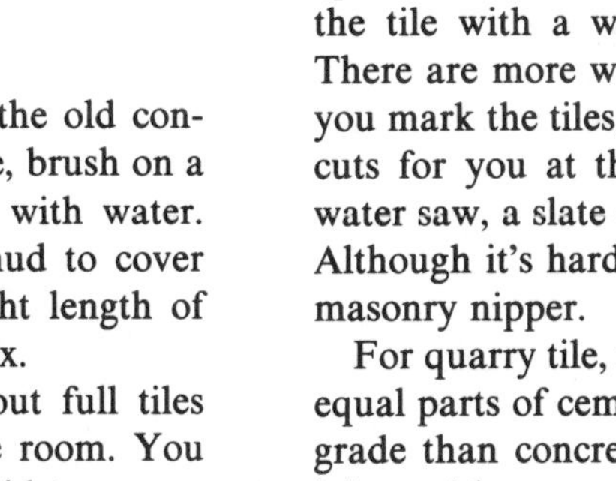

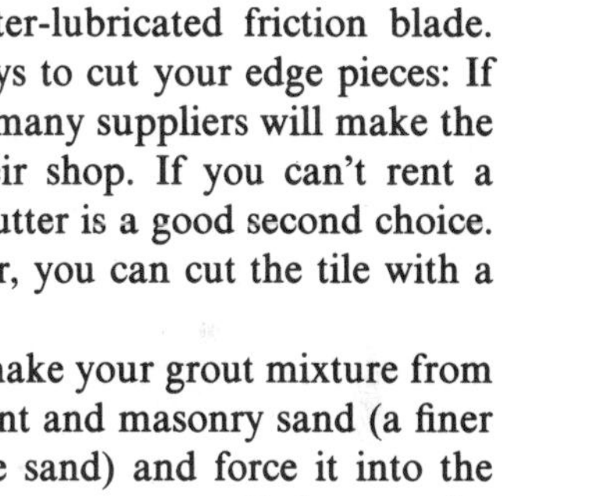

How to patch a hole in sheet flooring

THERE'S AN ADVANTAGE to having a tile floor. When a tile is damaged and must be replaced, there's no need to try making the "patch" invisible—you want it to be seen since it contributes to the over-all grid pattern of the floor. Replacing it requires little more than carefully breaking out the bad tile, chiseling away the hardened cement and cementing the new tile in place.

Making a patch in sheet flooring is different. This patch must be as invisible as possible to keep it from standing out like a sore thumb. While it's possible to make such a patch hard to spot, this depends on how carefully and accurately you cut the patch and the recess.

The six steps shown here are similar to those used in marquetry work in which outlines of both the patch and the recess are cut at the same time. Here's how you can do it.

Assuming you can obtain a piece of the same flooring, cut a square somewhat larger than the damaged area. Place it over the worn spot and align the pattern of the patch and the floor precisely. Before it shifts, hold the oversize patch on the floor with masking tape around all four edges. Then, cut through both thicknesses of linoleum. Use a thin-blade knife that's razor sharp and a metal straightedge. Extend the outline of the patch well beyond the damaged section.

Now peel off the tape and discard the scrap, keeping the square patch. If you find you didn't cut completely through the flooring, retrace the cut with the knife, being careful to stay on the line. Remove the old linoleum within the scored lines, scrape the recess clean of old adhesive, and dust clean. Check that the patch fits and that it's flush with the surface. Coat the back of the patch sparingly with linoleum cement. If too much is applied, it will ooze out around the edges. Press the patch in place and lay a wax-paper sheet over it. Place a flat board over the paper. Rest a heavy weight on this overnight; then wipe up any cement smears with a damp cloth.

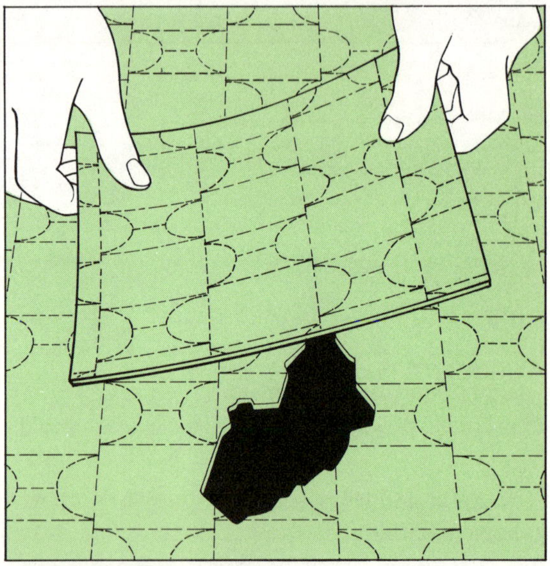

1. OBTAIN A PIECE of identical linoleum and from it cut a square somewhat larger than the damaged area. Then place the square over the spot and carefully align the two patterns exactly in both directions.

4. IF YOU SCORED THE LINES CAREFULLY, the patch should fit perfectly. To assure that the patch will be level with the surrounding surface, chisel and scrape out any old hardened cement, then brush it clean.

SEE ALSO

Adhesives . . . Home improvement . . . Tile, floor

2. WHEN IN POSITION, tape the scrap to the floor with strips of masking tape around the four edges. Mark a square outline and, with a sharp knife and a straightedge, cut through both thicknesses of linoleum.

3. LIFT OUT THE PATCH and peel off the tape. Throw away the leftover scrap. If you find that you didn't cut completely through the second layer, retrace the scored lines with a knife, keeping on the lines.

5. APPLY CEMENT SPARINGLY to the back of the patch; too much will take longer to dry and continue to ooze out at the joints when you step on the patch. Use linoleum cement and apply with a notched trowel.

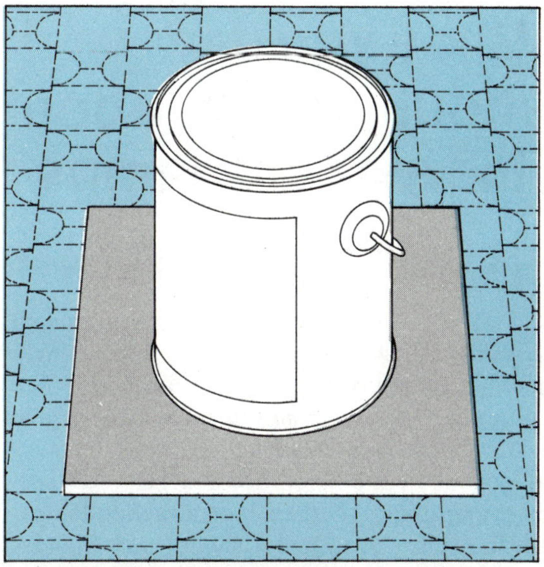

6. PRESS THE PATCH IN PLACE and keep it flat by weighting it with something heavy. Use a board under it to distribute the weight evenly. Place wax paper over the patch so the board won't stick to the flooring.

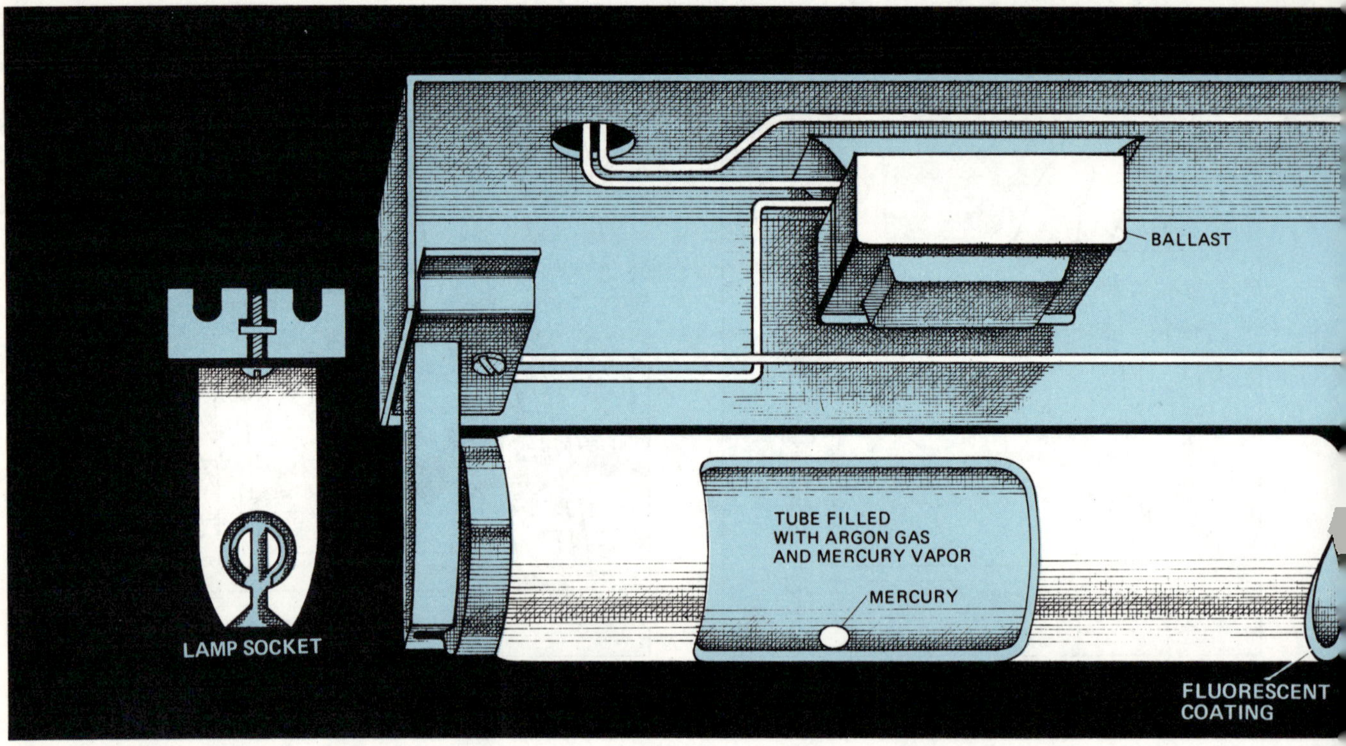

What you should know about fluorescent lamps

by ED FRANZESE

■ THE FACT THAT IT saves energy—as well as money—makes fluorescence an increasingly popular alternative to incandescence in office and home. Energy-saving fluorescent lamps give two to four times as much light per watt of power as incandescent bulbs. They also have low surface brightness. Unlike incandescent lamps, which are bright in just a single spot, fluorescents have a lower brightness over a larger area, resulting in fewer shadows, less eyestrain and better distribution.

Tubular in form, fluorescent lamps are usually called tubes and come in straight and circular styles. Straight fluorescents vary in length from 4¼ to 96 in. and from 4 to 215 watts. Circular fluorescents are known as Circlarc or Circline lamps and are available in outside diameters of 8¼, 12 and 16 in. with popular powers of 22, 32 and 40 watts.

The ends of each tube contain a cap with two terminals as shown above. These terminals connect to an internal tungsten filament inside each end of the tube. Inside the tube is a small amount of argon gas and a drop of mercury; the inside surface is coated with a fluorescent chemical.

In addition to the tube, the circuit contains a switch, ballast (transformer) and starter. A pull-chain toggle or pushbutton switch turns the circuit on and off. The ballast provides the high voltage necessary to start the mercury-vapor arc inside the tube and stabilizes the circuit by keeping the operating current at a steady value, as shown in the two-lamp circuit diagram on page 1253.

The starting switch closes the circuit between the two filaments when the lamp circuit is energized. It also opens the circuit between the two filaments after sufficient time has passed to heat

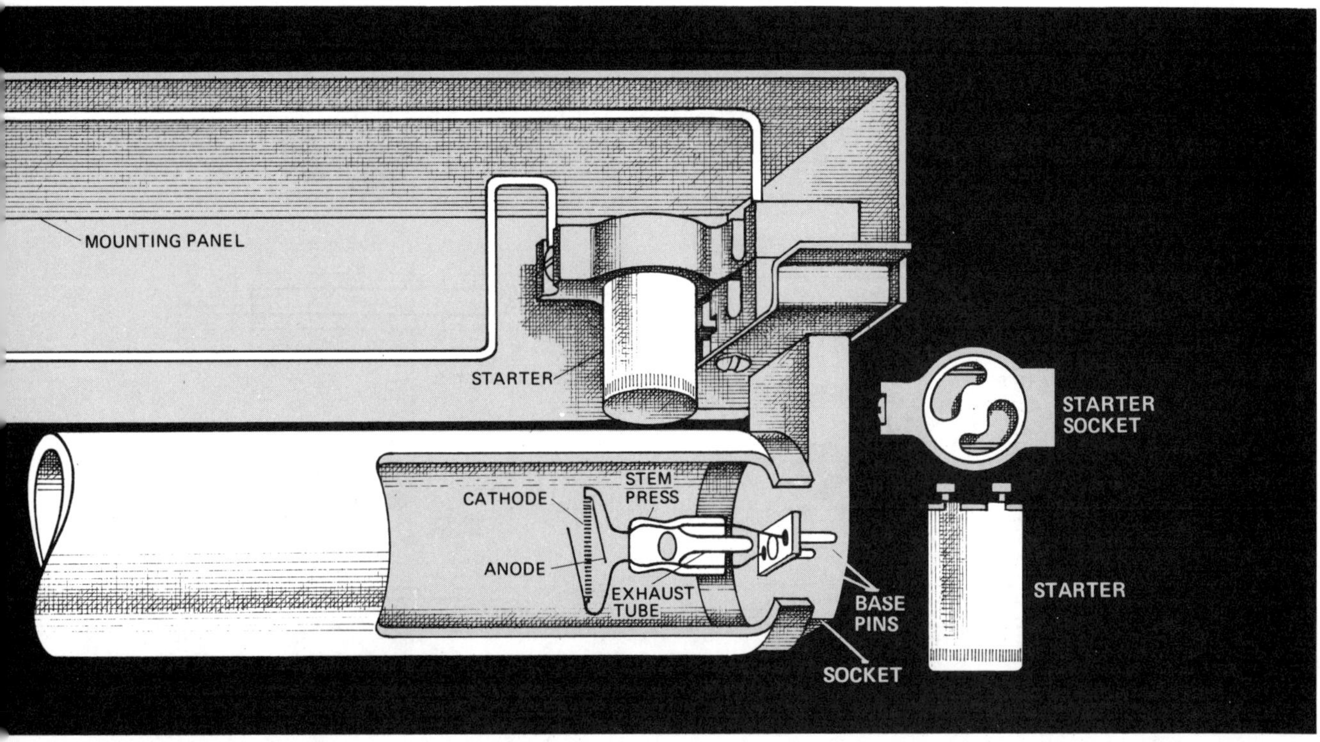

Blackening

POSSIBLE CAUSES	WHAT TO TRY
1. Mercury deposit inside of tube.	Normal.
2. Lamp failure.	Replace lamp.
3. Frequent starting.	Limit number of times lamp is turned on and off. Allow three to four hours of lamp operation.
4. Wrong-size ballast.	Check fluorescent specifications.
5. Low line voltage.	See "Lamp slow in starting," page 99.

Swirling and spiraling inside of lamp

POSSIBLE CAUSES	WHAT TO TRY
1. Lamp failure.	Replace lamp.
2. Improper or defective starter.	Check starter against fluorescent lamp circuit specifications. Replace defective starter.
3. Wrong-size ballast.	Check fluorescent specifications.
4. Low line voltage.	See "Lamp slow in starting," page 1253.

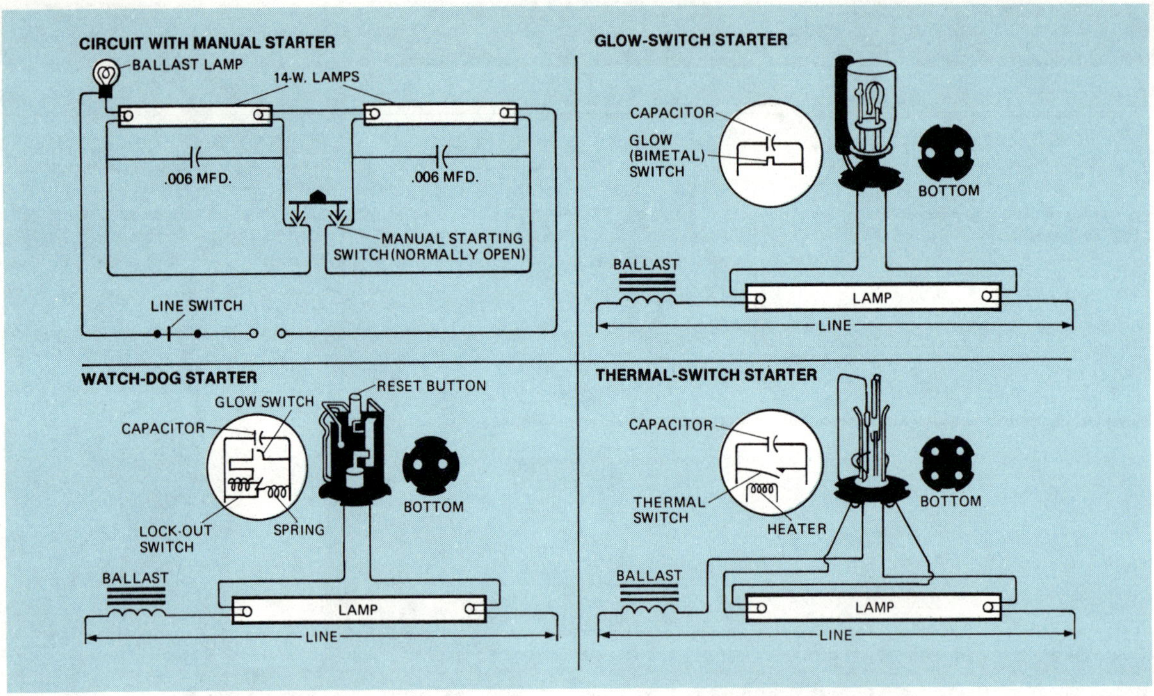

Four different starter circuits available for fluorescent lamps are shown. When you "turn on" a lamp by throwing a line switch, the circuit is closed, but the light does not appear immediately

The job of the starter element is to hold up the flow of electrical current until it has heated the two filaments in each lamp on the circuit to their proper temperature. The delay may take a second

LAMP WATT/LENGTH RATIO

Watts	Length (in.)
15	18
20	24
30	36
40	48
100	60

the filaments to the proper temperature. There are four different starter circuits available: manual, automatic glow-switch, automatic watchdog and automatic thermal-switch.

A circuit for a fluorescent tube is illustrated in the upper detail on page 1253. Here a ballast is connected in series with the lamp. The automatic starter switch is in closed position when no current is flowing through the circuit, though the starter element is heating (diagram A, "Glow-switch operation," page 1253). When the circuit is closed (diagram B), the two lamp filaments are connected in series through the starter to supply voltage. Since the automatic starter short-circuits the path, no current will flow in the lamp. Thus, the filaments are cold, and argon gas cannot conduct.

As the current begins to heat the lamp filaments to a certain temperature, the mercury in the lamp begins to vaporize. A few seconds later, the automatic starter opens (diagram C), breaks the circuit and causes the ballast to produce high voltage between the filaments. This voltage strikes an arc through the argon gas and mercury vapor. The mercury-vapor arc then causes the fluorescent chemicals inside the tube to fluoresce, emitting a brilliant light which illuminates the lamp.

Fluorescent lamps are available in many colors and "whites." Colors are used for decorative purposes; whites for general lighting. These whites offer the most efficiency per dollar of cost, the best color-rendering per-dollar cost, the best color-rendering properties.

The life of fluorescent lamps is not only affected by voltage and current, but also by the number of times they are started. Homeowners can prolong this life by following these suggestions:

- Operate lamps continuously for a three to four-hour period for maximum life. Turning the lamp on and off cuts its life considerably.
- Room temperature should be at least 50° F. For colder rooms, special fluorescent lamps and starters can be used.
- The right starter should be used with fluorescents. Check replacement starter numbers against numbers stamped on the original starter.
- Be sure the ballast has the catalog or type number specified for the fluorescent lamp unit.

BASIC SINGLE-LAMP CIRCUIT

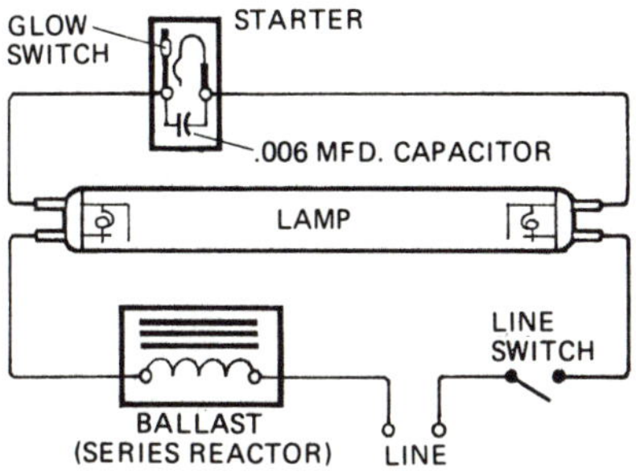

GLOW-SWITCH OPERATION

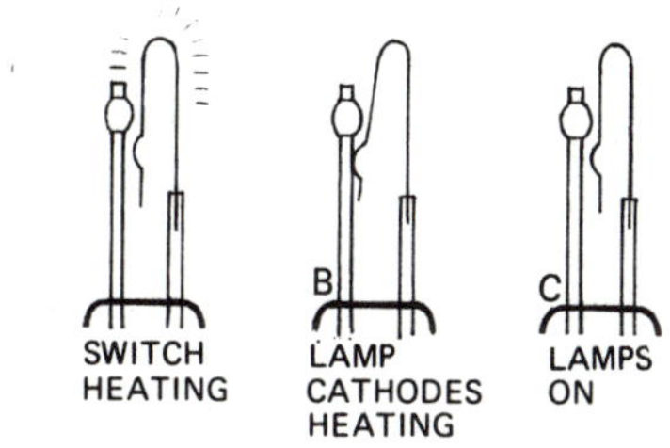

SINGLE-LAMP CIRCUIT WITH AUTOTRANSFORMER BALLAST

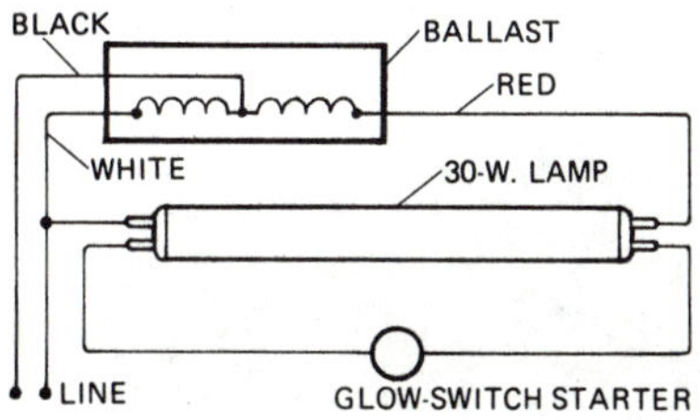

TWO-LAMP CIRCUIT

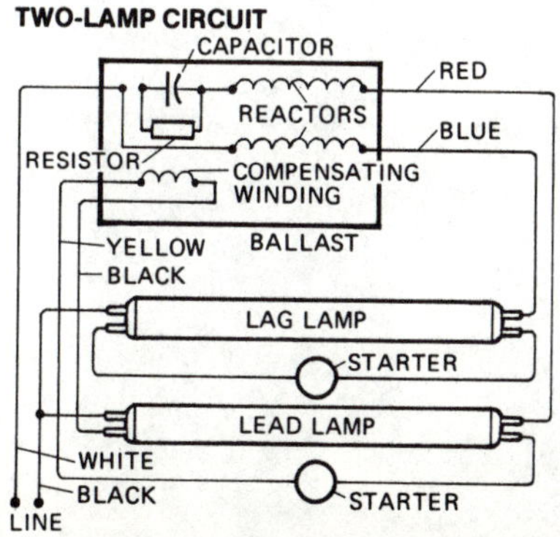

Ends of lamp remain lighted

POSSIBLE CAUSES	WHAT TO TRY
1. Shorted starter.	Replace starter.
2. Lamp failure.	Replace lamp.
3. Incorrect wiring.	Check wiring against manufacturer's schematic.

Lamp does not start

POSSIBLE CAUSES	WHAT TO TRY
1. Lamp not seated in sockets.	Reseat lamps firmly in sockets.
2. Defective starter.	Replace starter.
3. Defective lamp.	Replace lamp.
4. Defective switch.	Disconnect power. Place a continuity tester across switch. Turn switch on. A reading should exist. If not, replace switch.
5. Defective ballast.	If all of the above check good, then replace the ballast.

Lamp slow in starting

POSSIBLE CAUSES	WHAT TO TRY
1. Defective starter.	Replace starter.
2. Wrong-size ballast.	Check fluorescent specifications.
3. Low line voltage.	Check voltage. It must be ±10 percent of 120 v. If not, check with power company.

Lamp blinks on and off

POSSIBLE CAUSES	WHAT TO TRY
1. Lamp failure.	Replace lamp.
2. Defective starter.	Replace starter.
3. Cold drafts or low temperature	Block drafts or heat room up to above 50°F.
4. Wrong-size ballast.	Refer to previous section.
5. Low line voltage.	Refer to previous section.

Learn fly casting in just 60 minutes

Follow these instructions, and you'll soon be able to cast a fish-catching fly. There are tricks to be learned, but even a novice can master them within an hour

By LAWTON CARVER

IT'S ABOUT TIME somebody exploded the fiction that it takes at least five years to become a competent fly fisherman.

Fully mastering the art of fly-casting can take years, and I know experts who have been at it most of their lives and are still learning. But a complete novice can learn enough in one hour to cast a fly out onto a lake or stream, and if the fish are rising he'll catch his share.

Ellis Newman, a soft-spoken, burly outdoorsman who divides his time between giving trick casting exhibitions at sportsmen's shows and operating a fishing camp at Livingston Manor, N.Y., has devised a teaching method that is simple and infallible.

The basic idea in fly-casting is to drop an imitation fly on the surface of the water so that it

SEE ALSO
Boat camping . . . Camping . . . Casting, fly . . . Fishing tackle . . . Ice fishing . . . Lures, fishing

EXHIBITION FLY-CASTER and teacher, Ellis Newman, works with a student, keeping the rod in the correct position for the overhead cast.

looks like the real thing to a wary but hungry trout. The rod and the line are the tools for getting the fly out there. The function of the reel is simply to store the line and to take up the slack as you fight the fish.

The fly line is specially designed for its task. It is heavy to compensate for the lack of weight on the end, and it is tapered down to the end where it attaches to the fine silk or monofilament leader to which the fly is tied. For fishing dry flies the line is treated to float on the water.

A fly rod is generally longer than a bait casting or spinning rod, the eyelets are larger to allow the line to run freely, and it has more "whip" to the end, increasing the catapulting action.

The beginner can equip himself with a complete outfit, rod, reel, line, leaders and an assortment of flies, for as little as $25. And with Newman's simple system, which we illustrate here, you can teach yourself. You don't even need a stream or a lake. You can practice on a lawn or a rooftop in the city.

The proper stance is of primary importance. Make believe you are going to make a cast. The left foot goes out, as though you are going to throw a ball, and the body twists slightly to the right. This is wrong!

Rather stand with your feet planted on an imaginary line about 12 in. apart. Move the right foot forward until the heel is level with the toe of the left foot. Now go through an imaginary cast. Note how the arm goes straight up and down and there is no twisting of the body. This position will also eliminate the possibility of the excess line, which is held in the left hand, getting tangled with the rod or reel.

This stance is vitally important for the beginner. *The right foot always forward of the left.* This, of course, is reversed if you are left-handed.

Now you are ready to take up the rod. Hold it lightly, but firmly, in the right hand, the thumb resting on the top. Point it straight out before

you, the tip angled slightly above the horizontal. Now strip some line off the reel with the left hand, holding it in loops about 18 in. long.

By flipping the tip of the rod and letting loose of some of the line, you can get about 20 ft. of line out on the water. Take up the slack with your left hand.

You are now ready to attempt your first cast which will be a *roll* cast.

This is a technique used on streams or lakes where trees and heavy brush prohibit the use of the overhead cast. Most fly fishermen add this cast to their repertoire after they have experienced the problem of insufficient casting room, but Newman uses it as a starter because it is easy and enables the beginner to get the feel of both the rod and the line.

Standing with the right foot advanced, the rod held out horizontal to the ground and about 20 ft. of line floating directly out ahead of you,

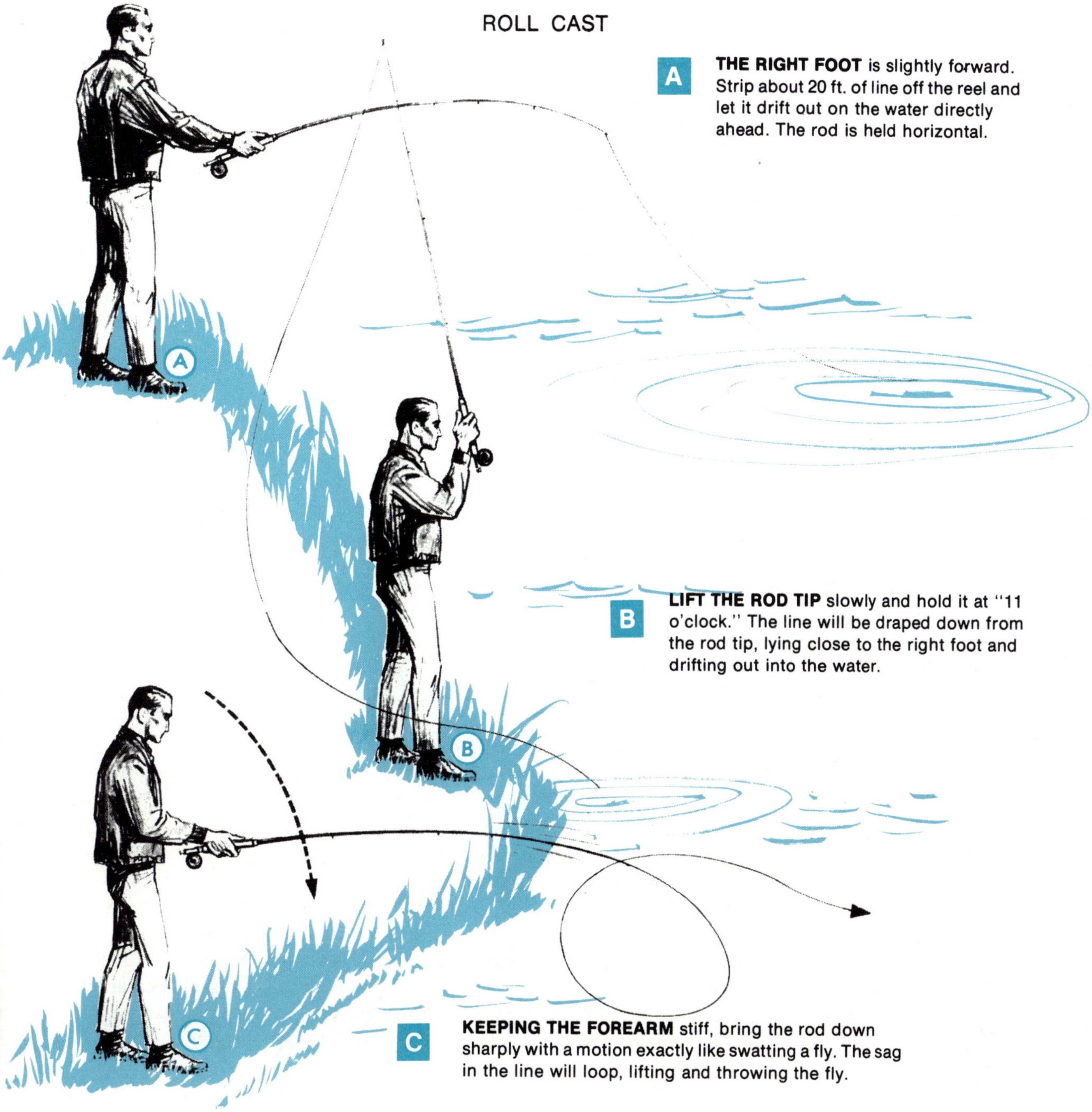

slowly lift the tip of the rod, drawing the line toward you. Hold the rod so that the tip is above and behind your head, in a position that would be pointing to the numeral "11" if it were the hand of a clock. The line will drape down from the tip of the rod and run close to your right foot. (See illustration B on this page.) Press your right elbow close to your side. Now, with the forearm and wrist as rigid as possible, bring the rod down sharply with exactly the same motion as you'd use swatting a fly. *Do not bring it down below the horizontal.* The sag in the line will go into a loop, neatly picking the fly off the water and dropping it again well beyond the rod tip.

That's all there is to the roll cast. It sounds easy and it is. It is also an extremely practical cast used by the experts in close quarters.

The overhead cast is almost entirely a matter of timing, and you can learn it in a few minutes.

What you are attempting to do is pick the fly

off the water, swing it back over your head, and then shoot it out over the water, letting it drop like a live insect touching down on the surface.

Slack line can be a problem in the overhead cast because it is line that is not under control. Learn to avoid this in the beginning and it will not become a problem as you gain in casting proficiency. Instead of yanking the fly into the air from wherever it and the line might be, lower the rod tip and take up the slack in loose coils with the left hand until the rod tip and line are as near as possible in a straight line toward the fly. Then slowly pull the fly toward you by lifting the rod tip to the proper position—angled slightly above the horizontal.

Now try the overhead cast. The right foot is advanced. The rod is slightly above the horizontal (Fig. A, page 1256). About two rod lengths of line are out before you. There is no slack in the line.

The following movements will seem exaggerated, but they are Newman's method, designed to teach control from the very beginning.

Press the right elbow tightly against the side, the upper arm perpendicular from shoulder to waist. Bend slightly forward from the waist (Fig. B). The forearm and wrist are kept rigid. There is no bending of the wrist.

count aloud

Count, "One!" Shout it aloud. Snap your body erect, throwing your head back. This will automatically bring the rod up, concentrating any movement in the elbow. Stop the rod in the position that would have the tip pointing to the numeral 10 on the face of a clock (Fig. C).

Freeze in that position!

The line is in the air and traveling back over your head.

Shout, "And!" This gives the line a full second to get fully straightened out behind you (Fig. D).

Shout, "Two," and snap your body forward, bending slightly at the waist, the elbow still tight against your side. The rod automatically returns to the position, angling slightly above the horizontal (Fig. E). The line descends to the water, the fly following it to land like a bug from the blue.

The timing is everything. "One—And—Two." If the line is snapped back before it has fully straightened, the result will be like cracking a whip. The line will not go out and the fly could snap off. If you wait too long the line drops behind you.

Run through the overhead cast until you get the feel of the timing. You can do this by making false casts. Before the line and fly hit the water bring it back up again, counting aloud, keeping the line in the air and working up a rhythm. "One—And—Two—And—One—And—Two."

When you have this down to your satisfaction, take a few loops of line in the left hand. Repeat the overhead cast, keeping the fly in the air, but now let out a little more line from the left hand on each false cast. As the length of line increases so must the length of the pause that allows it to straighten out. When all the slack is in the air, send it out and let it hit the water. This is the whole reason for the overhead cast, working the line out to the desired length that will place the fly where you want it to land.

Don't try to put out too much line. A fly line is 90 ft. long, but most stream fishing is done within a distance of 50 ft.

When you have the feel of the timing you can stop the exaggerated body movements and cast with just the arm. But remember: *no wrist movement!* The arm, from shoulder to hand, must be used like two rods with a hinge at the elbow.

gentleness is an art

A principle of fly casting is to lay the line on the water as gently as possible, so as not to frighten the fish. This is where you are getting into the "art" of fly casting, and it comes from practice.

You will also want to put the fly on target. This is the part that makes fly casting more pleasurable than other types of fishing. Catching fish becomes secondary to the fun of learning to put the fly where you want it. You can practice this on the lawn or rooftop, with a teacup as target.

In one hour you'll be able to fish with a fly. After that there is no limit to how skillful you may become—by practicing.

Ellis Newman can put out the full 90 ft. of line without a rod, using only his bare hands. He can cast with two rods in one hand. I've watched him cast simultaneously with a rod in each hand, and then alternate the rods so that he's in the back cast with one and the forward cast with the other.

This is the epitome of the art, but Newman is the first to admit that it doesn't impress a fish. Dropping a fly in the current so it looks like a free lunch is the important thing—and the easiest.

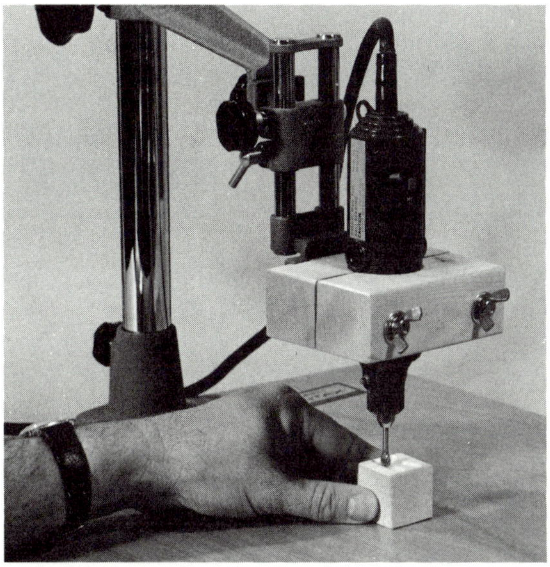

GET DOUBLE DUTY from a photographic copy stand by equipping it with blocks to hold a hand grinder. It not only becomes a miniature drill press, but also makes a dandy overarm router with fine adjustment for accurate work on small pieces.—*Ken Patterson, Regina, Sask.*

DRAWER PULLS, knobs and other furniture hardware are easier to paint when screwed to stiff cardboard that serves as a handle for them, and a convenient place for them to dry.—*William Swallow, Brooklyn, NY.*

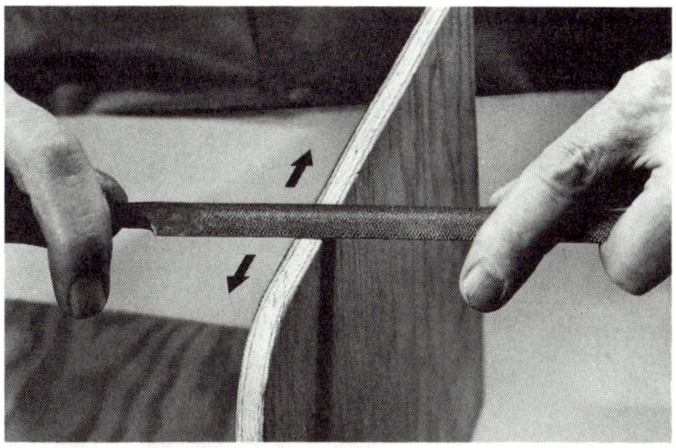

TO REDUCE SPLINTERING when smoothing the edge of a plywood panel with a wood rasp, use the rasp like a draw file. Hold it as shown above and move it back and forth parallel to the edge.—*Walter E. Burton, Akron, OH.*

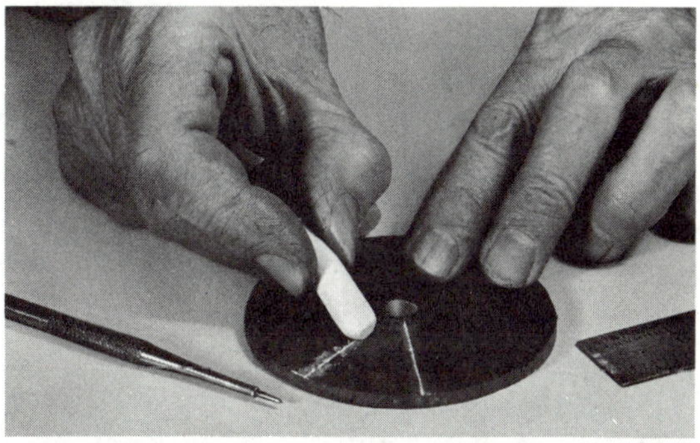

IF LAYOUT LINES scratched with a scriber on a dark-colored surface are difficult to see, try rubbing chalk crosswise into each line, removing excess with a finger.—*W. B. May, Oak Park, IL.*

TO SAVE TIME opening and closing the jaws of my lathe chuck, I use a reversible variable-speed drill with a socket drive instead of the regular chuck key. It works on a four-jaw chuck as well.—*Wilson Moore, Lexington, KY.*

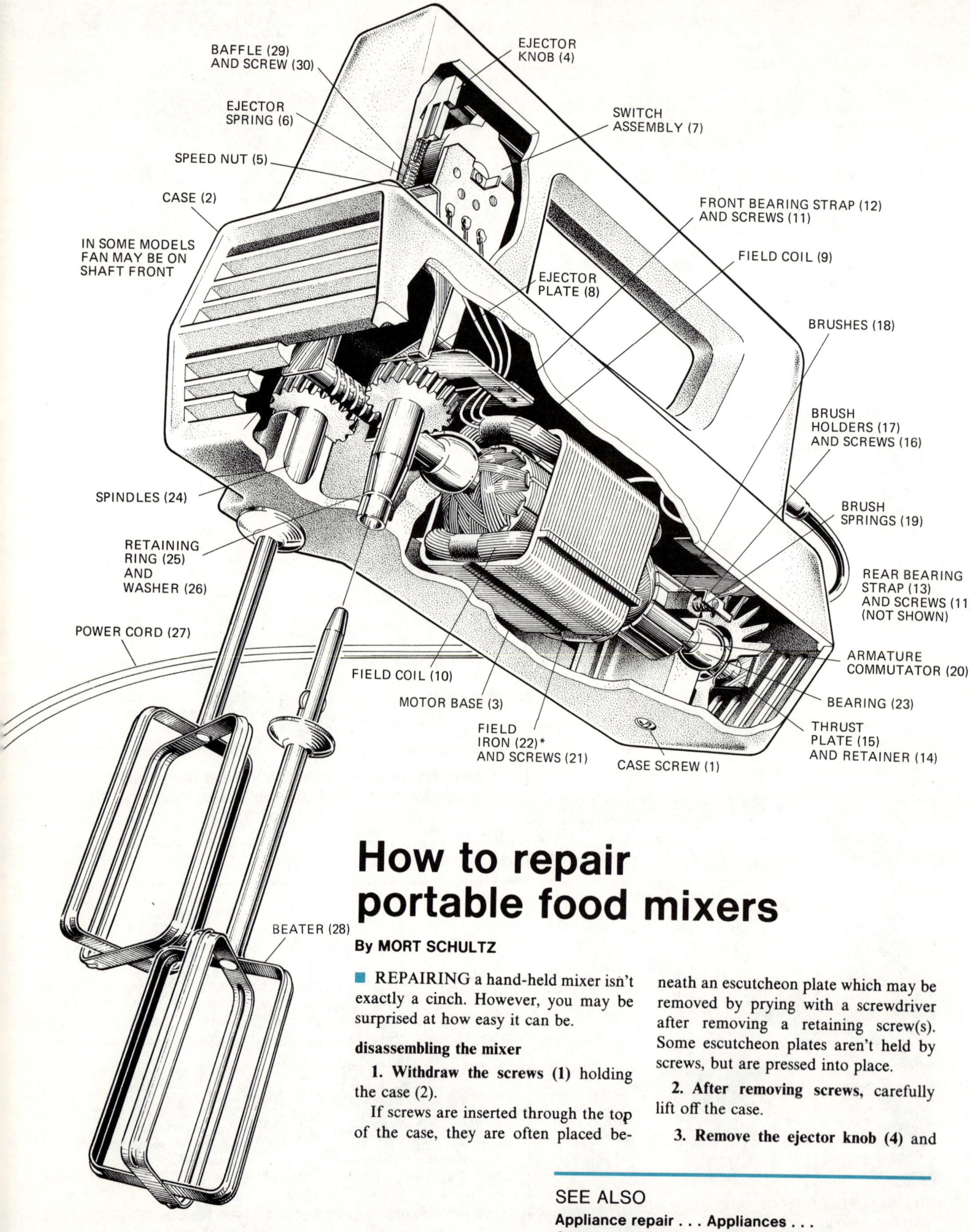

How to repair portable food mixers

By MORT SCHULTZ

REPAIRING a hand-held mixer isn't exactly a cinch. However, you may be surprised at how easy it can be.

disassembling the mixer

1. Withdraw the screws (1) holding the case (2).

If screws are inserted through the top of the case, they are often placed beneath an escutcheon plate which may be removed by prying with a screwdriver after removing a retaining screw(s). Some escutcheon plates aren't held by screws, but are pressed into place.

2. After removing screws, carefully lift off the case.

3. Remove the ejector knob (4) and

SEE ALSO

Appliance repair . . . Appliances . . .
Coffee percolators . . . Dishwashers . . .
Food processors . . . Irons . . . Mixers, food . . .
Oven hoods . . . Ranges . . . Toasters . . .
Vacuum cleaners . . . Washing machines

Motor won't run

POSSIBLE CAUSES	WHAT TO TRY
1. No voltage at the receptacle.	Check with a table lamp.
2. Damaged or defective power cord.	Inspect and/or test for continuity.
3. Bad switch.	Replace.
4. Other electrical breakdowns.	Check the circuit for continuity. If no open condition shows up, conduct checks outlined for a motor which has insufficient speed or power.

Motor has insufficient speed or power

POSSIBLE CAUSES	WHAT TO TRY
1. Bearing or spindle is binding.	Tap appliance in the vicinity of the front and rear bearing straps and field iron with a small hammer or the handle of a screwdriver as the motor is running. An increase in speed indicates a binding condition.
2. Brushes are worn.	Inspect.
3. Shorted armature.	Check armature resistance from segment to segment on the commutator. Field resistance is about 5 ohms and commutator resistance, bar to bar, should be about 3 ohms. If resistance is noticeably lower or higher, replace the armature.

Motor speed cannot be adjusted

POSSIBLE CAUSES	WHAT TO TRY
1. Bad switch.	Replace.
2. Shorted capacitor.	In those units that use a capacitor, replace.

Motor is noisy

POSSIBLE CAUSES	WHAT TO TRY
1. Dry spindles	Lubricate.
2. Worn spindles	Replace.
3. Worn bearing	Replace.
4. Bent fan	Replace fan, if possible—replace armature if fan is an integral part.
5. Defective armature	Replace.

switch assembly (7), held by a speed nut (5).

4. Unhook the ejector spring (6) and ejector plate (8).

5. Lift the ejector plate to disconnect it from the switch assembly. You may have to manipulate the switch so the ejector plate slips up past the switch knob. You may also have to force the ejector plate against the field coils (9 and 10) to slip the plate from its slot in the switch bracket.

Important: As you perform this step, carefully notice the way it's done. Reassembly is performed in reverse order.

6. Withdraw the screws (11)—in this model there are four—holding front and rear bearing straps (12 and 13), switch assembly, thrustplate retainer (14) and thrust plate (15). Remove these parts.

removing the brushes

7. Withdraw the screws (16)—in this model there are two—holding the brush holders (17). This releases the brushes (18), brush springs (19) and brush holders. There are two brush holders, two brushes and two brush springs. One assembly is positioned on each side of the armature commutator assembly (20).

8. Withdraw the screws (21) securing the field iron (22) to the case. Here there are three screws.

9. You can now remove the armature and replace the bearing (23) on the commutator end if necessary.

10. Remove spindles (24) by spreading the retaining rings (25). Slide the rings and washers (26) off spindle shafts, and lift spindles out of the top of the motor base.

11. If the power cord (27) has to be replaced, melt soldered joints. In all cases of electrical repair, make sure solder joints are made properly. Use the wiring schematic here as a guide in making electrical repairs, such as replacing the switch, field coils or power cord.

replacing beaters

12. Beaters (28) should be examined if the appliance runs but beaters don't revolve, spin sluggishly or whip. Look for bent rods and wear on beater tips. Replace them in pairs.

13. The baffle (29) may be replaced, if damaged, by removing the baffle screw (30).

Reassembling a portable food mixer is done the reverse of disassembly. Spindle shafts should be lubricated with appliance gear grease before they are put back in the motor base.

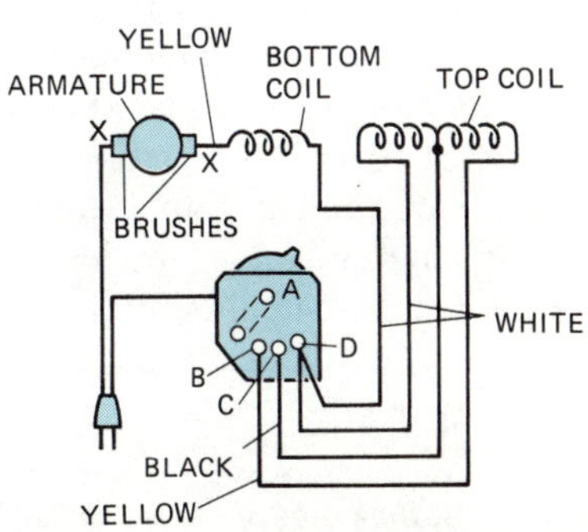

WIRING DIAGRAM

What to do when your food processor stops

By MORT SCHULTZ

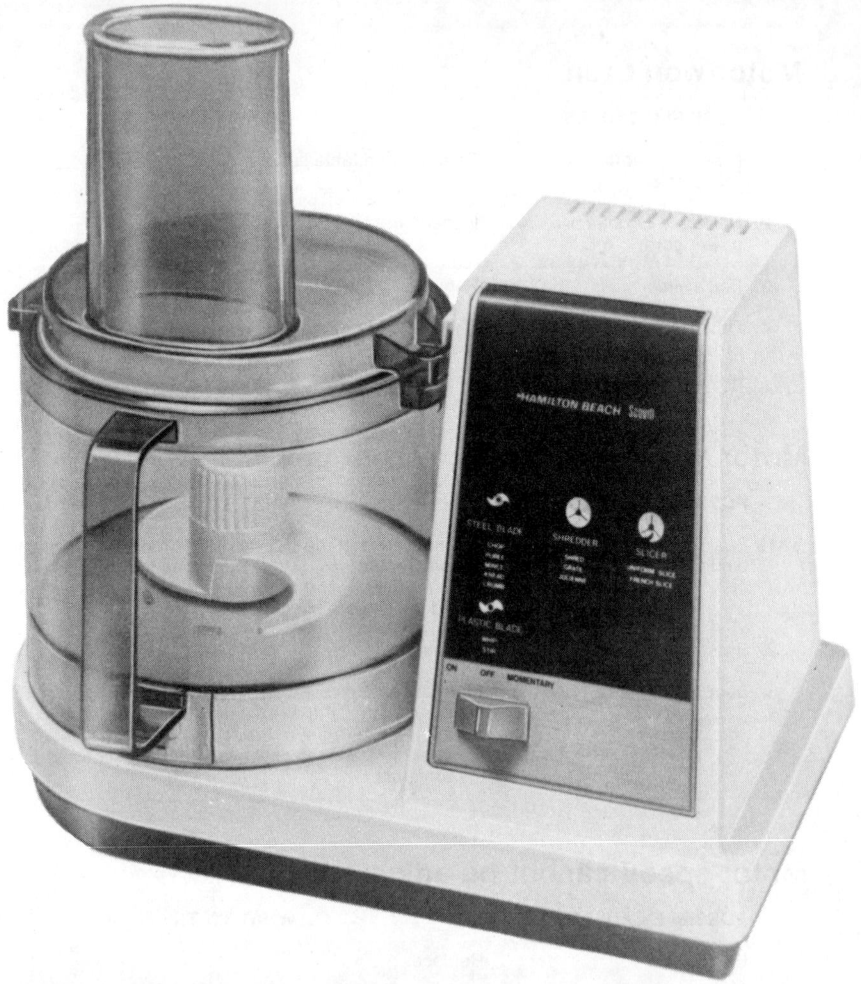

Electric food processors simplify many kitchen chores. When malfunctions occur, they are usually easy to repair. Here's what you need to know

■ ALTHOUGH FOOD processors have been selling like crazy, there is little talk about how to fix 'em when they break down. Many manufacturers are being close-mouthed about repair procedures. Here's some good news: Repairing a food processor is as easy as whipping egg whites in one.

Since replacement parts are somewhat hard to get, it would be a good idea to call your dealer to see if parts for your machine are available. If they aren't, you may be able to substitute a "universal" part. Disassemble the unit, find the defective part and take it to a store that's listed in the classified directory under "Electric Appliances—Small—Supplies, Parts."

SEE ALSO

Appliance repair . . . Appliances . . . Clothes dryers . . . Dishwashers . . . Food mixers . . . Freezers . . . Humidifiers . . . Irons . . . Kitchens . . . Ranges . . . Toasters . . . Vacuum cleaners

units are similar inside

Hamilton Beach is one maker that did provide us with useful information. There isn't much difference between their unit and most other makes when it comes to troubleshooting and repair. However, there is one notable difference between some units: Most use a cogged belt and two pulleys to drive the shaft, but some use a gear train.

Except for this, internal mechanisms are much the same from unit to unit. Parts include a universal motor; a rectifier (diode) that converts incoming a.c. to d.c., which is needed to run the motor; on-off and safety switches; and a power cord. These are the parts that cause problems.

two common problems

There are only two major problems that occur with any degree of frequency:

1. The motor won't run although the on-off switch is "on" and the bowl and bowl cover are locked in place. Locking the bowl and bowl cover

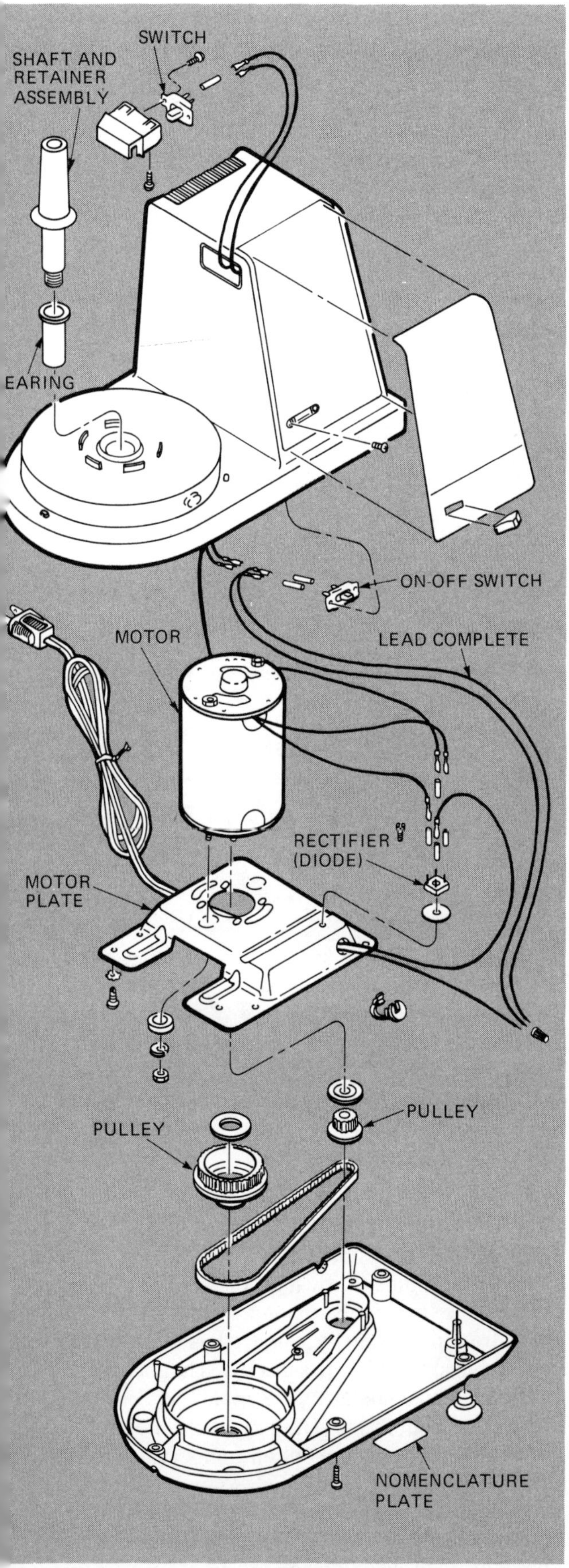

in place trips the safety switch to "on."

2. The motor runs, but the shaft and blades won't turn.

motor won't run

The causes are the following:

- No power
- Defective power cord
- Defective on-off switch
- Defective safety switch
- Defective rectifier
- Defective motor

Caution: Observe safety practices when troubleshooting and repairing. For example, don't leave a blade or disc attached.

Start by plugging the processor into another outlet in a different part of the house. If the motor starts running then your problem is with a defective house line—not with the unit.

Check the power cord for damage: Turn on the machine. If there's no sign of life, flex the cord over its length. If there's sporadic action, replace the cord.

Next, unplug the unit, remove the assembly screws from the underside of the bottom housing and separate the top and bottom housings. Don't force them apart. If they still hold tightly together, look for hidden screws—for example, under a nomenclature plate which you may have to pry off.

Check all connections for any that may have come loose. Also look for burned insulation on wire leads. Replace defective leads.

When you test the *on-off switch,* the power cord has to be plugged in with the safety switch engaged. When you test the *safety switch,* the power cord has to be plugged in and the on-off switch has to be "on." Test these switches by carefully using a jumper wire to bridge the switch terminals (or remove the switch leads and temporarily tape them together). If the processor comes to life in either case, replace the switch involved.

At this point, only a small rectifier and motor remain as causes for failure. Replace the rectifier. It isn't expensive. With luck, the motor will run now. If not, you probably need a new motor.

shaft won't turn

A bent shaft could cause this malfunction, but a bent shaft is not a common occurrence. It is more likely that the belt has broken or one of the pulleys has stripped. If your food processor uses a gear-driven shaft, one of the gears probably has stripped. The solution, in any case, is to find the defective part and replace it.

How to mount and frame fine pictures

Here's where to get low-cost prints, how to mat them and how to make 27 beautiful frames from standard wood moldings. You do the work inexpensively in your shop

By HARRY WICKS

GOOD ART PRINTS and frames don't have to be expensive. You can create frames which closely duplicate those found in the best museums. For example, the frame shown on the wall above would cost about $75 if purchased from a professional framing shop. We were able to build this frame ourselves for around $16. The print is an example of the high-quality prints that can be purchased from such sources as the Museum of Modern Art and the New York Graphic Society. This one is Wyeth's *Northern Point* and sells for about $16.

SEE ALSO

Clamps . . . Fasteners . . . Finishes, wood . . . Joinery . . . Moldings . . . Mountings, photo . . . Picture frames . . . Sanding . . . Staining, wood . . . Wood finishes

All of the frames shown on these pages were created inexpensively in our shop. We have made framing easier by using a basic two-part assembly: surfaced-four-sides (S4S) lumber for a subframe and standard pine moldings for the decorative front frame. Happily, these moldings are available at low cost at all lumberyards.

How the frames were made, plus other picture-frame know-how, is detailed in the text and illustrations that follow. The concluding section tells how each was finished.

Gone for the Summer/Hamilton

Ballet Girls/Duteurte

Tiger with Red Background/Hug

Amber Field/Russel

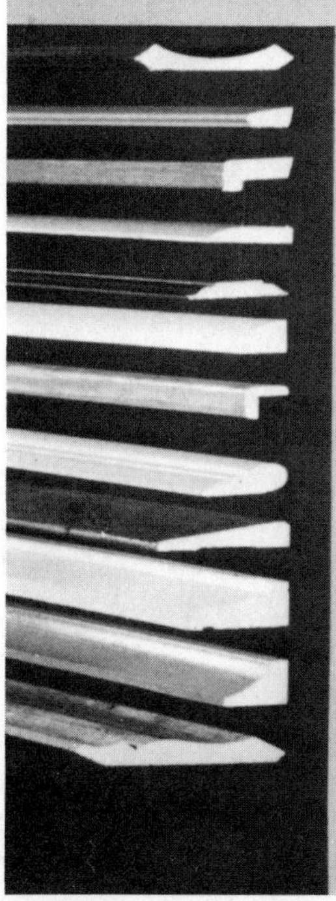

Island Silhouette/Ross

Passenger/Martin

ALL FRAMES were created using moldings for front frames, surfaced-four-sides (S4S) lumber for the subframes. Each of the 12 moldings at left was used on at least one of the frames. From top: cove (2¼ in.), glass bead, backband, clamshell stop, mullion casing, quarter-round, corner guard, picture mold, clamshell base, dripcap, solid cove and a 3¼-in. crown/bed molding. Using instructions given in the text, you can duplicate these or create your own frames.

Still Life with Pitcher/Chailloux

Ship in Drydock/Listri

Still Life/Salinas

World War II Tank Print

Pirate Treasure Map

Buddha/Lee

Courtyard/Felmart

Nature Morte Avec Three Fruits/Genis

Sailboats/Bria

PRINTS AND REPRODUCTIONS selected for use here are all available by mail order. Five pieces of art, such as the lithograph directly above, are original works. Complete details for making and finishing the frames (and where to buy prints) are given on these pages.

MAKING YOUR OWN FRAMES is just half the fun; creating attractive wall groupings is another reward. This wall features old-time posters, a woodcut and tools (from the author's collection) mounted on burlap.

If you are interested in any of the reproductions that we have framed, you'll be happy to know that they are available by mail. Sources are listed on page 1276

Tools and materials. Because construction techniques have been kept simple, the frames can be made using hand tools only. If you own power tools, the job will go faster, but the techniques remain unchanged.

Selecting stock. Standard pine moldings are the key to creating a good-looking frame; this factory-shaped stock eliminates the need for a router or shaper, or having to pay to have this work done by a cabinet shop. If possible, when you buy your moldings, pick out the materials yourself. Or at the least, take a sighting along each length of molding to assure its being straight and free of twists and bows. If you don't, you will quickly learn that warped moldings will give you trouble when you attempt to close a mitered joint. Also, avoid moldings that are excessively sappy; these will not take stain evenly, and you'll be disappointed with the finished product no matter how fine your carpentry.

BASIC FRAME

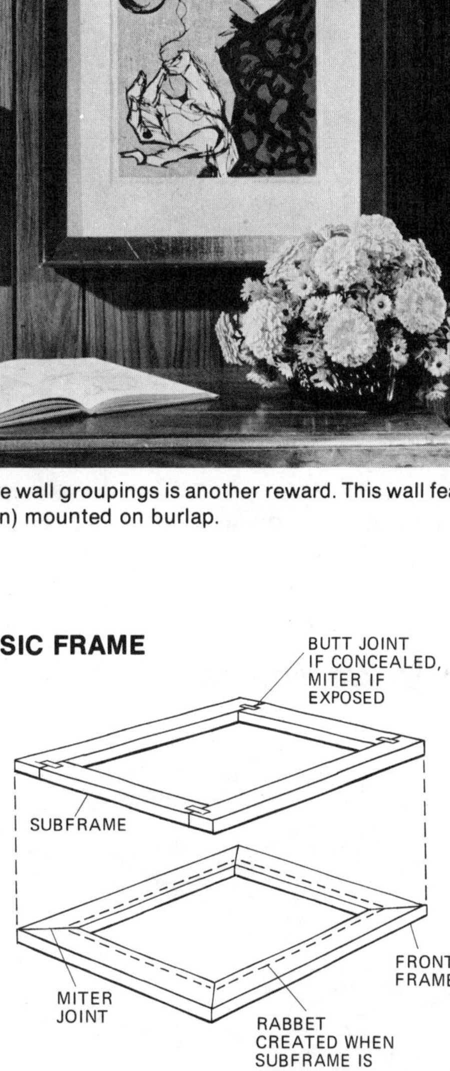

BUTT JOINTS are used on the subframe and mitered corners on the moldings. The rabbet is formed when they are joined.

Selecting the right frame for the picture. Since styles and tastes are constantly changing, you do have considerable "artistic license" when it comes to creating a frame. The basic rule to keep in mind is that the frame should complement the picture it will contain. Thus, a wide frame utiliz-

THIS WALL GROUPING features a Charlie Chaplin and three other posters. Most are available at bookstores or by mail.

HOW TO MAT PICTURES

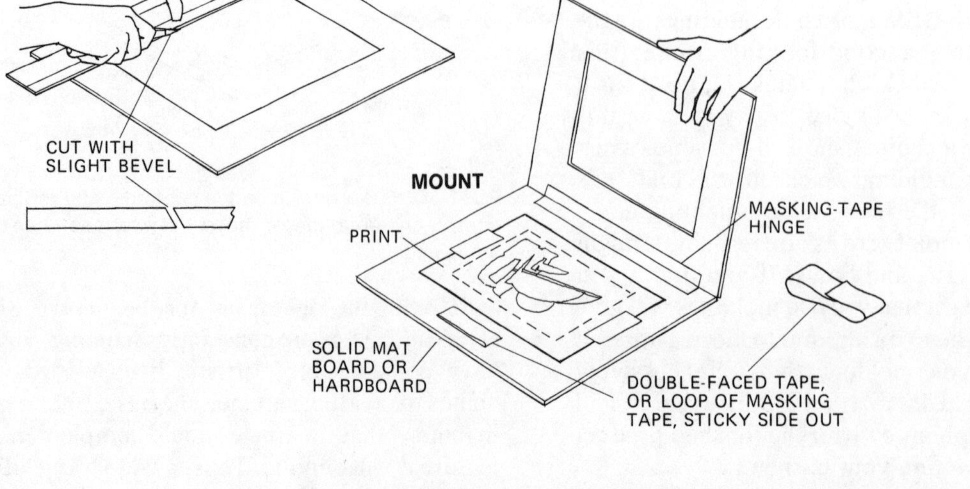

ing bold moldings is best suited to heavy, bold prints and oil paintings; narrow, simple frames should be used on small, delicate pictures.

To focus attention on a decorative object or display, such as the antique hand tools , use either an appropriately textured backing or make a frame with shadow-box effect (that is, with the front frame protruding an inch or so from the framed objects). A decorator rule-of-thumb (and in my opinion a correct one) is that *any picture will look good—in any room decor—if properly framed.*

How to mat. In general, delicate prints, watercolors and fine reproductions are enhanced by the addition of a mat. Mat board comes in 30x40-in. sheets in a variety of colors and textures from smooth to grass cloth in shiny or dull finish. If you decide that your picture needs a mat, it is the first step in picture framing because its outside dimensions will determine frame measurements.

Two "musts" when cutting a mat: First, the bottom horizontal is *always* slightly wider than the top horizontal and the verticals. The average mat is usually 3 in. wide at sides and top and 3½ in. wide at bottom. Second, the cutout should always be made with bevel cut as shown on page 1268. The sloped edge enhances the picture and also visually minimizes any minor irregularities if your cutting tool should wander from the straightedge even slightly.

Measure the picture to be framed and transfer the marks to the mat board. Make the cutout as

PICTURE-FRAMING TOOLS AND SUPPLIES

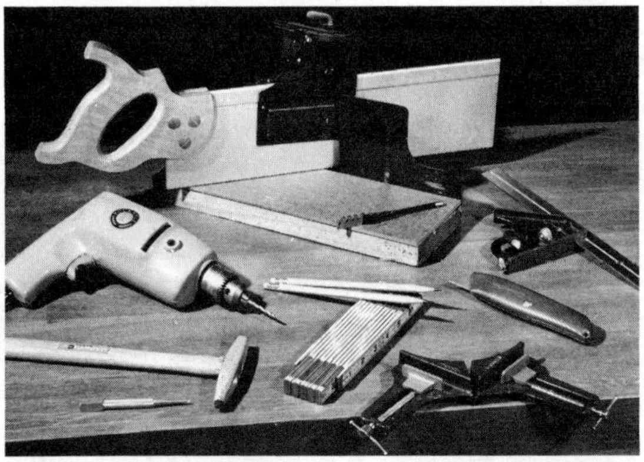

TOOLS YOU'LL NEED include a backsaw, miterbox, glass cutter, combination square, utility knife, corner clamp, ruler, pencils, nailset and light hammer. An electric drill, optional, is a desirable addition.

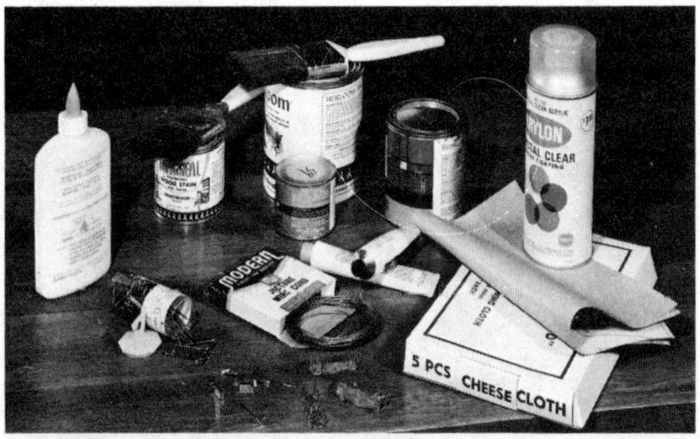

BUILDING AND FINISHING SUPPLIES: White glue, oil (or water) stain, varnish, assorted brushes (bristle for oil paints, nylon for latex), filler, paint, clear spray finish, sandpaper, cheesecloth, Skotch connectors, picture hangers, brads, picture wire and, for "antiquing," tubes of burnt umber and black.

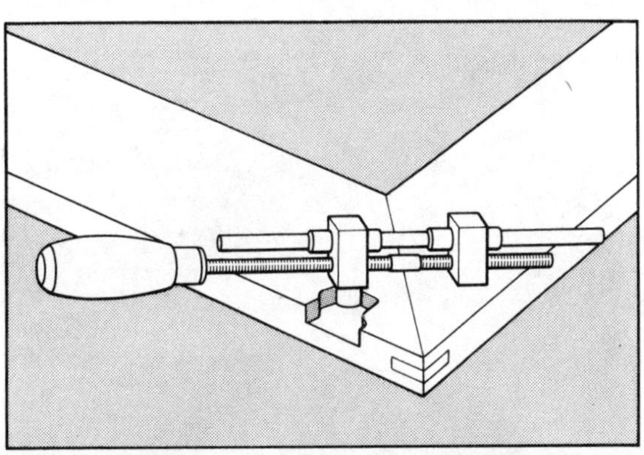

MITER CLAMPS are designed for use on flat stock (S4S). You must drill two ⅝-in. holes in back of the frame for seating each clamp. All clamps shown here are available at hardware suppliers. If you cannot find one locally, write to Adjustable Clamp Co., 422 North Ashland Ave., Chicago, IL 60622.

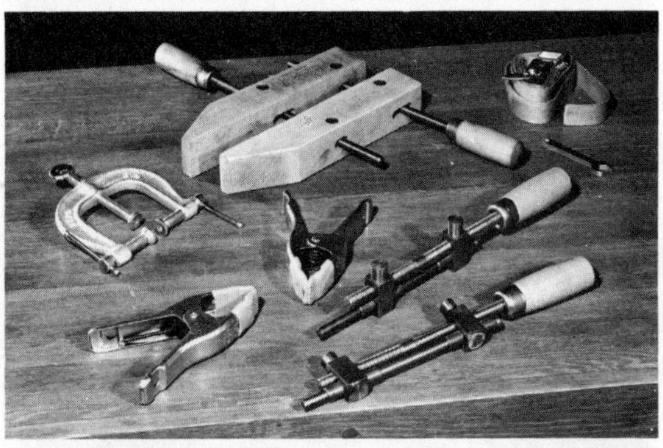

A GOOD VARIETY of clamps is nice to have around; they're a sound investment if you are planning to make a lot of frames. The clamps shown here are spring-type (center), three-way edging, handscrew, web and a pair of miter clamps—which hold a frame square.

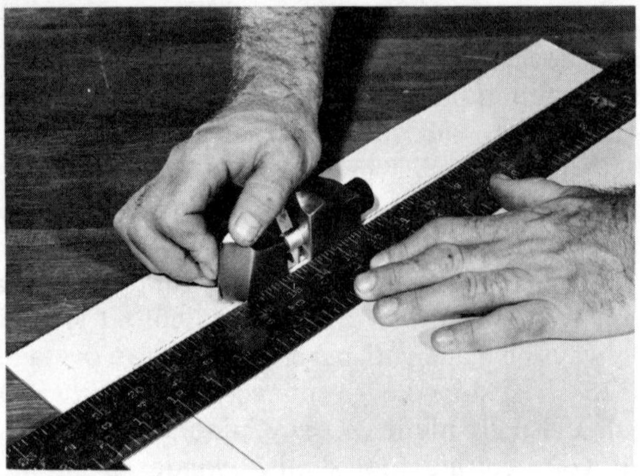

THE MAT CUTOUT should be made with a slight bevel toward the surface of the print. The cutter shown here lets you do this accurately and quickly.

shown, then decide the mat's width. Don't forget to add ½ in. in height and width to allow for the portion which will be in the ¼-in. rabbet. Cut a backing board, tape the print to its center and secure the mat.

THE CUTTER, called a Dexter Mat Cutter, costs about $6 at artists' supplies stores. It's made by the Russel Harrington Cutlery Co., Southbridge, MA 01550.

As a rule, matted pictures are covered with nonreflecting glass. When you buy picture glass, make certain it is clear and free of any bubbles or waves. And, because picture glass is particularly fragile, handle it with care. Work on a clean, flat

MAKING A PICTURE FRAME

TO ASSEMBLE THE SUBFRAME, use glue and Skotch connectors on the back side. If the subframe will be seen from the front, use mitered (instead of butt) joints.

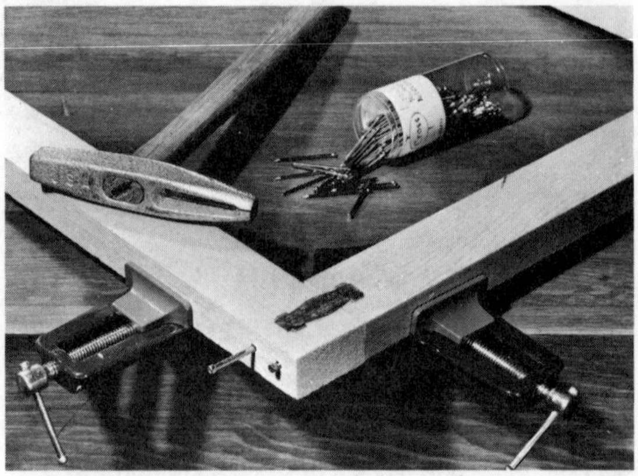

AFTER ASSEMBLY, drive in two finishing nails at each corner. Allow the nails to protrude 1/16 in. above the surface and then set them 1/16 in. deep.

CUT THE FRONT-FRAME molding using a miterbox and backsaw. For stability, clamp the miterbox to the workbench.

FASTEN THE FRONT FRAME to the subframe with glue and suitably sized brads. Molding overhang forms the rabbet.

surface; preferably your workbench after it has been covered with cardboard. Take accurate measurements of the frame's rabbet opening, and don't forget to subtract ⅛ in. in length and width so that the glass won't shatter when you insert it. (If you prefer, let glazier do the cutting.)

Making a picture frame. Most frames have a rabbet to contain the picture (all of those shown do). In some cases, a single molding such as back band—used on a simple poster—does the job. But for more sophisticated frames, you make a two-piece frame consisting of a back (subframe) and front frame (with an opening ½ in. less in width and height to create the ¼-in.-wide rabbet).

A subframe can be joined using simple butt joints if it will be fully covered by the front frame, Bainbridge board or cloth. If the subframe will be in view, however, miter-cut these corners as well as the moldings.

Use a miterbox to make the cuts and assemble the frames using a corner clamp as shown in

FINISHING TIPS AND HINTS

TO "ANTIQUE" A STAINED FRAME, darken the corners with burnt umber. Use a clean cheesecloth to blend the umber carefully into the adjacent stained wood.

TO COLOR-TONE A PAINTED FRAME, apply a wash of the second color (above, blue over white). After a few minutes, wipe off the color with a clean cheesecloth.

MOUNTING AND HANGING PICTURES

AN OIL PAINTING on stretchers is held in the frame by driving 4d nails through stretchers into the frame.

MOUNTED PRINTS (on cardboard or hardboard) are secured in the rabbet with eight brads (two per side).

INSTALL PICTURE WIRE below the top of the frame so that the picture hanger on the wall will not show. A simple jig assures correct wire length every time.

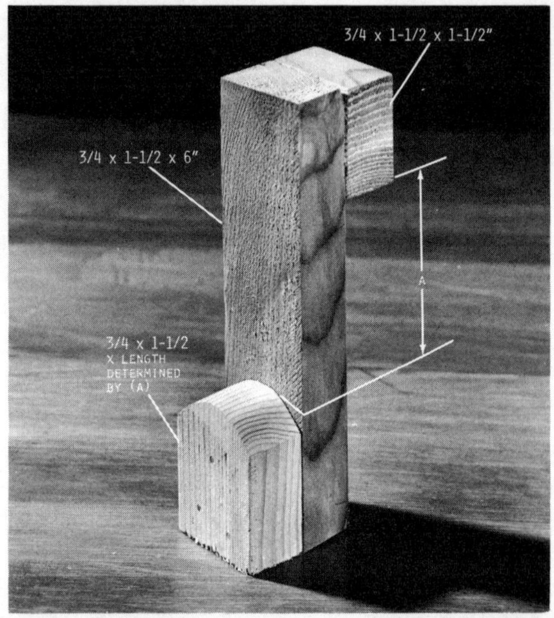

A PICTURE-WIRE JIG is quickly fashioned from scrap. Distance A must suit the frame to be fitted with wire.

A STRIATING "TOOL," conceived by the author, consists of 8d finishing nails through a ¾-in. pine strip.

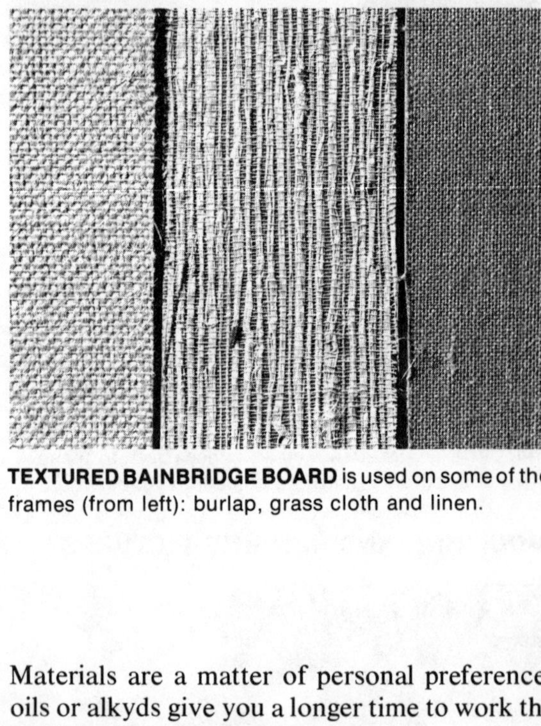

TEXTURED BAINBRIDGE BOARD is used on some of the frames (from left): burlap, grass cloth and linen.

photos. The clamp is fastened to the workbench and when the moldings are secured in its jaws, they're held square while you do the gluing and nailing. When all four sides are assembled, check the frame with your square and temporarily tack two diagonals across the frame back to hold it square while the glue dries. Finally, set all nails 1/16 in. below the surface, fill and sand.

Next, attach the front frame to the subframe with glue and appropriate-size nails. When the glue is dry, sand frame well with a fine-grit sandpaper and dust it thoroughly before finishing.

Finishing a frame. There are three basic finishes you can use: natural, stained and painted. Materials are a matter of personal preference; oils or alkyds give you a longer time to work the finish (when rubbing off an antiquing wash, for example), but latex materials let you do the job a bit faster and with less cleanup to be done when you have completed the job.

Natural finish. Apply either thinned shellac or varnish. Allow to dry overnight, rub lightly with 4/0 steel wool, wipe off dust and apply a second, nonthinned coat of the same finish. After 24 hours, apply wax and buff to a sheen.

Stained finish. Apply a stain of your choice, allow it to set 15-20 minutes, then wipe off the excess. Let this dry at least 24 hours, then apply a coat of shellac thinned 50-50 with alcohol. Wait a day, then rub lightly with steel wool, dust and apply a finish coat of varnish.

"Antiqued" stain finish. Follow the same steps described above, but after staining apply burnt umber directly from the tube, using a cheesecloth. Corners and crevices should appear darkest and the umber should be carefully blended to "disappear" as you work it toward the center. Then, you can proceed with finishing as indicated above.

Paint finish. Apply a wash-coat of shellac (thinned 50 percent with alcohol) and let it dry. Rub lightly with steel wool, dust and apply color of your choice. You can use oil-base enamel or, if you prefer, latex. The latter, though, should be followed with a coat of varnish. *Caution:* use *varnish only* over latex paint or the paint will lift off. As you prefer it, the varnish finish can range from dull to high gloss.

"Antiqued" paint finish. After applying the basic color, allow it to dry overnight. Then, mix a black paint with appropriate thinner to a *slightly heavier than water* consistency. Apply this wash to the frame, wait five minutes and wipe it off with a clean cloth. If desired, the antiquing can be done with another color instead of black. (For example, the frame surrounding the Tiger with Red Background (page 1274) was finished by wiping orange over Chinese red.) Finally, proceed with an appropriate clear finish.

spray varnishes

In general, when limited quantities will be needed, I've found that spray varnishes, lacquers and the like are easier to use than their brush-on counterparts. They eliminate a great deal of clean-up time and they set faster, which means that there's less time for dust to settle on your new frame during the drying time.

Hanging pictures. The easiest way to hang a picture is to use two screw eyes no longer than three-quarters of frame's thickness. Insert them about a quarter of the distance from top to bottom of the frame. Attach picture wire as shown and the picture is ready to hang. To keep picture from tilting, use a pair of picture hooks on the wall—spaced 6 in. or so apart—instead of just one. Make certain that the screw eyes, wire and hooks are strong enough to hold the weight of the picture.

Instructions for all of the frames shown in the photos are given. Bold type at the start of each caption refers to the picture's size. Following the size is a number in parentheses that refers to a where-to-buy source listed on page 1276.

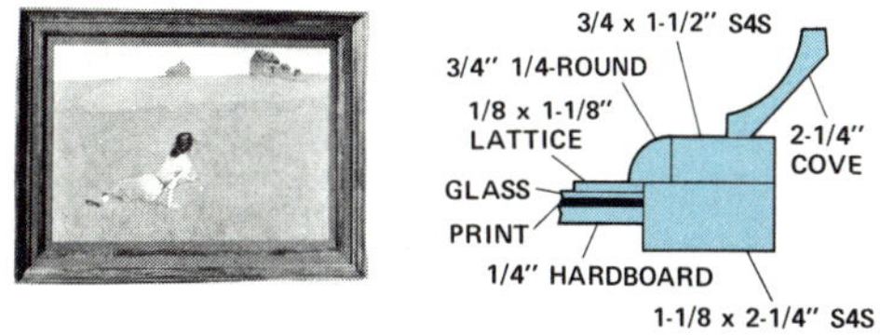

24x36 in. (1). Assemble subframe using the dimensioned stock shown. Cut and fit all moldings, and temporarily tack them in position. When you're satisfied with fit, remove moldings from the subframe. Striate the quarter-round and cove molds (see page **1272**), sand thoroughly and wipe off dust. Stain moldings dark walnut, let them dry; then finish with varnish. Seal the lattice and subframe with shellac wash. Apply charcoal gray latex paint to lattice and dark green (latex) to subframe. When parts are dry, permanently assemble the frame using glue and brads.

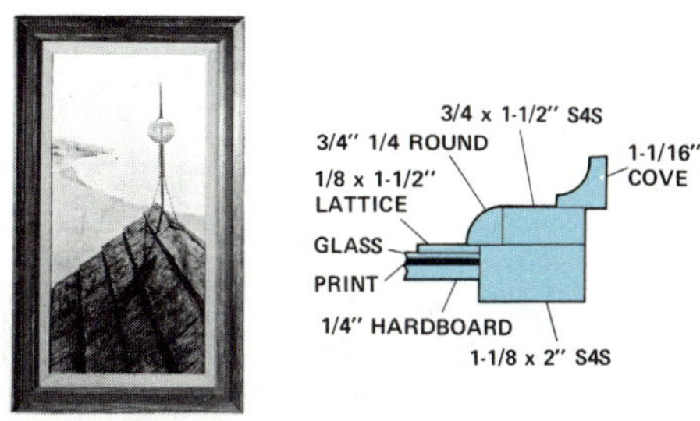

18x36 in. (2). Follow construction details above. Finishing details are also the same as above, except for a driftwood stain on moldings and dark blue latex on subframe.

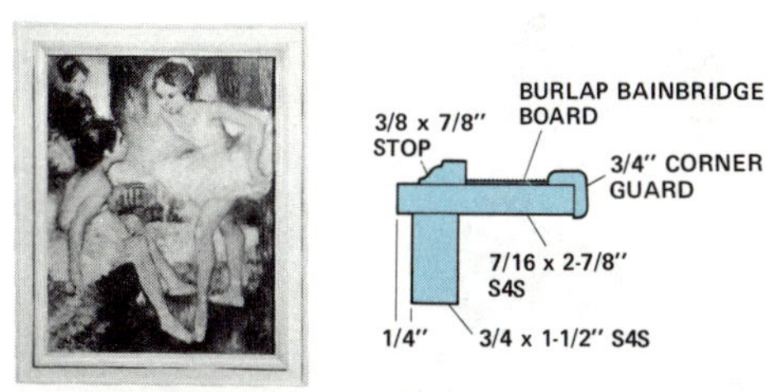

22x28 in. (3). Assemble the subframe and glue on white burlap board. Cut and fit moldings, remove and seal with shellac. Apply white latex, let it dry, antique with pink latex. Varnish and permanently assemble.

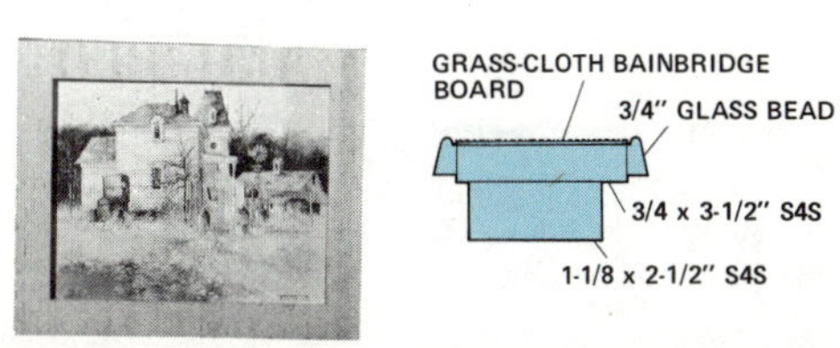

22x28 in. (3). Assemble the subframe, then glue and tack ¾-in. stock to the frame. Cut and temporarily tack bead moldings in position to check fit, then remove. Apply sandalwood grass-cloth board to frame, stain and varnish moldings, then permanently attach them to frame's inside and outside edges as shown.

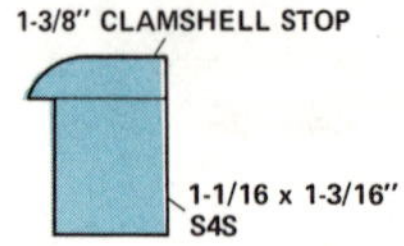

18x28 in. including mat (4). Assemble frame; sand, dust and apply a driftwood stain. After 15 minutes, wipe off the excess. When dry, size the frame with shellac, brush on a yellow latex paint, wait 5 minutes and wipe off frame. Finish frame with varnish.

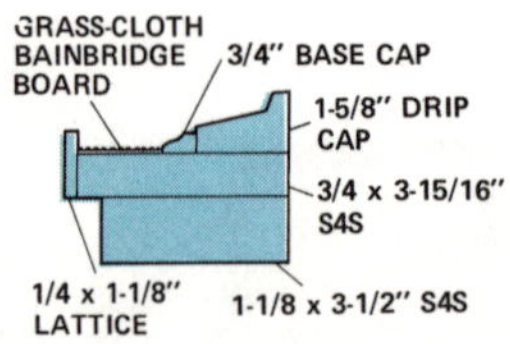

22x28 in. (3). Assemble subframe and ¾-in. stock. Cut, fit and temporarily assemble the moldings; then remove them. Cover frame with tan grass-cloth Bainbridge board. Striate and sand the drip cap, then apply a dark pine stain. Seal the lattice with a shellac wash; paint it mustard yellow. Finish moldings with varnish; permanently attach them to frame.

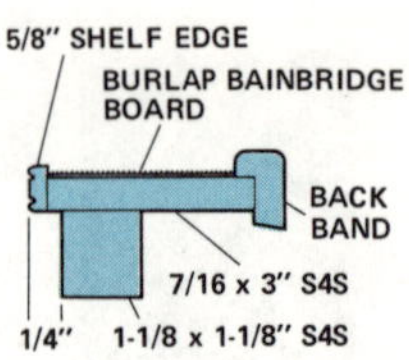

22x28 in. (3). Assemble subframe and $^7/_{16}$-in. stock. Cut and fit moldings, then remove. Size the frame with thinned shellac, allow it to dry, then cover it with gold burlap board. Seal moldings with shellac and apply Chinese red latex. When dry, antique with yellow latex, tinted slightly with black. Varnish moldings and permanently attach them to the frame.

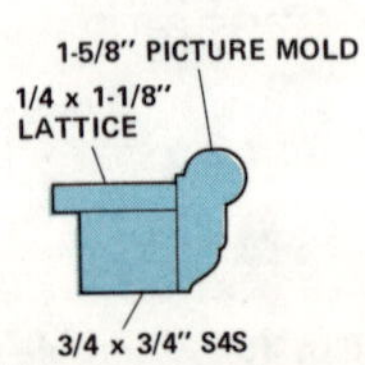

18x32 in. including mat (4). Assemble all parts and size with thinned shellac. Finish the frame using buttercup yellow and chocolate brown on picture molding and lattice, respectively. Whey dry, antique the yellow with an avocado green and varnish frame.

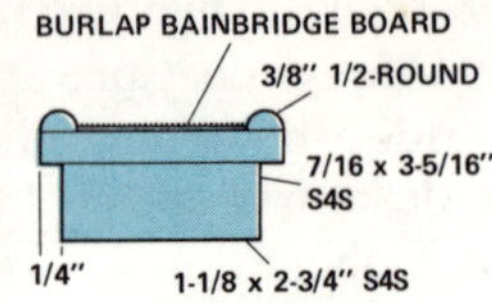

22x28 in. (3). Assemble the subframe and $^7/_{16}$-in. stock. Glue rust-colored burlap board to the frame, using brads where necessary. Miter cut and fit half-round moldings, then remove them. Size moldings with thinned shellac, then apply white latex paint. When dry, finish with varnish and attach moldings.

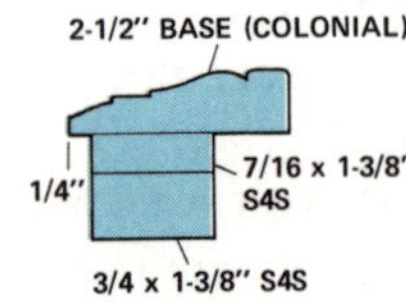

22x28 in. (3). Assemble the subframe, attach front-frame moldings (miter corners). Seal wood with a thinned shellac. Brush on colonial blue latex and let it dry. Next, apply a slightly thinned white latex and, after five minutes, wipe it off with clean cloth. When completely dry, finish wood with varnish.

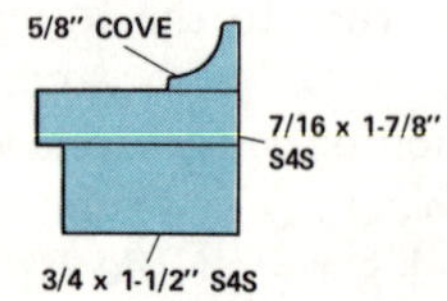

15x20 in. (5). Glue print to ¼-in. hardboard. Assemble frame and size it with shellac. Using latex paints, brush on olive green, allow it to dry, then antique with thinned red latex paint. Use varnish as a finish and picture glass to protect the print.

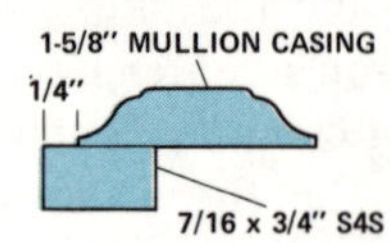

15x21 in. (6). Assemble the subframe and mullion casing. Brush on pine stain, wait 15 minutes and wipe off excess. Antique corners with burnt umber; allow 24 hours to dry. Finish the frame with lacquer.

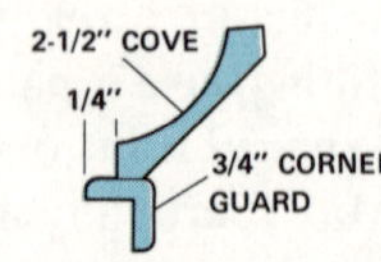

21x27 in. including mat (4). Assemble the frame from moldings, using miter cuts at all corners. Size the frame with a thinned shellac and allow it to dry. Apply a mustard yellow latex paint to the liner (corner guard) and use avocado green latex paint on the cove. Apply varnish to the frame for a finish.

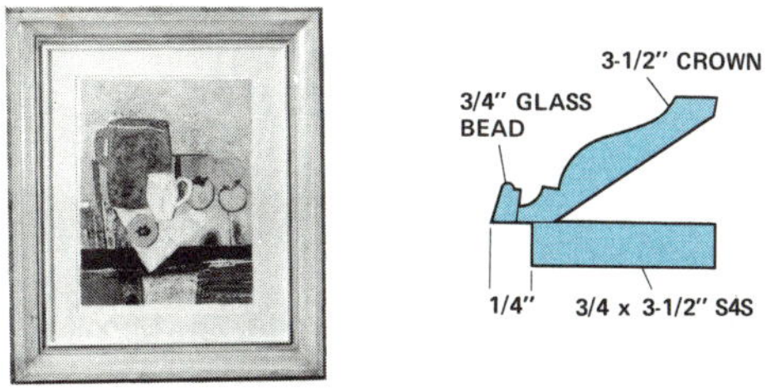

23x28 in. including mat (4). Because the subframe is visible, use miter joints, throughout. After assembling frame, apply dark walnut stain to subframe. Next, seal entire frame with thinned shellac. Paint crown molding and bead (liner) with white latex and let it dry. Then apply thinned orange paint to *crown only,* wait five minutes, wipe. When dry, spray on varnish.

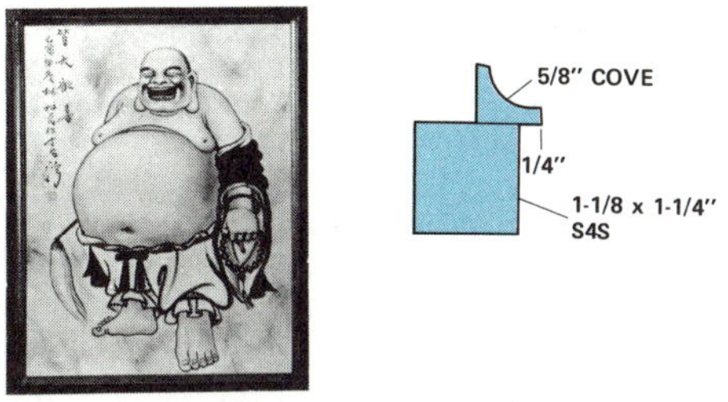

22x28 in. (3). Assemble the frame using miters on all corners. Size entire frame with a thinned shellac and set it aside to dry. Next, using latex paints, apply a dark yellow to the cove molding and a flat black to the subframe. When dry, antique cove molding with a thinned black. Finally, varnish all parts.

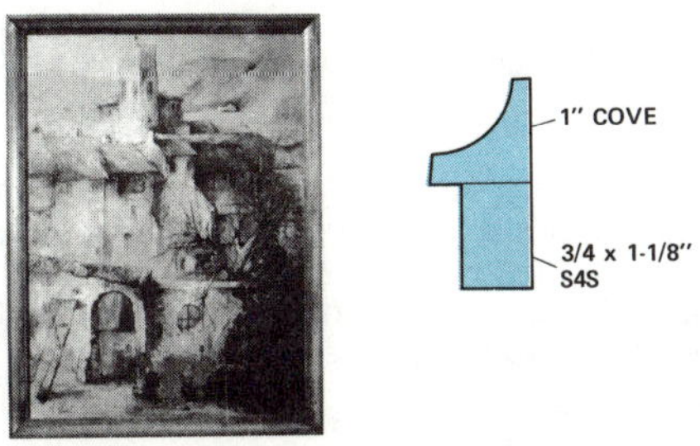

17½ x 23½ in. (3). Assemble frame, fill holes and sand thoroughly. Apply a walnut stain, wait 15 minutes and wipe off. Finish with two coats of a semigloss lacquer. Rub lightly with 4/0 steel wool between coats. Wait 24 hours; rub on paste wax and buff to sheen.

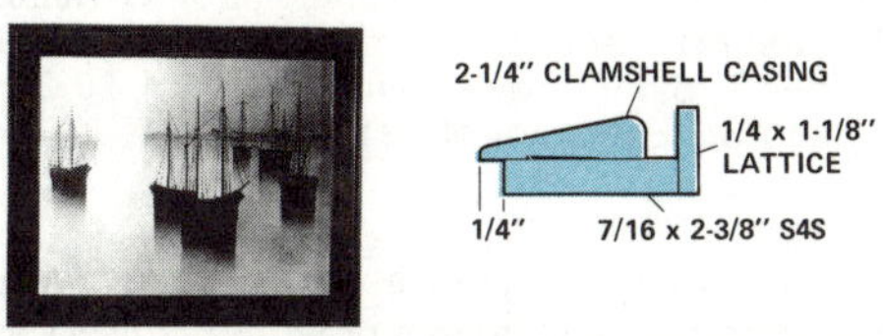

22x28 in. (3). Assemble the frame as shown above. Set all nails, fill nail holes and thoroughly sand wood. Size with thin shellac, allow to dry. Brush on dark green latex paint and let dry. Antique frame with thinned black latex. When dry, finish with varnish.

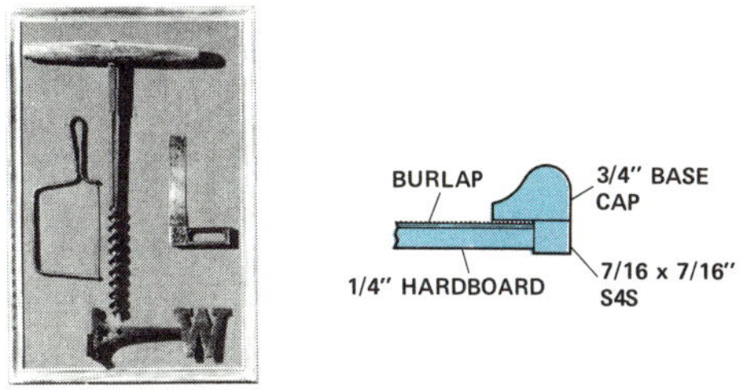

15x22 in. (framing a collection). Arrange objects to determine size of ¼-in hardboard. Glue red burlap to hardboard using staples at edges. Assemble the frame, striate wood moldings and sand. Apply driftwood stain, then wait 15 minutes and wipe off excess. When dry, apply lacquer. To hold objects, drill holes through board (bracketing a part of each object). Run thin copper wire around objects and through holes; knot wire on back of board. Wire each object in at least two places.

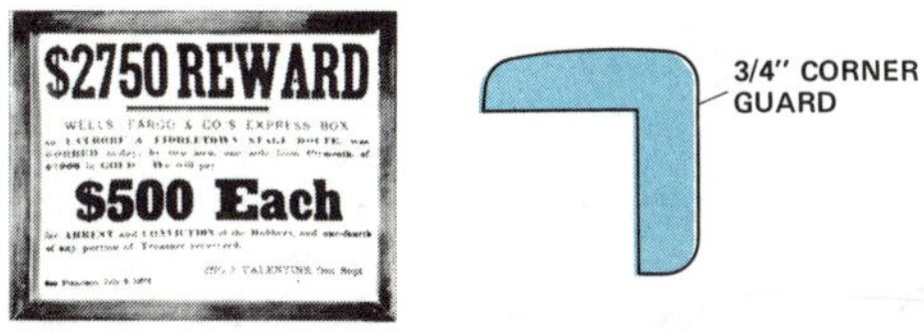

8x10 in. (7). Simple object, extra simple frame; assemble it with glue and brads at mitered corners. Apply pine stain, antique with burnt umber and finish with lacquer. Back up the print with cardboard.

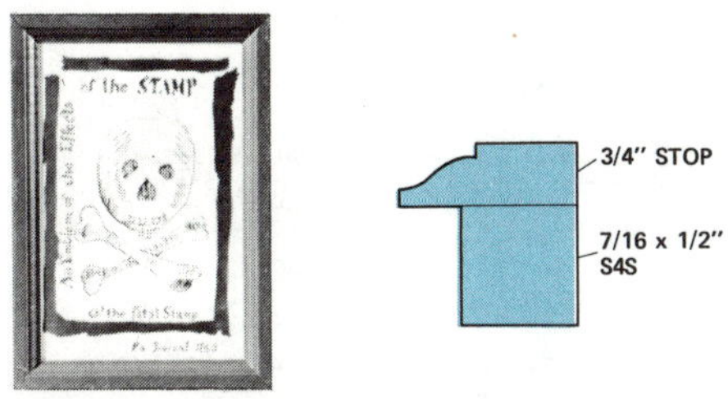

6½ x 9½ in. (7). Assemble the subframe and add stop molding at front. Size all wood with shellac and allow to dry. Sand it lightly and brush on avocado green latex paint. Let dry, finish with varnish. Print should be backed with cardboard and, if desired, covered with glass.

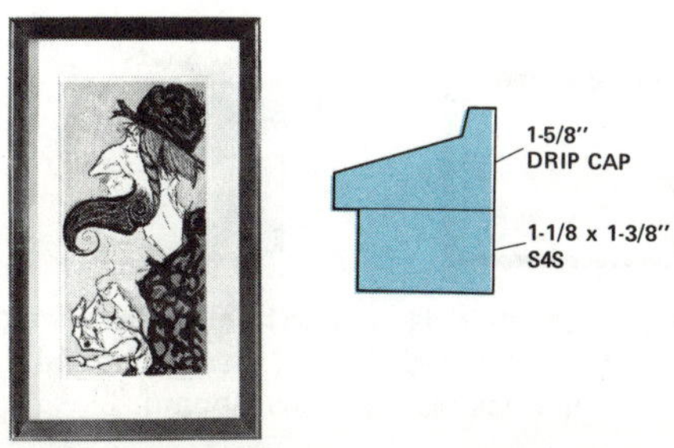

18x29 in. including mat (4). Assemble the subframe and frame using stock shown. Fill holes, sand, seal with shellac wash. Apply dark red latex paint, allow to dry and then antique with black-latex wash. Finish with two coats of varnish, protect the woodcut with picture glass.

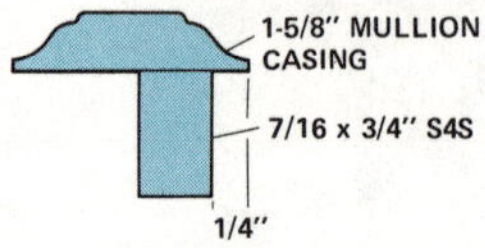

12x16½ in. (8). Assemble the frame, sand and seal with a shellac wash. Brush on reddish-orange latex, let dry, antique lightly with burnt-umber wash. Varnish when dry; use hardboard backing, glass to protect print.

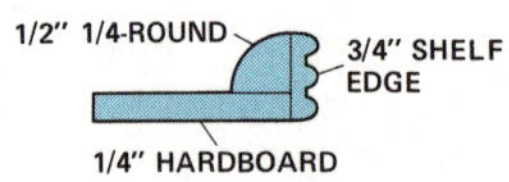

19x28 in. (9). Glue poster to piece of ¼-in. hardboard cut to the same size. Use a straightedge and clean cloth to assure that the poster will be perfectly flat and that there will be no air bubbles under it. Assemble the frame directly to hardboard and seal it with thinned shellac. Apply mustard yellow latex paint to the frame, let this dry and antique it with burnt-umber wash. Use this same wash to *slightly* antique the print around its edges. For a finish, apply a spray-type varnish (dull) to the frame as well as the poster.

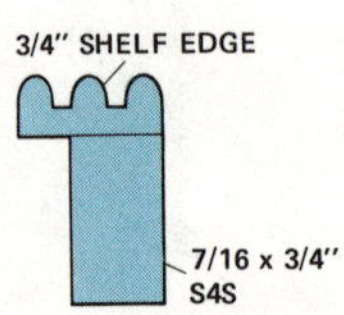

12x16 in. (8A). Using a white glue, affix poster to same-size piece of hardboard. Assemble frame and size with thinned shellac. Brush on orange semigloss enamel and allow to dry overnight. If desired, frame can be antiqued with burnt-umber wash, but make sure you follow this with a varnish finish.

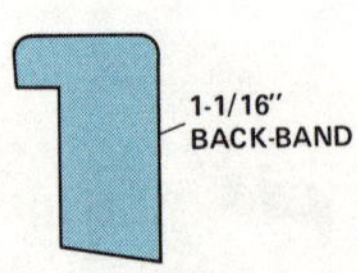

8x10 in. (7). Assemble back-band frame with mitered corners, seal it with thinned shellac, then finish with bright green enamel. Back print with cardboard.

12x16 in. (8B). This first-performance opera poster has the same frame construction and finish as that used for Reward poster. Glue reproduction to hardboard and cover poster with picture glass if desired.

WHERE-TO-BUY-IT INFORMATION

1. Print *Christina's World* (Wyeth). The Museum of Modern Art, Publication Sales, 11 West 53 St., New York, NY 10019.

2. Print *Northern Point* (Wyeth). For nearest source, write New York Graphic Society, Print Dept. PM, 140 Greenwich Ave., Greenwich, CT 06830. (Nine other Wyeth prints are also available.)

3. Oil painting reproductions: varnished canvas on stretchers or rolled canvas. Specify name of reproduction and artist when ordering. The Donald Art Co., Dept. PM, 90 South Ridge St., Port Chester, NY 10574.

4. Original woodcuts and signed lithos. Specify name of work and artist. Associated American Artists, Dept. PM, 663 Fifth Ave., New York, NY 10022.

5. World War II tank prints, four styles available. Mar-Star Enterprises, Box 724, Wheaton, IL 60187.

6. Pirate treasure map. Virgil Hammonds, 23735 Donald-C, East Detroit, MI 48201.

7. *Reward, Join or Die, Stamp Act* reproductions. Hinsdale Craftsman, Box 282, Elmont, NY 11003.

8. Temple rubbing, 10 styles available. (8A). 1911 Packard advertisement, 10 old-time posters available. (8B). First-performance opera posters, 12 styles available. Fiesta Arts, Inc., Greenvale, NY 11548. Free brochure on all styles available.

9. Chaplin poster; limited quantity available. Write Marboro Books, Dept. PM, 205 Moonachie Rd., NJ 07074, for poster catalog listing 350 styles available and prices.

Bainbridge board, textured and smooth. Available at art-supply and department stores, or write Charles T. Bainbridge's Sons, Dept. PM, 20 Cumberland St., Brooklyn, NY 11205.

Frame-making tools (shown on page 1301). Available at hardware suppliers or write Stanley Tools Div., The Stanley Works, 195 Lake St., New Britain, CT 06050, for nearest source.

Build a floater picture frame

By AL NUNES-VAIS

STEP 1: To make a floater frame, you will need 1 x 2 stock (the stock's actual dimensions will be ¾ x 1½ in.). Using a radial saw or bench saw, cut out a strip approximately ½ x ⅝ in.

■ FLOATER FRAMES are a popular way to display art. The illusion is created by a groove running between the outer frame and an inner frame where the art rests.

Use 1 x 2 stock (actual dimensions will be about ¾ x 1½ in.) to make your frames.

First figure the size for the frame you need and cut the stock to four lengths for top, bottom and sides. Make each member several inches longer than necessary for the finished frame.

Then remove a strip approximately ½ x ⅝ in. from each piece by making two rip cuts with a bench saw or radial saw (Step 1).

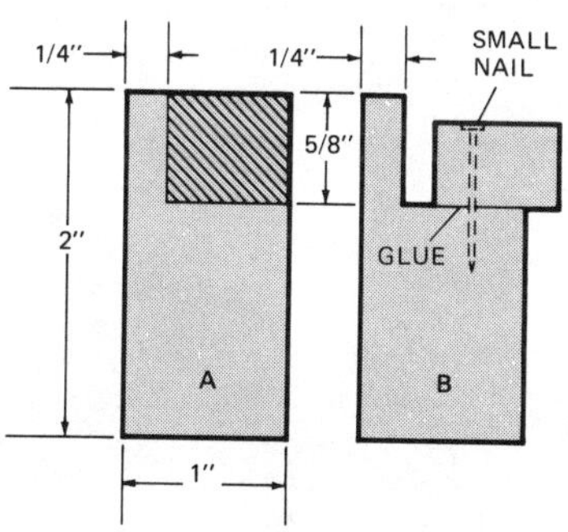

STEP 2: Take removed strip (shaded area in A) and reattach it as at B, leaving ¼-in. gap between outer frame and floater strip. Use glue and small nails. Strip is blade thickness lower.

STEP 3: Miter frame members to size so picture perimeter will coincide with outer edge of replaced strip. Assemble frame with glue and nails.

After you remove the strips, use white glue and nails to replace them, leaving a ¼-in. gap or groove between the outer frame and the floater strip (Step 2).

Now miter each side of the frame to the exact size, keeping in mind that the picture will rest on the outer edge of the floater strip. Assemble the frame (Step 2) using white glue and 1-in. finishing nails.

Once the frame is assembled (Step 4), the nail holes can be filled with wood filler and the frame sanded and finished to suit. You might want to paint, stain or varnish the frame. Regardless of your choice, black paint in the groove between the two raised surfaces will accent the isolation of the picture and give it the desired floating effect.

You can mount the art to a piece of mat or art board using dry-mount tissue or photo cement. Next cement the mounted picture to the frame's inner rim (Step 5).

STEP 4: Two frames are assembled, ready to be sanded and finished with paint, stain or varnish. Black paint in the groove will accent isolation of art and help give floating effect.

STEP 5: Mount picture on a mat or art board, then cement it to inner frame surface. Picture can easily be replaced by detaching entire mount and cementing new art in place.

SEE ALSO
Antique reproductions . . . Candle stands . . . Fasteners . . . Gifts, Christmas . . . Joinery . . . Letter racks . . . Mirrors . . . Miter joints . . . Moldings . . . Weekend projects

How to repair fancy picture frames

By ROBERT S. TOPPER

When a fancy picture frame with corner overlays is broken, it doesn't need to be replaced. If one of the corners is good, you can repair it yourself

1 **REBUILD THE** partially missing corner as close to the original as possible with water putty. Let this dry about 30 minutes

4 **CHIP OFF** the old overlay to the bare wood. Then make undercuts with a chisel to help anchor the new overlay casting to the frame.

7 **IF MORE** than one corner needs to be replaced continue to use the mold since it shrinks as it becomes thoroughly cured

■ ORNATE PICTURE FRAMES with fancy overlays can be repaired even if much of the composition overlay is missing. All you need is one overlay intact or partially intact and repairable. The frame shown had corners which were badly damaged but one of them could be repaired by building it up with water putty so that a mold could be taken of it to recast the other three.

After the corner is repaired, it's surrounded with a wood form. I used InstaMold (available at craft stores) to fill the form. It's a powder you mix with water to a fairly thin consistency so it can be brushed into crevices and valleys of the overlay without leaving air pockets. It dries in approximately 30 minutes, after which the form can be removed. Remove the form first, then gently lift off the mold.

I used water putty which dries rock hard. I mixed it to a thick cream and poured it into the mold. Then I placed the frame corner upside down on top of the mold, pressed down to force out excess putty and left intact for 12 hours. When you lift off the mold, a facsimile of the missing overlay remains which is difficult to tell from the original.

2 **ASSEMBLE** a wood frame around the corner overlay. Fit it as close to the picture frame as you can and dam with wet paper wads

3 **MIX CASTING** powder with water, fill the mold, let it harden. Then carefully lift the casting from the frame overlay

5 **POUR THE** water-putty mixture into the inverted mold level with the top. Mix the putty until it reaches the consistency of thick cream

6 **PLACE THE** filled mold right side up under the face side of the frame corner. Press down into the wet putty to force out the excess

8 **WHEN THIS** much of an embossed overlay is missing, the overlay must be replaced with a new casting. It's beyond repair

9 **COAT THE** new overlay with a clear sealer (Deft), wipe the frame with a lacquer thinner, then spray the entire frame with a gold paint

Concrete patch didn't hold

Last summer I patched a step on my concrete stoop, a corner that broke away. It didn't hold; just fell out of place. I'd like to try again, as I don't want to replace the stoop. Can you tell me the right procedure?—C.T., R.I.

Did you use a concrete patcher especially prepared for the purpose? New concrete won't always bond to old, even though you may have cleaned out all dirt and loose material. Obtain a concrete-patching material which comes as a dry mix and add water in a measured proportion. Again clean the area to be patched thoroughly and make an L-shaped form, bracing or staking the form so it will stay in place until the concrete mix sets. When mixing, be sure to follow instructions on the container in *all* details. After troweling the mix in place, cover with burlap or coarse cloth and keep damp several days.

Painting basement floor

I want to paint part of my basement floor, but I'm confused about the paints and methods. My floor is in good condition, smooth and with no cracks. Can you start me in the right direction?—E.J. Long, Fort Worth, Tex.

Manufacturers generally recommend a latex-alkyd paint (water- emulsion) for concrete floors. Follow the rather detailed instructions for application on the container. In all cases, the floor should be thoroughly washed and scrubbed beforehand to remove all dust and debris. You can use a brush, but a roller with a stand-up handle is better and faster, with less chance of laps showing. Provide adequate ventilation, using a fan if necessary to move air and blow out fumes.

If your floor has a near glass-smooth finish, the instructions may recommend that the surface be etched before applying paint. This is done with a muriatic acid solution; follow directions to the letter.

Painting steel basement sashes

I want to paint the steel sashes and frames of my basement windows. To paint the frames I must take out the sashes, but how? The frames are welded at the corners and so far I don't have the "combination."—R. Masters, Birmingham, Ala.

All basement metal sashes I know of are designed to be lifted out of their frames. I have such windows and to get them out they must be tilted inward about halfway, then one end is raised until one "ear," or lug, clears the frame. This requires a careful, controlled maneuver, but once the lug is clear, the sash is easily lifted out.

'Numbered' roof

My house is to be reroofed. The contractor says he will use a No. 235 asphalt shingle, that this is a standard shingle and that he would not recommend a heavier covering on my "roof deck." What's he talking about?—N.H., Wis.

If you have the number correct, he means he's installing a shingle that weighs 235 pounds for each 100 square feet of roof area, that is, an area 10x10 feet. I assume that the new shingles are to be laid over the old. Your contractor has undoubtedly examined the roofing and checked the deck and the rafter size and he feels that this is the heaviest shingle he can use as an "over-roofing." This weight shingle is expected to give at least 15 years' service, usually more except under extreme conditions. The term "roof deck" refers to the boards that are laid over the rafters.

You might ask the contractor if he intends to use a shingle of the self-sealing type. It's recommended because the undersides of its tabs are coated with a self-sealing adhesive to keep them from being turned up and torn during high winds.

'Cold' siding

I want to cover my old wood siding with new aluminum siding, but I've been told that this siding is "cold"—that my old house will be cold and difficult to heat. Right or wrong?—D.F., Kans.

To me, "cold" is a new term applied to house siding. Much would depend on what your informant meant by it. Perhaps he is right in what he meant to say. But I don't think application of aluminum siding will make your home colder temperaturewise, or more difficult to heat, provided that it is installed according to accepted practice and that your heating installation is adequate to cope with winter temperatures in your locality.

Remover doesn't

I always work with paint and varnish removers outdoors. Often the remover doesn't "remove." The residues seem to harden and dry up on the surface and won't strip off easily. I must be doing something wrong, but what?—Jerry Bates, Canton, Ohio.

You may be brushing the remover too thinly. It works best when laid on in a one-direction stroke, using a full brush at each sweep. Also, in the open on a dry day, remover tends to evaporate more rapidly, even though a retarder is included in its formulation. Try laying a thickness of waxed paper over the surface immediately after applying remover.

METRIC CONVERSION

Conversion factors can be carried so far they become impractical. In cases below where an entry is exact it is followed by an asterisk (*). Where considerable rounding off has taken place, the entry is followed by a + or a - sign.

CUSTOMARY TO METRIC

Linear Measure

inches	millimeters
1/16	1.5875*
1/8	3.2
3/16	4.8
1/4	6.35*
5/16	7.9
3/8	9.5
7/16	11.1
1/2	12.7*
9/16	14.3
5/8	15.9
11/16	17.5
3/4	19.05*
13/16	20.6
7/8	22.2
15/16	23.8
1	25.4*

inches	centimeters
1	2.54*
2	5.1
3	7.6
4	10.2
5	12.7*
6	15.2
7	17.8
8	20.3
9	22.9
10	25.4*
11	27.9
12	30.5

feet	centimeters	meters
1	30.48*	.3048*
2	61	.61
3	91	.91
4	122	1.22
5	152	1.52
6	183	1.83
7	213	2.13
8	244	2.44
9	274	2.74
10	305	3.05
50	1524*	15.24*
100	3048*	30.48*

1 yard =
.9144* meters
1 rod =
5.0292* meters
1 mile =
1.6 kilometers
1 nautical mile =
1.852* kilometers

Fluid Measure

(Milliliters [ml] and cubic centimeters [cc or cu cm] are equivalent, but it is customary to use milliliters for liquids.)

1 cu in = 16.39 ml
1 fl oz = 29.6 ml
1 cup = 237 ml
1 pint = 473 ml
1 quart = 946 ml
= .946 liters
1 gallon = 3785 ml
= 3.785 liters
Formula (exact):
fluid ounces × 29.573 529 562 5* = milliliters

Weights

ounces	grams
1	28.3
2	56.7
3	85
4	113
5	142
6	170
7	198
8	227
9	255
10	283
11	312
12	340
13	369
14	397
15	425
16	454

Formula (exact):
ounces × 28.349 523 125* = grams

pounds	kilograms
1	.45
2	.9
3	1.4
4	1.8
5	2.3
6	2.7
7	3.2
8	3.6
9	4.1
10	4.5

1 short ton (2000 lbs) =
907 kilograms (kg)
Formula (exact):
pounds × .453 592 37* = kilograms

Volume

1 cu in = 16.39 cubic centimeters (cc)
1 cu ft = 28 316.7 cc
1 bushel = 35 239.1 cc
1 peck = 8 809.8 cc

Area

1 sq in = 6.45 sq cm
1 sq ft = 929 sq cm
= .093 sq meters
1 sq yd = .84 sq meters
1 acre = 4 046.9 sq meters
= .404 7 hectares
1 sq mile = 2 589 988 sq meters
= 259 hectares
= 2.589 9 sq kilometers

Kitchen Measure

1 teaspoon = 4.93 milliliters (ml)
1 Tablespoon = 14.79 milliliters (ml)

Miscellaneous

1 British thermal unit (Btu) (mean) = 1 055.9 joules
1 calorie (mean) = 4.19 joules
1 horsepower = 745.7 watts
= .75 kilowatts
caliber (diameter of a firearm's bore in hundredths of an inch) = .254 millimeters (mm)
1 atmosphere pressure = 101 325* pascals (newtons per sq meter)
1 pound per square inch (psi) = 6 895 pascals
1 pound per square foot = 47.9 pascals
1 knot = 1.85 kilometers per hour
25 miles per hour = 40.2 kilometers per hour
50 miles per hour = 80.5 kilometers per hour
75 miles per hour = 120.7 kilometers per hour